בְּכָל לְבָבְךָ

BECHOL LEVAVCHA

With all your heart

בְּכָל לְבָבְךָ
BECHOL LEVAVCHA

With all your heart

by HARVEY J. FIELDS

UNION OF AMERICAN HEBREW CONGREGATIONS • NEW YORK

Feldman Library

The Feldman Library Fund was created in 1974 through a gift from the Milton and Sally Feldman Foundation. The Feldman Library Fund which provides for the publication by the UAHC of selected outstanding Jewish books and texts memorializes Sally Feldman who in her lifetime devoted herself to Jewish youth and Jewish learning. Herself an orphan and brought up in an orphanage, she dedicated her efforts to helping Jewish young people get the educational opportunities she had not enjoyed.

In loving memory of my beloved wife Sally
"She was my life, and she is gone;
She was my riches, and I am a pauper."

"Many daughters have done valiantly, but thou excellest them all."

Milton E. Feldman

© COPYRIGHT 1976 BY THE UNION OF AMERICAN HEBREW CONGREGATIONS

PRODUCED IN THE UNITED STATES OF AMERICA

9 10 11 12 13 14

FOR

Debra — Joel — Rachel

Each child carries its own blessing into the world
　　　　　　　　　　　(A Yiddish Proverb)

CONTENTS

Introduction *IX*

Some Words of Thanks *X*

About Bechol Levavcha *XI*

COMMENTARY *1*

    The Talit *2*

    Creating New Prayers — A Controversy: Old and New *4*

    Section One — Benedictions of Praise *9*

    Section Two — The Shema *23*

    Section Three — The Amidah *49*

    Section Four — The Reading of Torah *105*

    Section Five — The Conclusion of the Service *139*

    Finally, What Is Prayer? *158*

A Selected Bibliography *166*

Glossary *167*

INTRODUCTION

*W*E OFTEN assume that prayer and worship are purely emotional experiences, that it is enough to arouse in the worshiper the feelings of awe, reverence, gratitude, communion, and so on.

The *emotional* experiences of prayer and worship are surely necessary — but not sufficient. There is a strong *intellectual* element in Jewish prayer, as there is in Judaism itself. Understanding and insight are necessary too, especially *before* a worship experience — and, for these, knowledge and study are operationally necessary.

And so, in addition to the full play of the emotional aspect of prayer, Rabbi Fields has also given us, in *Bechol Levavcha*, a program for investigation, discussion, research, debate.

He has done more. We hear much nowadays about cognitive and effective learning and their confluence or convergence for better results than from either alone. We hear too little, however, about two other learning dimensions: the psychomotor, the development of habits and skills, and the conative, decision making among recognized choices. *Bechol Levavcha* provides ample scope for these two dimensions as well and is thus truly, as instructional material, a *kol bo*, a total approach.

It will be obvious to teachers and students that flexibility has been built into both format and procedure and that opportunity and encouragement for creativity abound.

We take pride in a work that, within its subject-matter field, is so complete and comprehensive, so versatile and multidirectional. We know it will find wide use on a variety of age levels from intermediate grades to adults and for teacher education programs.

Abraham Segal, *Director*
UNION OF AMERICAN HEBREW CONGREGATIONS
CENTRAL CONFERENCE OF AMERICAN RABBIS
COMMISSION ON JEWISH EDUCATION
June, 1975

SOME WORDS OF THANKS

THE CREATION of *Bechol Levavcha* is the result of many people and places. The Curriculum Committee of the Commission on Jewish Education and Rabbi Jack D. Spiro, a former director of the Commission, were among the first to urge that the idea for such a project be transformed into reality. One beautiful summer spent on Cape Cod, Massachusetts, and another on the banks of the Willamette River outside Portland, Oregon, provided the required blocks of concentrated time to formulate the text. An understanding congregation, Anshe Emeth Memorial Temple, New Brunswick, New Jersey, willingly encouraged its rabbi to pursue the project. Its religious school students and teachers experimented with the text, and their enthusiasm, critical evaluations, and reactions helped spark the direction and shape of the material.

A special debt of thanks is owed to Rabbis Joseph B. Glaser, Alexander M. Schindler, and Robert I. Kahn for their cooperation in publication; and to Rabbi Samuel Glasner, Arden Shenker, Samuel Nemzoff, and Rabbi Bennett F. Miller for their helpful comments and suggestions.

Abraham Segal, who was director of the Commission on Jewish Education during many stages of this project, has exercised the excellence of his editorial scalpel and the wisdom of his Jewish soul in giving good advice. Rabbi Daniel B. Syme, the acting director of the Commission, has creatively steered *Bechol Levavcha* through publication. Ralph Davis, whose devotion to the world of Jewish books is honored in *Bechol Levavcha*, has enriched the text with his creative and artistic understanding. My thanks to Leo Glueckselig who has added a variety of artistic renderings in order to suggest possible ways in which students might illustrate their own prayer books. To the UAHC copy editor, Esther Fried Africk, I am especially grateful. My secretary, Sharon Jankowski, also deserves a special thanks.

My wife, Sybil, has read and sensitively criticized each page of *Bechol Levavcha*. Her commitment to sharing a fresh insight into Jewish tradition and life with me has, more than anything else, made this project possible.

H.J.F.

ABOUT BECHOL LEVAVCHA

*T*HE CHASIDIC teacher, Rabbi Solomon of Karlin, once said: "The greatest of all miracles is to bring into the heart of a Jew the Holy Influence whereby he may be enabled to pray properly to his Creator." That, it would seem, is certainly an appropriate statement with which to begin a book or project on prayer.

On the other hand, I wonder what Rabbi Solomon meant by his observation. When one thinks about it for a moment, Rabbi Solomon's statement seems to raise more questions than it answers.

What, for instance, does Rabbi Solomon mean by "miracles"? What is a miracle? And what is the "Holy Influence"? Does he mean God or one power or aspect of God? And what could the good rabbi have had in mind when he used the words "to pray properly"? Is there a way to pray properly? How would you describe it? Who is to judge whether or not a person is praying properly?

And, with just a little חֻצְפָּה (*chutzpah*), one could even ask what Rabbi Solomon means by the phrase "the heart of a Jew." Is that different from the heart of a non-Jew?

WHAT IS BECHOL LEVAVCHA?

Bechol Levavcha has been created in order to answer the questions raised by Rabbi Solomon's observation and to help us discover and accomplish the "miracle" of prayer. That, of course, will not be easy or automatic. Prayer is an art requiring the full range of our emotional and rational sensitivities and abilities. *Bechol Levavcha* was conceived as a means which might open to us the rich possibilities of Jewish prayer. It is hoped that it will lead to investigation, discussion, research, debate, and creativity and that its results will be both enjoyable and exciting.

Throughout the *Bechol Levavcha Commentary*, you will find prayers and quotations from various sources. Wherever possible we have identified the authors or books quoted. The designation *HJF* indicates that the prayer has been written by the author of *Bechol Levavcha*. We are most grateful to the Central Conference of American Rabbis for permission to use portions of their new prayer book, *Gates of Prayer*. It is hoped that *Bechol Levavcha* will be a helpful companion to *Gates of Prayer* and to other prayer books used by Jews throughout the world.

Bechol Levavcha is divided into two parts. This division allows for a flexibility in the use of the material and many opportunities for individual and group creativity.

The first part contains the prayers of the traditional Shabbat morning service along with alternative selections from *Gates of Prayer*. Note that this entire volume contains perforated and punched pages. These should be removed and put into a loose-leaf notebook, thus allowing the readers to select their own order of worship and compose their own prayers. The printed cover may also be pasted onto the cover of the loose-leaf notebook. The translation of the prayers is as close as possible to the Hebrew original. This will enable students and teachers to compare and contrast the Hebrew and English. Hebrew words have been transliterated and translated the first time they appear. They are also listed in the Glossary starting on page 167. Wherever possible, in the translation, we have eliminated masculine references to God or human beings. This should be kept in mind when translating from Hebrew to English.

The use of the loose-leaf form provides an opportunity for introducing the new compositions or reading selections into the service. Creative musicians in the group may also wish to place their songs into this section. *Bechol Levavcha* is meant to increase sharing and enrich worship through mutual creativity and song.

You will notice that the Shabbat morning service, with the exception of two pages, is not illustrated. Obviously, it would have been easy to find pictures or to ask a talented artist to illustrate all the prayers. Instead, we preferred to let students create their own illustrations. For that reason, the designer has left space on most pages of the Shabbat morning service for their individual artistry, i.e., cutting out pictures from magazines or decorating the pages with their own designs. Looking at the *Commentary* for additional artistic suggestions will be helpful. Illustrating a prayer book is *not* a new idea. During the Middle Ages, Jews decorated their prayer books and *haggadot* in elaborate and beautiful ways. As a matter of fact, their illustrations tell us much about their lives and environment. You may wish to take a look in your synagogue library at some of their artistic achievements.

The second part of *Bechol Levavcha* contains the *Commentary* on all the prayer selections (which are repeated as they appear in the first part) and is fully illustrated. Hopefully, these illustrations will inspire students to try their own hands at illustrating their prayer books.

The purpose of the *Commentary* is to help us appreciate the development and artistry of Jewish prayer as well as the significant role it has played in the history and experience of the Jewish people. Because we wanted the *Commentary* to involve the student in a creative exploration of the meaning of Jewish prayer, we have filled it with questions, observations from Jewish tradition, and topics for consideration.

The *Commentary* asks many more questions than it answers. There are two reasons for that. First, the themes of our Jewish prayers often raise issues and insights that should be pursued and explored. Rather than closing off the opportunity to share ideas or to discover modern applications for ancient thoughts and convictions, the *Commentary* often leaves a subject open for continued speculation and argument. The readers are challenged to come to their own conclusions. Second, in many cases, where a problem or question is raised, there is not one simple answer. Instead, the *Commentary* offers a variety of Jewish approaches and responses. Hopefully, this will stimulate an exciting exchange which leads not only to new understandings but also to new questions.

The *Commentary* includes several additional prayers based on the themes of the traditional prayers. These are meant to be used within the worship service and to initiate the creation of new prayers by members of the group or congregation.

SUGGESTED WAYS TO USE BECHOL LEVAVCHA

The prayer and commentary material for *Bechol Levavcha* was developed so that it could be used with maximum flexibility by students of the widest possible range of ages. The following suggestions grow out of several years of experimenting with the material in a number of different ways. Some of them may fit your needs, others may not. Choose those which seem helpful and develop your own methods and approaches.

Suggestion one: *Bechol Levavcha* can be used very effectively within the Hebrew religious school setting by fourth through seventh graders. The students can be motivated to learn the Hebrew of the prayers by looking forward to leading their peers in Shabbat worship once a month. While the *Commentary* has been written for high school students and adults, teachers will find it very helpful in interpreting the meaning of the prayers with their intermediate grade students. Where *Bechol Levavcha* is used in the Hebrew religious school setting, congregations should be divided by various class levels. For example, all fifth graders would compose one congregation. In this case, one class group can be responsible for preparing and conducting the service each time the entire grade-level-congregation meets. Where such an arrangement is impossible, because numbers are either too small or too great, students could be combined and assignments divided up so that each one has the opportunity to participate. A congregation should be limited to no more than seventy-five persons. You can invite parents to be present and to participate. Maximum involvement is the goal.

Suggestion Two: *Bechol Levavcha* is an exciting way for high school students and adults, either together or separately, to experience and celebrate Shabbat morning. The *Commentary* provides a wide variety of subjects for sharing. You may wish to begin with a discussion of "What Is Prayer?" or with the controversy between fixed and creative prayer ("Creating New Prayers — A Controversy: Old and New"). When used by high school students and adults, it is suggested that different people be assigned the responsibility of leading the study and that the group decide the order and subjects for its discussion. Spend about an hour in study and sharing and then move on to your Shabbat morning worship.

Suggestion Three: *Bechol Levavcha* may be used for retreats, conclaves, or for summer camp programs. When utilized for a brief time, care should be given in selecting topics from the *Commentary*. The prayer book has been designed to allow a maximum of opportunities for inserting prayers written by participants.

Suggestion Four: *Bechol Levavcha* can also be adapted to a congregational Bar/Bat Mitzvah program. Not only will it acquaint students with the basic Hebrew of the Shabbat morning worship and its traditional sections, but it will also allow a Bar/Bat Mitzvah student to probe the meaning of Jewish prayer and, hopefully, enhance the Bar/Bat Mitzvah celebration. If it is possible, create a Shabbat *chug* (group) of Bar/Bat Mitzvah students (and parents!) which uses *Bechol Levavcha*, meets each Shabbat morning for study and prayer, and utilizes the opportunity creatively to prepare for the ceremonies.

Suggestion Five: You may want to use *Bechol Levavcha* for an adult education program on the meaning of Jewish prayer or as a part of your high school curriculum. If you do, it is suggested that each student gets a copy of *Gates of Prayer: The New Union Prayer Book* or the traditional *siddur*. This will allow a maximum opportunity for comparison and contrast and a valuable window into the evolution of Jewish prayer.

Shabbat Worship and the Use of Bechol Levavcha

Preparing for worship is a key to a beautiful prayer experience. As the group prepares to lead a service, first select the prayers that you are going to use. Not *every* prayer in *Bechol Levavcha* is meant to be included. For example, the first time you use the service you may wish to include the Hebrew and English of the *Yotzer* prayer. The next time, you may choose to use the Hebrew and one of the creative versions in the *Commentary* or a prayer written by someone in your group. Should a selection from the *Commentary* or a creative prayer composed by someone in your group be chosen for use, be sure to have enough copies made so that each person can insert it at the appropriate place in his or her copy of the service.

Parts of the service should be assigned at least two weeks in advance so that each participant has ample time to prepare. The amount of Hebrew utilized will, obviously, depend upon the level and ability of each reader. Beginners should read an opening line and closing line of Hebrew and then go on to English. Those more advanced will prepare more Hebrew. In assigning parts, decide which are to be read by leaders and which in unison by the whole congregation. The service of *Bechol Levavcha* contains very few directions. Leaders, therefore, will need to inform the congregation when to stand, sit down, read responsively, or join in song. A simple announcement of (for example) "We join together in the *Aleynu* on page 140" is all that is required.

Music is extremely important for the success of *Bechol Levavcha*. If possible, try to arrange for a music leader who can work with the group as it prepares its service and who will be present to lead singing when the congregation meets for Shabbat worship. Should you have a person who is talented in the area of dance, you may wish to add that lovely ingredient, on occasion, to some of your services. At times, the use of movies, slides, or recorded music can also be very enriching. Don't hesitate to use various media within the context of your prayer.

Carefully choose a place for prayer. You may be fortunate to have your own synagogue sanctuary or small chapel. On the other hand, you may want to create your own sanctuary by erecting such things as a reader's desk, ark, and eternal light. At times, you may wish to make your sanctuary outdoors taking advantage of the beauty of nature; or you may choose to meet for prayer in a home. Seating is also important. Experiment until you find the arrangement which seems to spark the most involvement from the congregation. Try placing the reader's desk in the midst of the congregation, the front of the congregation, or have everyone sitting in the round. If your group is small enough, you may find it better to have participants read from their seats and eliminate the reader's desk altogether.

The length of a service is of great importance, especially when it involves younger people. The following examples of services, utilizing *Bechol Levavcha Commentary*, should be helpful:

Shabbat Service: Fourth-Grade Level

Shabbat Songs
Praised Be the One p. 13
  (First five lines in Hebrew, rest in English)

Barechu p. 24
Yotzer p. 26
  (First paragraph in Hebrew, rest in English)

Shema p. 37
Veahavta p. 41
  (First paragraph in Hebrew, rest in English)

Geulah or Shabbat Song p. 46
Avot p. 68
  (First and last paragraphs in Hebrew and English)

Kedushat Hayom p. 82
  (First paragraphs in Hebrew and English, then sing Vetaher Libenu)

Birkat Shalom p. 97
  (First and last paragraphs in Hebrew and English)

Elohai Netzor p. 101
At the Ark p. 112
Taking the Torah from the Ark p. 116
The Aliyah p. 120
Returning the Torah to the Ark p. 135
The Derashah
The Aleynu (Part I) p. 140
The Kaddish p. 145
  (Final paragraph in Hebrew and English)
Concluding Shabbat Song

Shabbat Service: Seventh-Grade Level

Shabbat Songs
Benedictions of Praise p. 10
Creative Prayer
Barechu p. 24
Yotzer p. 26
  (First and last paragraphs in Hebrew and English)

Creative Ahavah Rabbah
Shema p. 37
Veahavta p. 41
Geulah or Shabbat Song p. 46
Avot p. 68
Creative Gevurot
Kedushah p. 78
  (First two sections)

Kedushat Hayom p. 82
  (Last two paragraphs in Hebrew and English, or creative Kedushat Hayom)

Birkat Shalom p. 97
Elohai Netzor p. 101
At the Ark p. 112
Taking the Torah from the Ark p. 116
The Aliyah p. 120
Returning the Torah to the Ark p. 135
The Derashah
The Aleynu (Part I) p. 140
Creative Aleynu
The Kaddish p. 145
Concluding Shabbat Song

Shabbat Service: High School or Adult Level

Shabbat Songs	
Psalm 100 or Psalm 135	p. 18
The Soul of Everything That Lives	p. 20
Barechu	p. 24
Yotzer	p. 26
(Hebrew, then creative English prayer)	
Shema	p. 37
Veahavta	p. 41
Geulah	p. 46
Avot	p. 68
(Hebrew, then creative English prayer)	
Creative Gevurot	
Kedushah	p. 78
Kedushat Hayom	p. 82
(First paragraph Hebrew, then creative English prayer, concluding with final Hebrew blessing)	
Avodah	p. 87
Hodaah	p. 93
(Final paragraphs in Hebrew and English)	
Birkat Shalom	p. 97
At the Ark	p. 112
Taking the Torah from the Ark	p. 116
The Aliyah	p. 120
Haftarah Blessings	p. 124
Returning the Torah to the Ark	p. 135
The Aleynu (Part I)	p. 140
The Kaddish	p. 145
Concluding Shabbat Song	

More Ideas

Assign one or two people the task of creating a large, decorative סֵדֶר הַתְּפִילָה (*Seder Hatefilah*), the Order of Prayer, poster which can be hung wherever your group meets for discussion and preparation for Shabbat worship. The poster should contain the following outline of the Shabbat morning service and space to record the participants' assignments. The poster will also serve as a helpful reminder of the order, sections, and prayers of the Shabbat service.

סֵדֶר הַתְּפִילָה

Pesuke Dezimrah
    a. Benedictions of Praise
    b. Praised Be the One
    c. The Soul Which You Have Given
    d. Of Courage and Truthfulness
    e. Psalm 100
    f. Psalm 135
    g. The Soul of Everything That Lives

Shema
    a. Barechu: The Call to Worship
    b. Yotzer: Former of Light
    c. Ahavah Rabbah: With Great Love
    d. Shema: Hear, O Israel
    e. Veahavta: You Shall Love the Lord
    f. Geulah: Redemption

Amidah
    a. Avot
    b. Gevurot
    c. Kedushah
    d. Kedushat Hayom
    e. Avodah
    f. Hodaah
    g. Birkat Shalom
    h. Elohai Netzor

Keriat Hatorah
    a. At the Ark
    b. Taking the Torah from the Ark
    c. Aliyah and Torah Service
    d. Haftarah Blessings
    e. The New Month
    f. Returning the Torah to the Ark

Siyum Haavodah
    a. The Aleynu
    b. The Kaddish
    c. Adon Olam
    d. En Kelohenu
    e. Yigdal
    f. Kiddush for Shabbat Day

Invite parents, grandparents, teachers, friends, and the rabbi to join at worship and, if possible, assign them parts in the service. For example, you may wish to ask a post-Bar/Bat Mitzvah to read a portion of Torah and Haftarah or invite a parent to come forward for the *aliyah*. On another occasion you may want to ask two or three people to prepare a dramatic interpretation of the Torah portion.

Plan a Kiddush just after the service. Serve wine and chalah. If there is time, you may want to include a special Shabbat program of singing, poetry reading, and folk dancing.

If you are meeting regularly for discussion and worship, you might want to consider dividing your group into the following committees:

A וַעַד עֲבוֹדָה (*Vaad Avodah*), Committee on Worship, could be responsible for the assignment of parts for the worship service and for the addition of special material on holidays or other occasions. This committee may also wish to choose and assign certain sections of the service for creative expression. It may also want to initiate projects to beautify the place of worship or to experiment with different seating arrangements.

A וַעַד תַּלְמוּד תּוֹרָה (*Vaad Talmud Torah*), Committee on Torah Study, might be responsible for choosing the areas of study in the *Commentary*. In some cases, the committee itself may wish to assign the discussion leaders or even plan the lesson. Within the *Commentary*, you will find suggestions for special projects. Here, too, the committee can set a project in motion and direct it.

A וַעַד קִדּוּשׁ (*Vaad Kiddush*), Committee for Kiddush, can plan your Kiddush with special programs and events. On one occasion you can have Shabbat singing; at other times, instrumental music, plays, or media presentations.

All of these committees ought to be rotating in membership so that everyone has a chance to serve in a different area of leadership responsibility.

Another Idea

The filmstrip/cassette program *Why Pray?* presents young people's emotional responses to a philosophical question. Rather than prescribing answers, the intention here is to stimulate uninhibited classroom discussion. The leader's guide by Rabbi Bennett Miller contains suggestions for fully exploiting the nuances of the dialogue and activities relevant to students from third grade through adult education programs. As an introduction to the subject of prayer, *Why Pray?* can be useful in challenging your students into articulating their perceptions of, and personal connections to, God. The *Commentary* often offers the gamut of Jewish responses to a particular question; *Why Pray?* effectively crystallizes the gamut of feelings of Jewishly involved young people. And just as *Bechol Levavcha* was developed to be used with maximum options, so too is *Why Pray?*; it can be incorporated into your unit at any point.

What's in a Name?

Why is this book called בְּכָל לְבָבְךָ, *Bechol Levavcha*?

Our title is taken from the well-known sentence which follows the words of the שְׁמַע (*Shema*) in the Torah (Deuteronomy 6:5) and in every prayer book. That sentence reads: "You shall love the Lord your God with all your heart (בְּכָל לְבָבְךָ), with all your soul, and with all your might."

Once some students asked their rabbi: "What does it mean to love God בְּכָל לְבָבְךָ, with all your heart?" He answered: "It means to serve God." "And what," they asked, "is the service of the heart?" The rabbi replied: "The service of the heart is prayer."

This book is called *Bechol Levavcha*, בְּכָל לְבָבְךָ, because it is hoped that it will help us discover and rediscover what it means to "serve God with all our hearts."

HARVEY J. FIELDS
Erev Shavuot 5736
June 3, 1976

The Commentary

The Talit

The talit with its fringes reminds us of the commandments of Torah and of our duty to remember and do them.

(Say as talit is put on)

בָּרוּךְ אַתָּה, יְיָ אֱלֹהֵינוּ, מֶלֶךְ הָעוֹלָם, אֲשֶׁר קִדְּשָׁנוּ בְּמִצְוֹתָיו, וְצִוָּנוּ לְהִתְעַטֵּף בַּצִּיצִת.

Praised be You, O Lord our God, Ruler of the universe, who enables us to attain holiness through the religious duty of wearing fringes.

Commentary

The טַלִּית (*talit*), prayer shawl, with its צִיצִית (*tzitzit*), or fringes, has been worn by Jews since biblical times. Today, many Jews continue to wear the טַלִּית. Among Reform Jews the wearing of a טַלִּית at worship is optional. The commandment to wear צִיצִית is found in the Torah, in the Book of Numbers.

> The Lord spoke to Moses saying: Speak to the Israelite people and instruct them to make for themselves fringes on the corners of their garments throughout the ages.... Look at it and recall all the commandments of the Lord and observe them, so that you do not follow your heart and eyes to do evil.
>
> (Numbers 15:37–39)

Why?

Why have Jews worn צִיצִית from biblical times until today?

We know that dress has always played an important part in the way people relate to one another. The Indian headdress, for instance, indicates the tribal position of the Indian wearing it. The uniform a soldier wears tells us his rank in the army. A Catholic priest is known by the white collar he wears.

Dress is also associated with various kinds of rituals. There is the white dress of the bride, the robes of the priest, and the animal masks worn by some Indians at special festive occasions.

Often ancient people wore special garments or charms because they believed that this would protect them from evil spirits, or be pleasing to the gods. Today, many people still wear what they call "good luck" charms believing that they will bring them safety, or good health, or success in their sport, or even protection from harm.

Originally the Hebrews, like other peoples, may have worn the צִיצִית either for protection from evil or for good luck. The Torah, however, transformed these superstitious practices and gave them a higher, spiritual meaning. The Torah teaches that the צִיצִית were meant to help us "recall all the commandments of the Lord." The Hebrew word for "commandment" is מִצְוָה (*mitzvah*). A מִצְוָה is a Jewish responsibility. In addition, the word מִצְוָה (מִצְווֹת, *mitzvot*, pl.), in a general sense, is also used for any good deed or act of piety or kindness. Later on (pages 33–36), we will discuss the variety of different מִצְווֹת in Jewish tradition.

The Talit and Prayer

The מִצְוָה of prayer is one of the most important responsibilities of the Jew. Prayer is our opportunity to share our Jewish faith; to express our love of God and humanity; to judge our actions and relationships with others; and to seek ways of improving ourselves and the world in which we live.

Putting on the טַלִּית with its צִיצִית is the unique way Jews "dress up" for prayer. Wearing the טַלִּית helps us get into the mood for Jewish worship.

When we put on the טַלִּית we do something that Jews have done for centuries when they prayed.

The Bratzlaver Rebbe, who was the great-grandson of the Baal Shem Tov, taught that "it is a מִצְוָה to be properly dressed for prayer." Would you agree with him? You may wish to arrange a discussion or debate on what is "proper dress" for prayer. Should you have such a discussion, be sure to include the טַלִּית and the wearing of the כִּפָּה (kipah), skullcap.

What about Women?

In the past it was only the men who wore the טַלִּית. The reason for this may have been that only the men were obligated to pray three times a day — שַׁחֲרִית (shacharit), morning; מִנְחָה (minchah), afternoon; and מַעֲרִיב (maariv), evening. Because of the duties of the home and the rearing of children, women were not expected to be at the synagogue at the special assigned times for prayer. This may explain why it became a custom for only men to wear the טַלִּית. There is, however, nothing in Jewish law which prohibits a woman from wearing the טַלִּית.

What do you think? Should both men and women "dress up" for worship by wearing a a טַלִּית? Do you find it meaningful to wear your best clothes to synagogue? Is there a benefit to "dressing up" for special occasions? You may wish to read: "Women Wearing a Talit," *Modern Reform Responsa*, chapter 8, by Rabbi Solomon B. Freehof, HUC Press, Cincinnati, 1971. Discuss some of these questions with friends, the rabbi and cantor, and with adults in your congregation. The differences in opinion might make an interesting debate.

Looking at the Talit

If you look carefully at each of the four corners of the טַלִּית, you will notice a long fringe. It is made in a very special way out of four threads.

The four threads are drawn through a small hole at the corner of the טַלִּית and tied in a double knot. Then one of the threads, called the שַׁמָּשׁ (shamash), or serving thread, is wound around the others seven times and knotted; and then eight times and knotted. Then it is wound another eleven times and tied; and finally another thirteen times and tied.

Why is the long fringe tied in such an elaborate way? Because it is a symbol. A symbol is an object which represents a special meaning. When we look at it, it is supposed to remind us of an idea, or hope, or great truth. For instance, the flag of our nation is a symbol. When we look at it, we are reminded of our country and of our responsibilities as citizens.

The long fringe of the טַלִּית is a symbol. The special way in which it is tied is meant to remind us of an important teaching of Judaism.

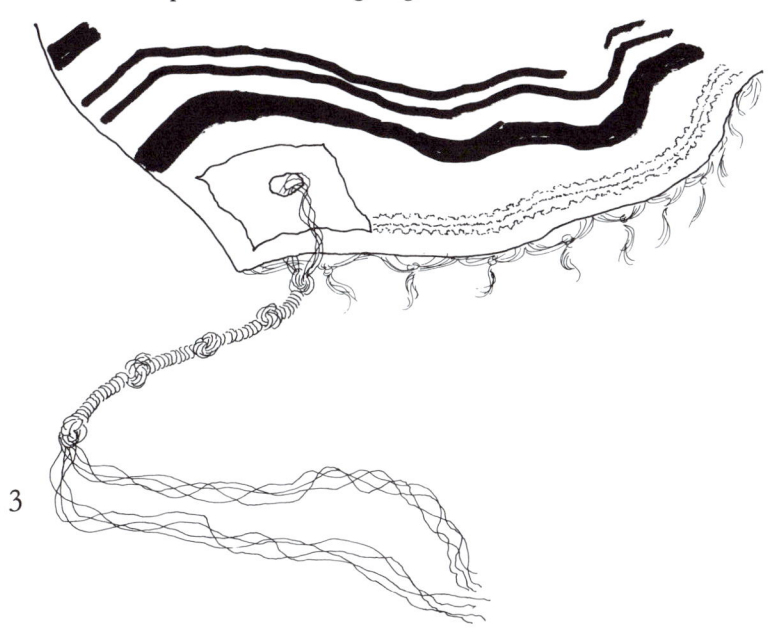

THE MATHEMATICS OF THE FRINGE

A little mathematics will help us understand the symbolic meaning of the long fringe. Look at the illustration and notice the following:

    The first winding equals   7
    The second winding equals 8
    which together equal   15
    In Hebrew letters, 15 could be יה.

The third winding equals 11. In Hebrew letters, 11 could be וה. All together they spell יהוה which means God.

The final winding equals 13. The Hebrew letters אחד also add up to 13, and the word אֶחָד (echad) itself means one.

When totaled together, the windings of the fringes remind us that יהוה אֶחָד, God is One. יהוה אֶחָד forms the last two words of the sentence of the שְׁמַע (Shema).

There is also another insight to be gained from the mathematics of the צִיצִת. The letter צ in Hebrew is equivalent to 90. The letter י is equivalent to 10, and the letter ת to 400. Added together the word צִיצִת has the numerical value in Hebrew of 600. If you add to that the five knots and eight strands of the completed fringe, your total will be 613. According to Jewish tradition, there are 613 מִצְוֹת, commandments, in the Torah.

When we put on the טַלִית, we are not only dressing up for Jewish prayer but we are recalling our people's belief in One God and their commitment to the מִצְוֹת of Jewish tradition.

THE TALIT KATAN

Traditional Jews not only wear the צִיצִית on a talit at times of prayer, they wear them as a special garment at all times!

The garment used for this purpose is called a טַלִית קָטָן (talit katan), small *talit* or אַרְבַּע כַּנְפוֹת (arba kanfot), four corners. It is similar to an undershirt with four corners.

Like the טַלִית, there are fringes on each of the four corners. Usually the fringes are left to hang out so that the wearer may see them and be reminded of the commandments of the Torah and that the God he serves is One.

CREATING NEW PRAYERS— A CONTROVERSY: OLD AND NEW

Should we use prayers written by others or only those we have composed ourselves? Should we use a prayer book which gives us a fixed order for prayer or create our own order of worship each time we wish to pray?

Can a congregation exist without some order of service that it uses each time it comes together for prayer? Does a congregation need its own special fixed prayers, as a nation needs its own special anthems, in order to express feelings of unity and common concern?

Which is better, fixed or spontaneous prayer? *These are not new questions.* The issue of whether prayers should be fixed or spontaneous was hotly debated by the rabbis of the Talmud over two thousand years ago. And the debate was never really resolved. In almost every age the controversy has continued between those who wanted a fixed prayer book and those who preferred newly created prayers.

Today, the debate is as alive as ever. All you have to do is ask a group of people which they prefer, fixed or spontaneous prayer — and the sides will quickly be drawn. Below are some of the arguments on each side of the debate. In other places on the next pages you will find quotations from Jewish sources which record the variety of opinions on the issue. The question before us is how we can resolve the debate within our own congregation.

ARGUMENTS FOR FIXED PRAYER

1.

We are a congregation, and, in order for us to feel a sense of unity with one another, we need to use the same words. The more we share, the closer we will feel.

2.

If we wait until we feel like composing a prayer, we might never pray or we might lose the ability to pray. Prayer demands the discipline of regular practice and the same words if we are to be successful at it.

3.

Not all of us are great poets or writers. It is silly not to make use of the outstanding poetry and prayers of our tradition that have been tested by time and many generations. They can express our feelings better than we ourselves can.

4.

When we use prayers composed by Jews throughout our history, we identify ourselves with the traditions and generations of our people. When we pray with the same prayers used by Jews throughout the world, we feel at one with our people no matter where they are. Fixed prayer insures the unity of the Jewish people.

5.

Often when an individual composes a prayer, it is self-centered and expresses only his own selfish concerns. Fixed Jewish prayer is concerned with the welfare of the community and has been carefully written so as to avoid selfish, fleeting needs.

6.

The rabbis teach us that a person should not be hasty to utter a word before God. That temptation is eliminated by fixed prayer. Spontaneous prayer is often hastily and carelessly composed. Prayer ought to be written with concentration by individuals possessing great skill. Fixed prayer fulfills this requirement.

> **Two Thoughts**
>
> Change not the fixed form in which the sages wrote the prayers.
>
> (Talmud)
>
> Be not rash with your mouth, and let your heart not be hasty to utter a word before God.
>
> (Ecclesiastes 5:1)

7.

Spontaneous prayer causes confusion among the worshipers. The talmudic sage, Rabbi Zeira, once said: "Everytime I added new words to my prayers, I became confused and lost my place." Such confusion takes away from the beauty and meaning of the prayer experience. A fixed order of worship solves this problem.

8.

Beautiful prayers, like great poetry, never lose their meaning through repetition. The more we read them with open minds and hearts, the more meanings we can discover. The cure for dull prayer experiences is in us, not in the creation of new prayers.

ARGUMENTS FOR SPONTANEOUS PRAYER

1.

While the fixed prayers may be beautiful, after you have said them over and over again, they become dull, repetitive, and lose their meaning. The rabbis recognized this and, in the Mishnah, they tell us: "Do not let your prayers be a matter of fixed routine but rather heartfelt expressions."

2.

Spontaneous prayer allows us to express our feelings, hopes, and concerns. If we are bound by a fixed text, we are prevented from making our worship as personally meaningful as it should be. The Bratzlaver Rebbe, a leading teacher of Chasidism, once said to his students:

"You must feel your words of prayer in all your bones, in all your limbs, and in all your nerves." When we use our own prayers we feel deeply about that for which we are praying.

3.

We are not machines and we can't be programed to be in the same mood as everyone else at the same time. Spontaneous prayer allows us the freedom to express our true feelings in the moment we pray.

4.

We should not forget that the fixed prayers of tradition were once spontaneous expressions of individuals and their communities. Throughout Jewish history, Jews have been composing new prayers and adding them to the prayer book. We need to continue that creative process for it has helped keep Jewish prayer meaningful, and even added to the survival of Judaism.

5.

In every generation our people has faced new problems and challenges. These should be expressed in our prayers. Obviously, if we are bound to a fixed text or style of prayer, we cannot include contemporary issues or forms in our worship.

CREATING NEW PRAYERS

The controversy over fixed and spontaneous prayer continues in our own day. There are those who oppose any changes either in the order of Jewish worship or in any of the traditional prayers. Others favor innovation and the creation of new prayers and worship experiences. *Bechol Levavcha* is an attempt at a compromise between the two positions. It combines the order and prayers of our tradition with new prayers and offers us the opportunity to create our own expressions.

Throughout Bechol Levavcha you will find themes entitled "Creating with Kavanah". Kavanah (כַּוָנָה) means inner feeling, devotion, concentration. Within the box will be a list of the themes of the prayers in that section.

You will also find the themes explained in the Commentary passages. You may use those themes for the creation of your own prayers.

You should first master the traditional prayer and its meaning. Then, use some of the other prayers in the section. Afterwards, with an understanding of the traditional prayer, you will be ready to create your own original expression.

At the time of congregational worship you can substitute the creative prayers for the traditional ones.

HOW DO WE CREATE OUR OWN PRAYERS?

Just as no one has ever given a successful recipe for writing beautiful poetry, no one has ever produced an easy recipe for creating meaningful and beautiful prayer. The challenge of writing outstanding literature is both exciting and demanding. It requires thoughtful consideration, skill, patience, discipline, and an understanding of the themes and ideas we want to express.

While Jewish tradition does not provide us with a simple method of how to create our own prayers, it does offer us some very useful guidelines. These guidelines give us direction and can serve as a check and balance against which we judge and evaluate our creative prayers.

Rabbinic Opinions

Only that person's prayer is answered who lifts his hands with his heart in them.
(Taanit 8a)

Rabbi Eliezer said: If a person prays only according to the exact fixed prayer and adds nothing from his own mind, his prayer is not considered proper.
(Berachot 28a)

Rabbi Abahu would add a new prayer to his worship every day.
Rabbi Aha in the name of Rabbi Jose said: It is necessary to add new words to the fixed prayers each time they are recited.
(Berachot 4a)

> **A Bouquet of Blessings**
>
> Every word of your prayer should be like a rose which you pick from its bush. You continue to gather the roses until you have formed a bouquet and can offer it as a beautiful blessing to God.
>
> (The Bratzlaver Rebbe)

GUIDELINES FOR CREATIVE PRAYER

LET YOUR WORDS BE FEW

Rabbi Meir said: "Let a person's words before God always be few." (Berachot 61a) A prayer does not have to be lengthy. It can be brief and still be beautiful. After you have written your first draft, study it and ask yourself which words might be eliminated in order to make the prayer easier to understand.

DON'T PRAY FOR THE IMPOSSIBLE

The rabbis teach us that "to pray for the impossible is disgraceful." (Tosefta Berachot 7) The chasidic rabbi, Leib Sassover, explained this guideline to his students by telling them: "It is not permissible to ask God to change the laws of nature to suit your desires."

DO NOT SEPARATE YOURSELF FROM THE COMMUNITY

We are members of many communities. Some are more immediate and important to us than others. Our prayers ought to reflect our responsibilities and relationships to our families, the Jewish people, our nation, and all humanity. The talmudic rabbis taught that "all Israel is responsible for one another." By this they meant to teach that, whenever another Jew is in danger or in need of help, our duty is to do all we can. Jewish prayer stresses our role in seeking peace and security for the people of Israel and for all the world. The prayers we compose should remind us of our responsibilities as human beings and inspire us to actions of love, charity, helpfulness, concern, and peace.

JUDGING OURSELVES AND OUR SOCIETY

The Hebrew word לְהִתְפַּלֵל (lehitpalel), to pray, can mean "to judge oneself." One of the important purposes of prayer is to help us understand and improve ourselves and our society. We accomplish this purpose when our prayers remind us of the ideals and values of our tradition and challenge us to evaluate ourselves ethically. The Koretzer Rebbe taught: "If you feel no sense of improvement after you have worshiped, then your prayer was in vain." The prayers we create should encourage us toward the ethical examination of ourselves and the society in which we live.

DON'T PRAY FOR THE HURT OF OTHERS

We are taught: "It is forbidden to ask God to send death to the wicked." (Zohar Hadash 105) Our prayers may express our anger or our feelings of not being loved or appreciated. We may even want to express our desire not to share the company of those who have caused us or others pain. To ask God, however, to bring pain or destruction to others, even though they may be our enemies, is forbidden by Jewish tradition. We are taught to have sympathy and respect for all people as children of God.

GIVE THANKS

Perhaps the earliest form of prayer was thanksgiving. The Psalmist says: "It is good to give thanks unto the Lord." (Psalms 92:2) Life is a sacred and wonderful gift from God. Our prayers should reflect our sensitivity to everything from the drop of rain to the miracle of growth, from the natural laws which make life possible to the human mind which is able to explore the universe and its mysteries.

MAKE MUSIC AND DANCE BEFORE THE LORD

Words are not the only form of prayer in Judaism. During Temple times all forms of musical instruments were used to enhance worship. Dance and song were also an important part of the Temple service. Sometimes an idea, a hope, or a feeling can be better expressed through music or dance than through words. This is also true of art, slides, or films. Often a good picture will highlight an idea and help people understand something in a new way. Creating our own prayers, then, can include the forms of dance, instrumental music, song, and the use of art and film.

EMPHASIZE SHARING

Have you ever wondered why most Jewish prayers are written in the plural? ("*Our* God, and God of *our* fathers"; "*We* give thanks"; "Let *all* bless You.")

Jewish worship is a community experience which is meant to include and involve everyone who wishes to participate. When you are creating a prayer, you may want to ask yourself how others in the congregation will be involved in this prayer.

There are several ways to include the congregation in worship. One is the *responsive reading*, where the leader reads a line and the congregation answers. Another is the *antiphonal reading*, where one side of the congregation reads and then the other responds. Perhaps the most common form of involvement is the *congregational prayer*, where everyone reads together. A final form, and perhaps the most loved, is *congregational singing*.

This emphasis upon sharing is not meant to exclude prayers read by one person. At times we share best when listening thoughtfully to another person's feelings. The most successful worship is usually a balanced combination of individual and group participation.

PREPARATIONS FOR PRAYER

The Tanzer Rebbe was asked by a follower: "What do you do in order to prepare for prayer?" The rebbe replied: "I pray that I may be able to pray properly!"

The pious of old used to wait an hour before praying in order to concentrate their thoughts on God. (Berachot 5:1)

Throughout the centuries Jews have created a variety of meditations which are meant to aid us in preparing for prayer. These have been collected and placed into a section at the beginning of the prayer book called פְּסוּקֵי דְזִמְרָה (*Pesuke Dezimrah*), Verses of Song.

The פְּסוּקֵי דְזִמְרָה include Psalms 100, 145–150, and many prayers written by Jewish poets over the last two thousand years. On the Sabbath and festivals, Psalms 19, 34, 90, 91, 135, 136, 33, 92, and 93 are added in this order to this section of preparations for prayer.

In the following pages, you will find a selection of meditations from the פְּסוּקֵי דְזִמְרָה. Use some of them, or their themes, in the creation of your own service.

Section One

פְּסוּקֵי דְזִמְרָה

BENEDICTIONS OF PRAISE

Pesuke Dezimrah

    a. Benedictions of Praise *10*
    b. Praised Be the One *13*
    c. The Soul Which You Have Given *15*
    d. Of Courage and Truthfulness *16*
    e. Psalm 100 *18*
    f. Psalm 135 *18*
    g. The Soul of Everything That Lives *20*

Benedictions of Praise

בָּרוּךְ אַתָּה, יְיָ אֱלֹהֵינוּ, מֶלֶךְ הָעוֹלָם, שֶׁעָשַׂנִי בְּצַלְמוֹ.

Praised be You, O Lord our God, Ruler of the universe, who has created me in Your image.

בָּרוּךְ אַתָּה, יְיָ אֱלֹהֵינוּ, מֶלֶךְ הָעוֹלָם, שֶׁעָשַׂנִי בֶּן חוֹרִין.

Praised be You, O Lord our God, Ruler of the universe, who has made me free.

בָּרוּךְ אַתָּה, יְיָ אֱלֹהֵינוּ, מֶלֶךְ הָעוֹלָם, שֶׁעָשַׂנִי יִשְׂרָאֵל.

Praised be You, O Lord our God, Ruler of the universe, who has made me a Jew.

בָּרוּךְ אַתָּה, יְיָ אֱלֹהֵינוּ, מֶלֶךְ הָעוֹלָם, פּוֹקֵחַ עִוְרִים.

Praised be You, O Lord our God, Ruler of the universe, who opens the eyes of the blind.

בָּרוּךְ אַתָּה, יְיָ אֱלֹהֵינוּ, מֶלֶךְ הָעוֹלָם, מַלְבִּישׁ עֲרֻמִּים.

Praised be You, O Lord our God, Ruler of the universe, who provides clothes for the needy.

בָּרוּךְ אַתָּה, יְיָ אֱלֹהֵינוּ, מֶלֶךְ הָעוֹלָם, הַנּוֹתֵן לַיָּעֵף כֹּחַ.

Praised be You, O Lord our God, Ruler of the universe, who gives strength to the weak.

בָּרוּךְ אַתָּה, יְיָ אֱלֹהֵינוּ, מֶלֶךְ הָעוֹלָם, אֲשֶׁר הֵכִין מִצְעֲדֵי גָבֶר.

Praised be You, O Lord our God, Ruler of the universe, who guides the steps of human beings.

Commentary

When the Israeli author, Shmuel Y. Agnon, was told that he had been awarded the Nobel Prize for literature, he recited the prayer for hearing good news. And, when he arrived in Stockholm to receive the Nobel Prize from the king of Sweden, Agnon recited the blessing appropriate for that occasion. In both instances, the form of the prayer recited by Agnon is known in Jewish tradition as the בְּרָכָה (berachah), benediction of praise.

Throughout the centuries Jews have developed and used בְּרָכוֹת (berachot), benedictions of praise, for almost every occasion in life. Why? Why should a religious Jew, according to the talmudic sage, Rabbi Meir, say at least 100 בְּרָכוֹת each day? What difference do you think it would make if you said a prayer of thanks for every experience you had during the course of one day?

Try It Out for One Day! Make a list of your experiences and, if you can, a record of what you said by way of thanks. After you have composed your list, ask yourself what effect the whole experience has had upon you. Then share it with the members of your study group.

What Is a בְּרָכָה?

Prayer is meant to heighten our sensitivity to all the experiences in life. The word בְּרָכָה is derived from the Hebrew ברך which means to "bend the knee." "Bending the knee" is the ancient Jewish way of showing respect and gratitude to God.

The religious Jew sees God in every aspect of existence. God is in the beauty of the sunset, in the morning dawn, in the love we feel for another person, in the desire we have to provide for the poor, in the help we experience in times of trouble, in the gratefulness we sense in satisfying our hunger, and in our struggles to overcome evil and suffering. The בְּרָכָה is a means through which Jews give thanks and praise to God and remind themselves that life is a sacred opportunity.

Three Kinds of בְּרָכוֹת

According to Moses Maimonides (1135–1204), one of the greatest of all Jewish scholars, there are three kinds of בְּרָכוֹת.

a. First, there are the בִּרְכוֹת הַנֶהֱנִין (*birchot hanehenin*). These are benedictions of praise in gratitude for the pleasures we derive from eating, drinking, or smelling a pleasant odor. An example of this kind of בְּרָכָה would be the blessing a Jew recites before eating.

בָּרוּךְ אַתָּה, יְיָ אֱלֹהֵינוּ, מֶלֶךְ הָעוֹלָם, הַמּוֹצִיא לֶחֶם מִן הָאָרֶץ.

Praised be You, O Lord our God, Ruler of the universe, who brings forth bread from the earth.

b. Second, there are the בִּרְכוֹת הַמִצְווֹת (*birchot hamitzvot*). These are benedictions of praise recited at the time of doing *mitzvot* which are commanded by the Torah or tradition. Notice that this kind of בְּרָכָה includes the words אֲשֶׁר קִדְּשָׁנוּ בְּמִצְווֹתָיו וְצִוָּנוּ, "who had made us holy with *mitzvot* and commanded us...." An example of a benediction recited at the time of performing a *mitzvah* would be the בְּרָכָה made at the time of placing a *mezuzah* on the door post.

בָּרוּךְ אַתָּה, יְיָ אֱלֹהֵינוּ, מֶלֶךְ הָעוֹלָם, אֲשֶׁר קִדְּשָׁנוּ בְּמִצְווֹתָיו וְצִוָּנוּ לִקְבּוֹעַ מְזוּזָה.

Praised be You, O Lord our God, Ruler of the universe, who has made us holy with *mitzvot* and commanded us to attach the *mezuzah*.

c. Finally, there are the בִּרְכוֹת הַפְּרָטִיוֹת (*birchot hapratiyot*). These are benedictions of praise recited at personal or private occasions. These may be at times of joy, such as when Agnon received the Nobel Prize. And they may also be said at a moment of sadness as an expression of affirmation and love of God. For instance, at the time a Jew hears of the death of a loved one, he or she says:

בָּרוּךְ אַתָּה, יְיָ אֱלֹהֵינוּ, מֶלֶךְ הָעוֹלָם, דַּיַּן הָאֱמֶת.

Praised be You, O Lord our God, Ruler of the universe, Judge of truth.

The בְּרָכָה and Jewish Prayer

Many of the prayers in the prayer book begin or end with the Hebrew words בָּרוּךְ אַתָּה יְיָ. Some historians of Jewish prayer believe that this formula of the בְּרָכָה was developed by the Men of the Great Assembly during the time of Ezra and Nehemiah (421 B.C.E.). The בְּרָכָה formula, however, may be much older than that.

The Hebrew Bible reports that when King David prayed before the Israelites he used the words בָּרוּךְ אַתָּה יְיָ, "Praised be You...." (I Chronicles 29:10) It could be, then, that this form of the בְּרָכָה is one of the oldest Jewish formulas of prayer.

Commenting on the formula of the בְּרָכָה, Rabbi David ben Joseph once said: "We begin the בְּרָכָה with the words בָּרוּךְ אַתָּה יְיָ אֱלֹהֵינוּ, 'Praised be You, O Lord our God,' in order to remind ourselves that the God we worship is *our God* and the *God of all people*. Then we say מֶלֶךְ הָעוֹלָם, '*Ruler of the universe*,' to remember that *our God* is also the *Power which sustains all of nature*."

Praised Be the One and Praised Be Them That Praise the Lord

בָּרוּךְ שֶׁאָמַר וְהָיָה הָעוֹלָם.

Praised be the One who spoke, and the world was created.

בָּרוּךְ הוּא.

Praised be the Lord.

בָּרוּךְ עוֹשֶׂה בְרֵאשִׁית.

Praised be the Source of creation.

בָּרוּךְ אוֹמֵר וְעוֹשֶׂה.

Praised be the One who speaks and does.

בָּרוּךְ גּוֹזֵר וּמְקַיֵּם.

Praised be the One who announces and fulfills.

בָּרוּךְ מְרַחֵם עַל הָאָרֶץ.

Praised be the One who has compassion for all the earth.

בָּרוּךְ מְרַחֵם עַל הַבְּרִיּוֹת.

Praised be the One who has compassion for all human beings.

בָּרוּךְ מְשַׁלֵּם שָׂכָר טוֹב לִירֵאָיו.

Praised be the One who rewards the goodness of those who have faith.

בָּרוּךְ חַי לָעַד וְקַיָּם לָנֶצַח.

Praised be the One whose life giving power is for ever.

בָּרוּךְ פּוֹדֶה וּמַצִּיל.

Praised be the One who redeems and frees.

בָּרוּךְ שְׁמוֹ.

Praised be the Lord's name.

Commentary

The בָּרוּךְ שֶׁאָמַר (*Baruch She'amar*) was formulated sometime during the ninth century. It became so popular as a praise of God that it was placed at the very beginning of the פְּסוּקֵי דְזִמְרָה section.

THE CREATOR

Some prayers not only give thanks and praise to God, they also help us understand what Jewish poets believed about God. In the בָּרוּךְ שֶׁאָמַר, we find the outlines of a description of God.

The author begins his prayer by praising God as the Creator of the universe. His words recall the first chapters of the Torah where we are told about the creation of the world. The Torah and our prayers do not mean to give us a scientific explanation of creation. Those who wrote the first chapters of the Torah and the poet who composed the בָּרוּךְ שֶׁאָמַר sought to help us understand the wonder of the world and God's creative power in making possible all that we see and experience.

Compare the first five sentences of בָּרוּךְ שֶׁאָמַר with the following from the first chapter of Genesis.

> God said: "Let there be light." And there was light.
> God said: "Let the earth put forth grass and fruit-bearing trees." And it was so.
> God said: "Let the earth bring forth living creatures." And it was so.
> God said: "Let us make man." And it was so.

Why do you think that the authors of Genesis and the בָּרוּךְ שֶׁאָמַר thought of God as being able to create by "speaking" or "announcing"? Can a person "create" with speech? Rabbi Asher ben Yechiel once said to his students: "Do not allow an unworthy coin to go forth from your lips — weigh and judge carefully all your words." What do you think he meant?

THE MERCIFUL ONE

The second part of the בָּרוּךְ שֶׁאָמַר speaks of God's power of compassion. The Hebrew word for compassion is רַחֲמִים (rachamim). It is derived from the Hebrew root רחם which can mean love, tenderness, and concern. רֶחֶם can also mean womb, the place in the mother's body in which the child is nurtured before its birth. In Jewish tradition, God is thought of as הָרַחֲמָן (Harachaman), "the Merciful One" who constantly sustains and cares for the universe.

Do we have evidence that God really "sustains and cares" for the world or human beings? What about the development of our bodies, or the order a scientist discovers in our universe, or the process of growth we find in nature? What about the way in which a child is nurtured in the womb of its mother?

A CHALLENGE

Jewish tradition challenges us to imitate God. The Torah tells us that God is "merciful and gracious, long-suffering, and abundant in goodness and truth." (Exodus 34:6) The task of the Jew is to strive to incorporate all of these ethical traits into his or her behavior.

During the lifetime of the prophet Micah (about the eighth century B.C.E.), men and women, especially the comfortable, failed to live up to the ethical ideals of Judaism. They treated the poor with contempt, and they disregarded the rights of widows, orphans, and the impoverished sick. One day Micah went to the Temple and angrily protested against the corruption and evil he saw all about him.

He asked the people questions that they would have preferred not to hear. And he told them what God really wanted from them.

> Hear this, I pray you,
> You heads of the house of Jacob,
> And rulers of the house of Israel,
> You who hate justice and pervert all that is right....
> It has been told you, O man, what is good,
> And what the Lord requires of you:
> Only to do justice, and to love mercy, and to walk humbly with your God.
>
> (Micah 3:9; 6:8)

What has Micah's statement to do with the בָּרוּךְ שֶׁאָמַר prayer?

How can a person imitate God? When a person works to free a captive or someone who is being persecuted by others, how is he imitating God? Turn to Exodus 34:6, and discuss with your congregation or group some of the ways we can imitate the attributes of God in our relationships with one another, our parents, and with our teachers.

What do you think the rabbi meant when he said: "God is really God when human beings decorate themselves with good deeds"?

The Soul Which You Have Given

אֱלֹהַי, נְשָׁמָה שֶׁנָּתַתָּ בִּי טְהוֹרָה הִיא.

My God, the soul which You have given me is pure.

אַתָּה בְרָאתָהּ, אַתָּה יְצַרְתָּהּ, אַתָּה נְפַחְתָּהּ בִּי.

You created, formed, and breathed it into me.

מוֹדֶה אֲנִי לְפָנֶיךָ, יְיָ אֱלֹהַי וֵאלֹהֵי אֲבוֹתַי, רִבּוֹן כָּל הַמַּעֲשִׂים, אֲדוֹן כָּל הַנְּשָׁמוֹת.

I am grateful before You, O Lord my God, and God of my ancestors — the Lord of all creation and all souls.

Commentary

This prayer was composed by the talmudic rabbis (Berachot 60b), and it is a part of the daily morning service.

What do we mean by נְשָׁמָה (*neshamah*), soul?

The נְשָׁמָה is a person's uniqueness. It is comprised of our character, our personality, and our spiritual qualities. It is all of our feelings, attitudes, and expressions. Just as each of us has a thumbprint unlike any other in the world, so too each of us possesses a soul unlike any other in the world.

Judaism teaches that God gives each person a נְשָׁמָה טְהוֹרָה (*neshamah tehorah*), pure soul, at the time of birth. Jews do not believe that human beings are born in sin or evil. The soul of every person can be good or evil depending upon the way he chooses to live. The task of every person is to develop his talents and his sense of right and wrong so that his soul may become a beautiful expression of God's creation.

Creating with Kavanah

Themes:

a. The uniqueness of each human being.
b. The variety of abilities and feelings we possess.
c. The responsibility we have to develop the content and shape of our souls.
d. The wonder of our souls being a part of God — a gift from the Source of all souls.

Rabbi Abraham Neuman once remarked: "Man's supreme and final battles are to be fought out in his soul." What do you think he meant by his observation?

Of Courage and Truthfulness

Leader

לְעוֹלָם יְהֵא אָדָם יְרֵא שָׁמַיִם בַּסֵּתֶר וּבַגָּלוּי, וּמוֹדֶה עַל הָאֱמֶת, וְדוֹבֵר אֱמֶת בִּלְבָבוֹ.

A person should always serve and respect God in secret or in public by acting honestly and speaking truthfully.

Everyone

לְפִיכָךְ אֲנַחְנוּ חַיָּבִים לְהוֹדוֹת לָךְ, וּלְשַׁבֵּחֲךָ, וּלְפָאֶרְךָ. אַשְׁרֵינוּ, מַה טוֹב חֶלְקֵנוּ, וּמַה נָּעִים גּוֹרָלֵנוּ, וּמַה יָּפָה יְרֻשָּׁתֵנוּ. אַשְׁרֵינוּ שֶׁאֲנַחְנוּ מַשְׁכִּימִים וּמַעֲרִיבִים, עֶרֶב וָבֹקֶר, וְאוֹמְרִים פַּעֲמַיִם בְּכָל יוֹם:

It is our duty to thank, bless, and praise You, O Lord, for we are fortunate to be Jews. How beautiful and pleasant is our heritage and tradition. Happy are we who, each morning and evening, are able to proclaim:

שְׁמַע יִשְׂרָאֵל, יְיָ אֱלֹהֵינוּ, יְיָ אֶחָד.

בָּרוּךְ שֵׁם כְּבוֹד מַלְכוּתוֹ לְעוֹלָם וָעֶד.

Hear, O Israel, the Lord our God, the Lord is One.
Praised be the name of God, whose glory is for ever and ever.

Commentary

Rabbi Judah ha-Nasi (135–220 C.E.) was the editor of the first great collection of Jewish law called the Mishnah. He taught that a person should strive for the truth in private and in public — alone and with others. And he knew that the pursuit of truth was not always the easiest path to take.

Being honest with oneself is a challenge. It means recognizing faults and being ready to accept responsibility for one's actions, choices, and words.

But being truthful with oneself can mean something else as well. Often we find ourselves put into situations where we are tempted to conform to the opinions or behavior of others. Rather than doing what we may believe best for ourselves, we find that we are imitating someone else.

The founder of modern Zionism, Theodor Herzl, once wrote: "The greatest happiness is to be that which one is." What do you think he meant by that observation?

Fortunate to Be Jews

Many of our prayers are not only beautiful expressions of faith, they also reflect the history of the times in which they were written. The paragraph of our prayer which begins with "It is our duty..." was composed while Jews were living under the harsh rule of the Persian King, Yazdergerd II, in about 452–6 C.E.

Yazdergerd II sought to destroy Judaism. He forbade worship services in the synagogue and sent spies to report on the activities of Jews. He wanted to prevent Jews from reciting the *Shema* since it proclaimed the belief in one God while the Persians, who were Zoroastrians, believed in two gods — the god of good and the god of evil.

Rather than give in, and conform to Yazdergerd II, Jews met secretly for their services. They recalled the teaching of Rabbi Judah ha-Nasi and added to it the prayer "It is our duty...." Then, they recited the *Shema*.

This prayer became so popular as a prayer of defiance and courage that, even after the persecution had ceased, Jews included it in the פְּסוּקֵי דְזִמְרָה section.

Divide your group into (a) Jews living under Yazdergerd II; (b) Jews living under Hitler in 1939; (c) Jews living as Marranos in Spain; and (d) Jews living in Russia today. Have each group compose a prayer to be recited before the שְׁמַע, as did the Jews of Yazdergerd's time. Then compare the prayers and discuss their differences, similarities, and how they reflect the problems which the various Jewish groups faced.

Thoughts

You cannot find peace anywhere save in yourself.
(Simchah Bunam)

Happiness derived from falsehood, injustice, or lust is built on sand.
(Moses Maimonides)

Peace without truth is a false peace.
(Mendel of Kotzk)

Only when we respect ourselves as Jews, can we win the respect of others.
(Albert Einstein)

Psalm 100

הָרִיעוּ לַיְיָ כָּל הָאָרֶץ. עִבְדוּ אֶת יְיָ בְּשִׂמְחָה. בֹּאוּ לְפָנָיו בִּרְנָנָה.

Shout joyfully unto the Lord all the earth. Serve the Lord in gladness. Come before the Lord in happiness.

דְעוּ כִּי יְיָ הוּא אֱלֹהִים. הוּא עָשָׂנוּ, וְלוֹ אֲנַחְנוּ, עַמּוֹ וְצֹאן מַרְעִיתוֹ.

Know that God is the Lord. God created us. We are God's people, the sheep of the Lord's pasture.

בֹּאוּ שְׁעָרָיו בְּתוֹדָה, חֲצֵרֹתָיו בִּתְהִלָּה. הוֹדוּ לוֹ, בָּרְכוּ שְׁמוֹ. כִּי טוֹב יְיָ, לְעוֹלָם חַסְדּוֹ, וְעַד דֹּר וָדֹר אֱמוּנָתוֹ.

Come into God's gates with thanksgiving, and into the Lord's courts with praise. Thank the Lord. Bless God's name. For the Lord is good. God's mercy is for ever. God's faithfulness is to all generations.

Psalm 135

הַלְלוּיָהּ. הַלְלוּ אֶת שֵׁם יְהוָה.

Praise the Lord. Praise the name of the Lord.

הַלְלוּ עַבְדֵי יְהוָה שֶׁעוֹמְדִים בְּבֵית יְהוָה.

Praise the Lord all servants of the Lord who are standing in the house of our God.

הַלְלוּ יָהּ, כִּי טוֹב יְהוָה. זַמְּרוּ לִשְׁמוֹ כִּי נָעִים.

Praise the Lord, for the Lord is good. Sing of God's name for it is pleasant.

כִּי יַעֲקֹב בָּחַר לוֹ יָהּ, יִשְׂרָאֵל לִסְגֻלָּתוֹ.

The Lord has chosen Jacob and made Israel a special treasure.

Commentary

The Book of Psalms, סֵפֶר תְּהִלִים (*Sefer Tehilim*), is a collection of 150 prayers. Many of the psalms were sung or recited while the Temple in Jerusalem was still in existence. When the Temple was destroyed by the Romans (70 C.E.), the rabbis incorporated many of the psalms into the service of the synagogue.

The names of the authors of the psalms are not known. Some of them begin with the words "A Psalm of David," as if to indicate that they were written by King David. We know, however, that they were not all composed by David, but, perhaps, given his name by authors who wanted to dedicate their poems to him, or by editors who believed that David might have written the psalms.

Throughout the ages, the Book of Psalms has been considered among mankind's greatest literature. The hopes, faith, and feelings expressed in the psalms have not only shaped Jewish prayer but they have also contributed to the development of Christian worship.

Psalm 100

In Psalm 100, the poet calls upon the whole earth, all that lives, to thank and praise God. For him, prayer is a joyful experience. He appreciates life and all the opportunities for happiness it offers.

He also recognizes that it is only human beings who can appreciate God's relationship to nature and express thanksgiving. No other form of life, that we know of, is capable of such understanding or expression.

What do you think the poet meant by his words "His faithfulness is to all generations"? How does God's power extend to all generations?

How would you compare the ideas expressed in "Other Thoughts" to Psalm 100?

Psalm 135

In Psalm 135 the poet calls upon all who are standing in the house of God to join him in praising the Lord. By house of God, he meant the Temple in Jerusalem. Today when we use this psalm, we mean any place where people have gathered for prayer.

A Special People?

The poet refers to the Jewish people as a "chosen people" or a "special treasure." Does this mean that he believed that Jews were "better" or more favored by God than other people? Not at all!

When we speak of Jews as being "chosen" or "special," we have in mind our people's task to fulfill the commandments of the Torah and to help all people advance toward a day of justice and peace. To be "chosen" means to be selected for responsibilities — not for privileges!

Read the following Bible sections: Amos 5:4–15; Isaiah 42:1–6; and Deuteronomy 30:1–20. What do they tell us about the task of the Jewish people? For what are Jews "chosen"? Your study group might wish to discuss how your congregation should be fulfilling some of the tasks of the Jewish people. You may even wish to develop some projects of your own.

> **Other Thoughts**
>
> **As a house implies a builder, a dress a weaver, a door a carpenter, so the world proclaims God as its creator.**
> (Rabbi Akiva)
>
> **God's wisdom and power in creating an ant or bee is no less than in the making of the sun and its sphere.**
> (Judah ha-Levi)
>
> **In goodness God renews each day the work of creation.**
> (Yotzer prayer)

The Soul of Everything That Lives

נִשְׁמַת כָּל חַי תְּבָרֵךְ אֶת שִׁמְךָ, יְיָ אֱלֹהֵינוּ, וְרוּחַ כָּל בָּשָׂר תְּפָאֵר וּתְרוֹמֵם זִכְרְךָ, מַלְכֵּנוּ, תָּמִיד.

The soul of everything that lives shall praise Your name, O God. The spirit of every human being shall give You glory always.

אִלּוּ פִינוּ מָלֵא שִׁירָה כַּיָּם, וּלְשׁוֹנֵנוּ רִנָּה כַּהֲמוֹן גַּלָּיו, אֵין אֲנַחְנוּ מַסְפִּיקִים לְהוֹדוֹת לְךָ, יְיָ אֱלֹהֵינוּ.

Even if our mouths were as filled with song as the sea is filled with water, and even if our tongues could sing like the waves of the ocean roar, we would still be unable to thank You, O Lord our God, for all of the wonders and blessings of life.

עַל כֵּן, אֵבָרִים שֶׁפִּלַּגְתָּ בָּנוּ, וְרוּחַ וּנְשָׁמָה שֶׁנָּפַחְתָּ בְּאַפֵּינוּ, וְלָשׁוֹן אֲשֶׁר שַׂמְתָּ בְּפִינוּ, הֵן הֵם יוֹדוּ וִיבָרְכוּ אֶת שִׁמְךָ, מַלְכֵּנוּ.

Therefore, we will strive to give You thanks for the gifts You have given to us. We will praise You with clapping hands and dancing feet, with songs and words of our mouths, and with all our souls.

Commentary

This meditation is known as the נִשְׁמַת (*Nishmat*). It was written during Maccabean times and was recited as a part of the Temple service. The נִשְׁמַת was a favorite prayer of the rabbis who composed the Passover Haggadah. They recommended it as the concluding prayer for the seder.

It is difficult, if not impossible, to thank God for all the gifts of life!

Why is this so? Perhaps, because there are so many gifts of God that no list could contain all of them. For that reason the author of the נִשְׁמַת reminds us that, while we cannot name all of the things God does for us, we can give thanks for what we experience and for what we have.

THE SPIRIT OF EVERY HUMAN BEING

The נִשְׁמַת prayer speaks of every human being giving glory to God. Jewish tradition considers each person a unique reflection of God. The Torah teaches that man and woman were created in the image of God. (Genesis 1:27) The rabbis taught that just as an artist's painting is a reflection of his interests and abilities so, too, each human being is a representation of God's power, love, and creativity. This appreciation of each person's relationship with God has led to important conclusions about how human beings should treat one another.

> **Praise God for every drop of rain... for in it are all the waters of the earth!**

For instance, Rabbi Nehemiah taught that "God considers every human being equal in value to all of creation." (Avot deRabbi Natan, 31) In other words, the life of each person should be treated as if the future of the world depended upon it. How would you apply Rabbi Nehemiah's observation to the treatment of the elderly, the poor, the criminal, and those who may be considered enemies? What changes would we need to make in society in order to treat "every human being equal in value to all of creation"?

Once you have discussed the meaning of "The Soul of Everything That Lives," you may wish to create a prayer which incorporates your own ideas and feelings about how we should be treating others as precious images of God. In your prayer, try to contrast the ways you see people treated with the ways you believe they ought to be treated.

Compare the following psalm with the נִשְׁמַת. *What do both prayers have in common? Where do they differ?*

O Lord our God,
How glorious is Your name in all the earth!
When I behold Your heavens, the work of Your fingers,
The moon and the stars, which You have established;
What is man, that You are mindful of him?
And the son of man, that You think of him?
Yet You have made him little lower than Divine,
And have crowned him with glory and honor.
You have made him to have dominion over the works of Your hands;
And put all things under his feet.
O Lord, our God,
How glorious is Your name in all the earth!

(Psalms 8:2, 4–10)

Creating with Kavanah

Themes:
a. We praise God with our abilities.
b. It is impossible to thank God for all the gifts of life.
c. Every human being is a precious part of creation.

Section Two

שְׁמַע

THE SHEMA

a. Barechu: The Call to Worship *24*
b. Yotzer: Former of Light *26*
c. Ahavah Rabbah: With Great Love *30*
d. Shema: Hear, O Israel *37*
e. Veahavta: You Shall Love the Lord *41*
f. Geulah: Redemption *46*

Barechu: The Call to Worship

בָּרְכוּ אֶת יְיָ הַמְבֹרָךְ.

Praise the Lord, to whom all praise is due.

בָּרוּךְ יְיָ הַמְבֹרָךְ לְעוֹלָם וָעֶד.

Praised be the Lord to whom all praise is due for ever and ever.

Commentary

With the בָּרְכוּ (*Barechu*), we begin a new section of our service called the שְׁמַע (*Shema*). This section includes the יוֹצֵר (*Yotzer*), Creator; the אַהֲבָה רַבָּה (*Ahavah Rabbah*), Great Love; the שְׁמַע; the וְאָהַבְתָּ (*Veahavta*), You Shall Love; and the גְאוּלָה (*Geulah*), Redemption.

ORIGINS OF THE בָּרְכוּ

The בָּרְכוּ is a very ancient Jewish call to worship. We are told that when the Jewish people returned from Babylonian exile, sometime around 421 B.C.E., their leaders, Ezra and Nehemiah, called them together to hear the Torah and to pledge themselves to uphold it. At that time, the people were called to prayer with these words:

קוּמוּ בָּרְכוּ אֶת יְהוָה אֱלֹהֵיכֶם מִן הָעוֹלָם עַד הָעוֹלָם.

Stand and bless the Lord your God who is forever and ever.

וִיבָרְכוּ שֵׁם כְּבֹדֶךָ וּמְרוֹמַם עַל כָּל בְּרָכָה וּתְהִלָּה.

And say: Praised be Your glorious Name, and may it be exalted by every blessing and praise.
(Nehemiah 9:5)

Compare these words found in Nehemiah 9:5 with those of the בָּרְכוּ. At times you may wish to call your congregation to worship with the words in Nehemiah rather than the בָּרְכוּ.

Refer to the prayer in Nehemiah 9:6—10:1.

What do you learn from the prayer about the author's beliefs and his thoughts about the people of Israel? Are there parts of his prayer that you could use today?

After reading the prayer to the people, the leaders "set their seal" upon it. Why?

You might wish to write a prayer for your congregation, then read it and, afterwards, have everyone sign it.

24

What Is a Minyan?

Notice that the emphasis of the בָּרְכוּ, and the words found in the Book of Nehemiah, is upon *calling the congregation* together for prayer. Jewish tradition emphasizes praying with a community. The rabbis of the Talmud teach that "he who prays with the congregation will have his prayer answered."

What is meant by "congregation" or "community" in Judaism? And why does Jewish tradition consider prayer with a congregation superior to praying alone?

According to traditional Jewish law and practice, ten men past the age of 13 form a מִנְיָן (minyan), quorum. We are not sure when or where this tradition developed. Some say that the number 10 was taken from the first sentence in Psalm 82. It reads:

אֱלֹהִים נִצָּב בַּעֲדַת אֵל.

God is present in the congregation of the Lord.

The word עֵדָה (edah), congregation, is used here in its Hebrew construct form עֲדַת (adat), congregation of. So what does that have to do with the number 10? Well, the rabbis point out that עֵדָה is also used by the Torah (Numbers 14:27) when it refers to the 10 spies who were sent by Moses to explore the Land of Israel and then return with a report. Those 10 spies were called עֵדָה.

From the fact that עֵדָה was used in the spy story to refer to 10 men and עֲדַת in the psalm to refer to congregation [of], Jewish tradition defined a מִנְיָן as 10 adult men. Among Reform Jews, both men and women have always been counted as part of the מִנְיָן. Conservative Jews recently began to do so also.

Why Pray with a מִנְיָן?

There are several answers which can be given to this question. We will discuss some of them further on in *Bechol Levavacha*. One way of answering the question, however, is to make a list of the reasons why you prefer to share experiences with friends.

Make up such a list. Then, discuss it asking what reasons you have for praying with others. If someone wants to take the other side of the argument, you may want to arrange a debate. You may also wish to develop a sermon on the question and then present it at one of your services.

Another way of answering the question is to look at the answers given to us by other Jews. Here is one response written by the great Jewish poet, Yehudah ha-Levi. He lived in Spain during the years 1085 to 1140 and wrote many poems that have become a part of Jewish worship. In his book, called *The Kuzari*, he tried to answer many difficult questions about Jewish tradition, history, and faith. This is what he wrote about praying with a מִנְיָן.

> Praying with a congregation has many advantages. In the first place, a community will never pray for something which is harmful to the individual, while sometimes an individual will ask for things which can be harmful to others. That is why it is taught that a person should recite prayers with a congregation.
>
> A person who prays only for himself is like one who goes alone into his house and refuses to help others in the work of the community.... It is the duty of each person to bear hardships for the sake of the common good of all.

Why does Yehudah ha-Levi make the connection between praying alone and not fulfilling one's community obligations? Would you agree with him?

Is a person more apt to be selfish in his prayers while praying alone? How might the presence of others remind us that we have responsibilities to others?

Yotzer: Former of Light

בָּרוּךְ אַתָּה, יְיָ אֱלֹהֵינוּ, מֶלֶךְ הָעוֹלָם, יוֹצֵר אוֹר וּבוֹרֵא חְשֶׁךְ, עֹשֶׂה שָׁלוֹם וּבוֹרֵא אֶת הַכֹּל.

Be praised, O Lord our God, Ruler of the universe, former of light, creator of darkness, maker of peace, and creator of all things.

הַמֵּאִיר לָאָרֶץ וְלַדָּרִים עָלֶיהָ בְּרַחֲמִים. וּבְטוּבוֹ מְחַדֵּשׁ בְּכָל יוֹם תָּמִיד מַעֲשֵׂה בְרֵאשִׁית.

In Your mercy light shines over the earth and upon all who inhabit it. Through Your goodness the work of creation is daily renewed.

מָה רַבּוּ מַעֲשֶׂיךָ יְיָ. כֻּלָּם בְּחָכְמָה עָשִׂיתָ. מָלְאָה הָאָרֶץ קִנְיָנֶךָ.

How great are Your works, O Lord, in wisdom You have made all of them. The earth is filled with Your creations.

תִּתְבָּרַךְ יְיָ אֱלֹהֵינוּ עַל שֶׁבַח מַעֲשֵׂה יָדֶיךָ. וְעַל מְאוֹרֵי אוֹר שֶׁעָשִׂיתָ יְפָאֲרוּךָ סֶּלָה.

בָּרוּךְ אַתָּה יְיָ יוֹצֵר הַמְּאוֹרוֹת.

The works of Your hands, O Lord, our God, praise You. And the wonderous stars and planets of the skies glorify You.

Praised be You, O God, Creator of all the lights of the heavens.

Commentary

In Jewish tradition this prayer is called the **יוֹצֵר** which means "former" or "creator" because it praises God as the Creator and Maker of heaven and earth. The title **יוֹצֵר** is taken from the first Hebrew word after the opening phrase:

בָּרוּךְ אַתָּה, יְיָ אֱלֹהֵינוּ, מֶלֶךְ הָעוֹלָם, יוֹצֵר ...

Its theme is praise to God who restores light to the earth every morning. It was written over 2,000 years ago and may have been used as a part of the Temple service.

When we look at it carefully, we get a good insight into what its author had in mind when he created it.

Wonders of Nature

The wonder and order of nature have always stirred the imaginations of sensitive and poetic human beings. The Torah begins with the story of creation, and the prophets and psalmists all wrote songs of praise to God as the Creator and Source of all nature. They believed that just as the paintings of an artist reveal his talents so, too, do the beauties and wonders of nature reveal the powers of God.

The poet and philosopher, Moses ibn Ezra, who lived in Spain from 1070 to 1138, wrote the following poem about God's relationship to nature.

> O God, where shall we find You?
> We see You in the starry field,
> We see You in the harvest yield,
> In every breath, in every sound,
> An echo of Your presence is found.
> The blade of grass, the simple flower,
> Bear witness to Your wonderful power.

One of the important points made in the יוֹצֵר, in ibn Ezra's poem, and in Rabbi Joshua ben Karhah's statement is that God is not only the Creator of the huge and endless universe in which we live but that God's power extends to even the smallest blade of grass.

Today we are aware of atoms and many universes beyond ours. How might we express the ideas we find in ibn Ezra's poem in a modern prayer? Imagine yourself first studying the world through a microscope and then looking out into space through a telescope. What words of prayer might you use to express what you have seen and felt?

Creator of All Things

The opening sentence of the first line of the יוֹצֵר concludes with: "Former of light, Creator of darkness, Maker of peace, and Creator of all things."

These words, and this idea about God, were taken by the prayer's author from Isaiah. The prophet, speaking in the name of God, said:

> I am the Lord, and there is none else.
> I form light and create darkness,
> I make peace and create evil.
>
> (Isaiah 45:7)

Some ancient religions taught that there were two gods at war with one another for control of the universe. One was a god of light and good, the other was a god of darkness and evil. This idea is called dualism — belief in two gods. The followers of Zoroastrianism, a Persian religion founded about 600 B.C.E., believed that the world is a struggle between Spenta Mainya (the spirit of good) and Angra Mainya (the spirit of evil).

Judaism rejected dualism and taught that One God was the creative power responsible for everything.

Compare Isaiah's words with those found in our prayer. Notice how the author of the יוֹצֵר used all of Isaiah's words except for the last phrase: "create evil." For that phrase he substituted the words: "Creator of all things." Why did he make this change?

It could be that he did not want to refer to God as a "Creator of evil" in the midst of prayer. Perhaps there is another reason. He may have disagreed with Isaiah's belief that God creates evil and wanted to teach that nature is filled with many mysteries we may never fully understand. Can you think of any other reasons why the author of the יוֹצֵר deliberately changed

---

He Is in Every Place!

A man once asked Rabbi Joshua ben Karhah:

Why did God choose to speak to Moses through a common thorn bush?

Why not out of a great tree or from a noteworthy place?

The rabbi answered:

To teach us that there is no place, common or unusual, where God does not dwell!

(Exodus Rabbah 2:5)

Isaiah's words? Who or what do you think is responsible for the evils which we experience and encounter in life?

Light and Life

In the expression: "In Your mercy light shines over the earth and upon all who inhabit it," we see the sensitivity of the prayer writer to nature and, especially, to the part played in nature by the power of light.

Have you ever tried to grow a seed or flower inside your house? What are the conditions you must provide for it to grow? What part does light play in the growing process?

Modern science teaches us that no living thing can exist without the immediate or, at least, indirect influence of light. It is the power of light that sets the forces of life in motion.

Creation Is Daily Renewed

In Jewish tradition, God is not thought of as a far off machine which has nothing to do with nature and us. The author of the יוֹצֵר says that through God's goodness "the work of creation is daily renewed." What the poet is saying is that God is a Power, constantly at work, sustaining all the starry skies, the fields and forests, animal life, and the existence of human beings.

Can you think of examples in nature where renewal takes place? What about within the human body?

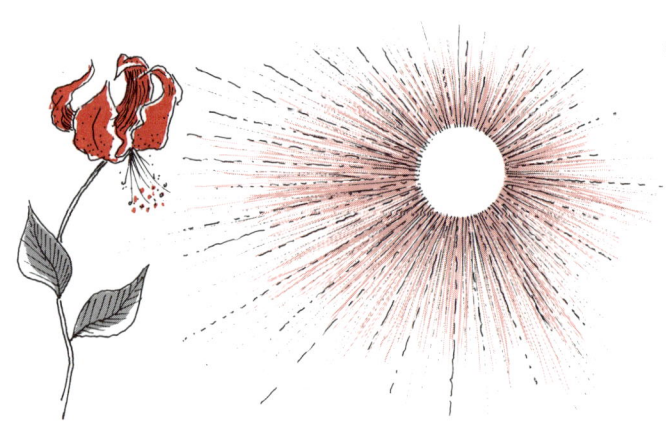

How Great Are Your Works

We have already mentioned that the Book of Psalms was one of the most important sources of prayer for Jews and Jewish poets. Often we find that the author of a prayer will borrow a line or a phrase from a psalm. Having called attention to the order and beauty of nature, the author of the יוֹצֵר quotes from one of the most lovely of all nature psalms. (Psalms 104:24) Look at the whole psalm and then compare it with the יוֹצֵר prayer.

Three Prayers on the יוֹצֵר Theme

I. How Glorious Is Your Name

O Eternal, our God, how glorious is Your name in all the earth.

When we see the heavens, the work of Your fingers,
The moon and the stars, which You have placed there;

The gold of the sun, the silver of the moon, and the diamond sparkle of the stars;

The cool, green grass, the gentle flowers, the freshness of flowing streams,

We give thanks to You, who made them all;

And put beauty and goodness within them.

All the world sings its song to You:

The song of the trees, when the wind stirs their leaves,

The song of the sea, when the waves kiss the shore.

The song of human praise to You, O God, for all the works of creation.

(Arranged by HJF)

II. Let Us Imagine

Let us imagine a world without the grace of color, where regal red or leafy green would never more be seen.

We give thanks for the colors of the rainbow, for eyes that see, for the gift of beauty.

Let us imagine a world in deathlike silence, never knowing the joy of sound.

> We give thanks for words that speak to our minds, for songs that lift our spirits, and for souls that know how to listen.

Let us imagine a world in which nothing can be known, where day and night, winter and summer, or the flow of the tides can never be predicted.

> We give thanks for nature's wondrous order, for the stars in the sky to the pulsebeat within us.

Let us imagine a world without love, where each person is alone and unable to share with others.

> We give thanks for the power of love within us. You, O God, have made it possible for us to know the joy of friendship and the benefit of reaching out to help those in need.

(Based on a prayer by Rabbi Henry Cohen)

III. The Blessed God

אֵל בָּרוּךְ גְּדוֹל דֵּעָה,
הֵכִין וּפָעַל זָהֳרֵי חַמָּה,
טוֹב יָצַר כָּבוֹד לִשְׁמוֹ,
מְאוֹרוֹת נָתַן סְבִיבוֹת עֻזּוֹ.
פִּנּוֹת צְבָאָיו קְדוֹשִׁים, רוֹמְמֵי שַׁדַּי,
תָּמִיד מְסַפְּרִים כְּבוֹד אֵל וּקְדֻשָּׁתוֹ.

The blessed God, great in knowledge,
Formed and made the sun's rays.
He created it in goodness, a glory to His name.
He set the lights of the skies rotating with His power.
All the hosts of heaven praise the Almighty.
They continually declare God's glory and holiness.

אֵל בָּרוּךְ (*El Baruch*) is a poetic acrostic. An acrostic is a poem in which the author uses the letters of the alphabet to develop his theme or, in some cases, to sign his name. An example of an acrostic in English is: *C*onsider *A*nd *R*espect *E*veryman.

The *El Baruch* was written by an eighth-century Jewish mystic who used the 22 letters of the Hebrew alphabet in their order from *alef* to *taf*. In doing so, the author cleverly reminds us that just as God is praised by all nature so should God be praised with every letter and word known to the human mind. For there is no end of thanking God for the gifts of life.

> **Two Thoughts**
>
> Prayer in Israel teaches man ... to think, not of what the world owes him, but what he owes the world and God.
> (Solomon Freehof)
>
> Our prayers are answered, not when we are given what we ask, but when we are challenged to be what we can be.
> (Morris Adler)

> **Created for His Glory**
>
> All of that, which the Holy One, blessed be He, has created in the world, was created for His glory.
> (Avot 6:2)

29

Ahavah Rabbah: With Great Love

אַהֲבָה רַבָּה אֲהַבְתָּנוּ, יְיָ אֱלֹהֵינוּ. חֶמְלָה גְדוֹלָה וִיתֵרָה חָמַלְתָּ עָלֵינוּ. אָבִינוּ מַלְכֵּנוּ. בַּעֲבוּר אֲבוֹתֵינוּ שֶׁבָּטְחוּ בְךָ וַתְּלַמְּדֵם חֻקֵּי חַיִּים.

With great love have You loved us, O Lord our God. Your compassion upon us has been abundant. Our ancestors put their trust in You and You taught them the laws of life.

כֵּן תְּחָנֵּנוּ וּתְלַמְּדֵנוּ. הָאֵר עֵינֵינוּ בְּתוֹרָתֶךָ. וְדַבֵּק לִבֵּנוּ בְּמִצְוֹתֶיךָ. וְיַחֵד לְבָבֵנוּ לְאַהֲבָה וּלְיִרְאָה שְׁמֶךָ.

Be gracious also to us, and teach us. Enlighten our eyes with Your Torah, and let us strive to do Your mitzvot. Unite our hearts to love and serve You.

כִּי בְשֵׁם קָדְשְׁךָ בָּטָחְנוּ. נָגִילָה וְנִשְׂמְחָה בִּישׁוּעָתֶךָ. כִּי אֵל פּוֹעֵל יְשׁוּעוֹת אָתָּה. וּבָנוּ בָחַרְתָּ וְקֵרַבְתָּנוּ לְשִׁמְךָ הַגָּדוֹל סֶלָה בֶּאֱמֶת. לְהוֹדוֹת לְךָ וּלְיַחֶדְךָ בְּאַהֲבָה.

בָּרוּךְ אַתָּה יְיָ הַבּוֹחֵר בְּעַמּוֹ יִשְׂרָאֵל בְּאַהֲבָה.

Because we trust in You, we will be glad and rejoice in Your saving power. For Your will, O God, works for the salvation of all. You have chosen us and drawn us to Your service that we might give thanks to You and proclaim Your unity in love.

Be praised, O God, who has chosen Israel to serve in love.

Commentary

The אַהֲבָה רַבָּה prayer takes its name from its first two Hebrew words. Its theme is love. It speaks of God's love for the Jewish people and of the people's devotion to God. Like the יוֹצֵר, the אַהֲבָה רַבָּה was composed during the existence of the Temple and was made a part of the Temple service by the rabbis of the Great Assembly.

LOVE, GOD, TORAH, AND ISRAEL

The highest expression of love is giving. When we give something which we prize and cherish to another person, we are giving more than an object, we are giving of ourselves and of our love.

Jewish tradition teaches that God, out of אַהֲבָה, chose to give the Torah to the people of

Israel. And the people of Israel, in accepting the Torah, chose to live according to God's *mitzvot*. Notice that the first and last words of the אַהֲבָה רַבָּה prayer are אַהֲבָה, love. In this way, the prayer reminds us of the loving relationship between God, Israel, and Torah.

What do you think Jewish tradition means when it speaks of God as loving and choosing Israel? Are Jews chosen for special privileges? Are they "superior" to others? Is that what being "chosen" or loved by God means?

According to the prophet Isaiah, "being chosen by God" was not a privilege but a task. The Jew was selected for special responsibilities. Speaking in the name of God, Isaiah said:

> But you, Israel, My servant. . . .
> You who I have taken hold of from the ends of the earth . . .
> And said unto you: "You are My servant, I have chosen you. . . ."
> I the Lord have called you in righteousness,
> And have taken hold of your hand,
> And kept you, and set you for a covenant of the people,
> For a light to the nations.
>
> (Isaiah 41:8, 9; 42:6)

What does Isaiah regard as Israel's task as a chosen people? What do you think it means to be a "servant" for God?

Some years ago, Zvi Kolitz discovered the story of Yossel Rakover, a chasidic Jew who died fighting the Nazis in the Warsaw Ghetto in 1943. Kolitz was deeply moved by Rakover's fate and tried to reconstruct what the thoughts of a pious Jew might have been in the last hours of his life. His beautiful "Testament of Yossel Rakover" provides a valuable insight into what Jewish tradition teaches us about Israel's task as a chosen people or "servant" of God.

The Testament of Yossel Rakover

I am proud that I am a Jew, not in spite of the world's treatment of us, but precisely because of this treatment. I should be ashamed to belong to the people who spawned and raised the criminals who are responsible for the deeds that have been perpetuated against us.

I am proud to be a Jew because it is an art to be a Jew, because it is difficult to be a Jew. It is no art to be an Englishman, an American, or a Frenchman. It may be easier, more comfortable to be one of them, but not more honorable. Yes, it is an honor to be a Jew.

I believe that to be a Jew means to be a fighter, an everlasting swimmer against the turbulent, criminal human current. . . .

I am happy to belong to the unhappiest peoples of the world, whose precepts represent the loftiest and most beautiful of all morality and laws.

I believe that to be a Jew is an inborn trait. One is born a Jew exactly as one is born an artist. It is impossible to be released from being a Jew. That is our godly attribute that has made us a chosen people. Those who do not understand will never understand the higher meaning of our martyrdom. If I ever doubted that God once designated us as the chosen people, I would believe now that our tribulations have made us the chosen one.

What does Zvi Kolitz's "Testament of Yossel Rakover" reveal the task of the Jew to be? What can it teach us about the meaning of being a "chosen people"? What does the "Testament of Yossel Rakover" have in common with the prophet Isaiah's understanding of the Jewish people and its task?

Unite Our Hearts

In the אַהֲבָה רַבָּה prayer we have the words, וְיַחֵד לְבָבֵנוּ (*veyached levavenu*), and unite our hearts. What does this expression mean?

We know that, in order for an artist or an athlete to perform with excellence, he must give total attention to his task. The same can be said about prayer or living as a Jew. It takes complete devotion or, what the rabbis called, כַּוָּנָה.

> The sage Rav once declared: "The *mitzvot* were given to the people Israel only in order that human beings should be purified through their fulfillment of them."
> (Genesis Rabbah)

There may be another meaning for יַחֵד לְבָבֵנוּ. Often, when we set out to do something that we believe is right, we meet obstacles. There may be people who laugh at us or call us foolish. It may be that, in doing what we feel is right, we will have to stand up against many who disagree with us. At such times, we are called upon to act with added courage and determination. Perhaps that is what is meant by the prayer's words: "unite our hearts to love and serve You."

The Purpose of the Mitzvot

The יוֹצֵר prayer praises God as the Creator of all the stars of heaven. For centuries, travelers have used the stars as guides for direction. Jewish tradition teaches us that there is another source of direction for human beings. The Torah provides us with ethical מִצְווֹת, commandments which help us to understand the difference between good and evil, right and wrong. For instance, the Torah teaches us about how we should treat the poor and the sick, and what our responsibilities are to parents, strangers, and our neighbors.

The rabbis of the Talmud believed that "if there were no Torah, the world would not continue to exist." (Nedarim 32a) What led them to such a conclusion?

Perhaps they thought it would be impossible to have a society without laws and people devoted to living according to them. And, perhaps, because they loved the Torah so much for what it taught them about justice, truth, the sacredness of life and peace, they could not conceive of a world existing without its wisdom.

The אַהֲבָה רַבָּה prayer speaks of the Jewish people's devotion to Torah. It emphasizes the special task of the Jew to study Torah and live according to its *mitzvot*.

> ### Creating with Kavanah
>
> Themes:
> a. Love of God for Israel.
> b. The special tasks of the people of Israel.
> c. The responsibility of being a Jew.
> d. The challenge of doing *mitzvot* with *kavanah*.

Three Prayers on the אַהֲבָה רַבָּה Theme

I. Eternal Love

אַהֲבַת עוֹלָם בֵּית יִשְׂרָאֵל עַמְּךָ אָהָבְתָּ. תּוֹרָה וּמִצְוֹת חֻקִּים וּמִשְׁפָּטִים אוֹתָנוּ לִמַּדְתָּ. עַל כֵּן יְיָ אֱלֹהֵינוּ בְּשָׁכְבֵנוּ וּבְקוּמֵנוּ נָשִׂיחַ בְּחֻקֶּיךָ, וְנִשְׂמַח בְּדִבְרֵי תוֹרָתֶךָ וּבְמִצְוֹתֶיךָ לְעוֹלָם וָעֶד. כִּי הֵם חַיֵּינוּ וְאֹרֶךְ יָמֵינוּ. וּבָהֶם נֶהְגֶּה יוֹמָם וָלָיְלָה. וְאַהֲבָתְךָ אַל תָּסִיר מִמֶּנּוּ לְעוֹלָמִים. בָּרוּךְ אַתָּה יְיָ אוֹהֵב עַמּוֹ יִשְׂרָאֵל.

With eternal love, You have loved the house of Israel as Your people. You have taught us Torah, *mitzvot*, laws, and judgments. Therefore, O Lord, our God, we will study Your laws at all times and rejoice in the words of Your Torah and *mitzvot*. For our lives depend upon them, and so does the length of our days. O may Your love never depart from us. Praised be You, O God, who loves Your people, Israel.

The אַהֲבַת עוֹלָם (*Ahavat Olam*) prayer is the evening version of the אַהֲבָה רַבָּה and was most likely composed by the same author or authors. Notice that its themes are parallel to those found in the אַהֲבָה רַבָּה.

II. Where Can We Find You?

O Lord, how can we know You? Where can we find You? We discover You in observing the beauty and order of nature. And we find You, O God, in the fulfillment of the *mitzvot* of Torah.

When we are moved to be loving to others, and to strive for truth, we discover You within us. When we are kind and give of what we have to those in need, we feel Your presence. And, when we heal another person's hurt, or give comfort, we sense Your goodness, O God, at work in our lives.

We give thanks to You for the Torah which teaches us that we can find You in the fulfillment of Your *mitzvot*.

(HJF)

III. The Challenge of Torah

With love, O Lord our God, You have given the gift of Torah to the people of Israel. Through it our people has sought to bring human cooperation and peace to the world. Often they were called upon to sacrifice their comfort, safety, possessions, and even their lives, in order to fulfill the *mitzvot* of Torah.

May we, O God, be worthy of the gifts of Torah and the devotion of our people. Help us to study Torah carefully and to apply its *mitzvot* to our lives. We praise You, O God, who in love has given us the responsibilities and challenge of Torah.

(HJF)

The Mitzvot of Torah

The אַהֲבָה רַבָּה and אַהֲבַת עוֹלָם, like many prayers within our prayer book and Jewish tradition, refer to the מִצְוֹת, the commandments of Torah. Just what are the מִצְוֹת?

According to the rabbis there are 613 מִצְוֹת in the Torah. They are divided into two categories. Those which begin with the words "You shall not . . ." are called the "negative מִצְוֹת" because they tell us what we should not do. Those which begin with "You shall" are called "positive מִצְוֹת," because they tell us what we ought to do. Most of the מִצְוֹת are found in Exodus, Leviticus, and Deuteronomy.

Jewish tradition also divides the מִצְוֹת into two other categories. There are the מִצְוֹת of ritual which are called מִצְוֹת בֵּין אָדָם לַמָּקוֹם (*mitzvot beyn adam lamakom*), commandments between the individual and God. These מִצְוֹת deal with the Jewish holidays, the Shabbat, religious practices, and what a Jew is allowed to eat. The other category is מִצְוֹת בֵּין אָדָם לַחֲבֵרוֹ (*mitzvot beyn adam lechavero*), commandments between the individual and other human beings. These are meant to help a person know the difference between right and wrong and live a just, truthful, and good life.

Here are some examples of the מִצְוֹת. You may want to compare and contrast them. After reading and discussing them, open your Bible to Leviticus, read Chapter 19, and then try to distinguish which מִצְוֹת are מִצְוֹת בֵּין אָדָם לַמָּקוֹם and which are מִצְוֹת בֵּין אָדָם לַחֲבֵרוֹ.

EXAMPLES OF מִצְוֹת בֵּין אָדָם לַמָּקוֹם

Shabbat

Remember the Shabbat day to keep it holy.
(Exodus 20:8)

Sukot

You shall keep the Feast of Tabernacles seven days.
(Deuteronomy 16:13)

Pesach

Observe the month of Aviv, and keep the Passover unto the Lord your God.
(Deuteronomy 16:1)

Rosh Hashanah

In the seventh month, in the first day of the month, shall be a solemn rest unto you, a memorial proclaimed with the blast of horns, a holy convocation.
(Leviticus 23:24)

Yom Kippur

On the tenth day of the seventh month is the day of atonement; there shall be a holy convocation unto you, and you shall afflict your souls. . . .
(Leviticus 23:27)

Food

These are the living things which you may eat among all the beasts that are on the earth. Whatever has a parted hoof, and is completely cloven-footed, and chews its cud — these you can eat.
(Leviticus 11:2–3)

The pig, because it has a parted hoof, and is cloven-footed, but does not chew the cud — it is unclean for you. Of its flesh you may not eat.
(Leviticus 11:7–8)

34

EXAMPLES OF מִצְווֹת בֵּין אָדָם לַחֲבֵרוֹ

Honor your father and your mother.
(Exodus 20:12)

You shall not murder.
(Exodus 20:13)

You shall not bear false witness.
(Exodus 20:13)

You shall not follow the majority to do evil.
(Exodus 23:2)

You shall not oppress the stranger.
(Exodus 23:9)

When you reap the harvest of your land, you shall not reap the corner of your field . . . you shall leave them for the poor and for the stranger.
(Exodus 19:9–10)

You shall love your neighbor as yourself.
(Leviticus 19:18)

You shall have just balances and just weights.
(Leviticus 19:36)

You shall not force judgment; you shall not respect persons in judgment; neither shall you take a gift; for a gift blinds the eyes of the wise and perverts the words of the righteous.
(Deuteronomy 16:19)

You shall not remove your neighbor's landmark.
(Deuteronomy 19:14)

Are the מִצְווֹת Too Difficult?

Can a person live according to the מִצְווֹת or are they too difficult or idealistic?

Someone must have asked Moses the same question, for the Torah contains his answer. Speaking to the people of Israel, he said:

> For this מִצְוָה which I command you this day is not too hard for you, neither is it far off. It is not in heaven, that you should say: "Who shall go up into heaven and bring it to us and make us hear it, that we may do it?" Neither is it beyond the sea, that you should say: "Who shall go over the sea for us and bring it to us, that we may do it?" But the word is very near to you; it is in your mouth and in your heart, that you may do it.
> (Deuteronomy 30:11–14)

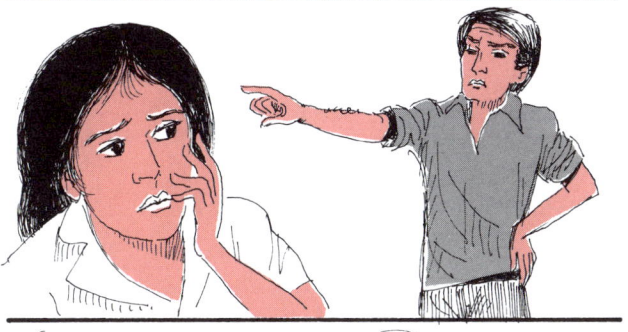

What do you think of Moses' statement about the מִצְווֹת? Are any of the examples of מִצְווֹת too difficult or impossible to do? Are some more easy to perform than others? Why? The rabbis of the Talmud summarize Moses' statement in the following way: "The מִצְווֹת were given that we might live by them." (Tosefta Shabbat 16a) What do you think that they meant by the phrase "live by them"?

The study of the מִצְווֹת is not the most important thing. Doing them is more important!

(Avot 4:13)

35

Do Them Every Day With All Your Heart

The rabbis loved to play with the meaning of numbers and words. They noticed that there were 365 negative מִצְווֹת and 248 positive מִצְווֹת. And so they taught:

> Moses was given 365 negative מִצְווֹת which correspond to the 365 days of the year.
>
> And he was given 248 positive מִצְווֹת which correspond to the 248 parts of the human body.
>
> This teaches that we should be doing the מִצְווֹת every day and with all our human powers.
>
> (Makkot 23b–24a)

A Story

A man died and was brought before the Heavenly Court. His sins and good deeds (מִצְווֹת) were placed on the scales, and the sins far outweighed the good deeds. Suddenly a fur coat was piled on the scale containing the good deeds, and, this side becoming heavier, the man was sent to Paradise.

He said to the Angel who escorted him: "But I cannot understand why the fur coat was brought in."

The Angel replied: "One cold wintry night you traveled on a sled and a poor man asked for a ride. You took him in, and, noticing his thin clothes, you placed your fur coat on him to give him warmth. This act of kindness more than offset your transgressions."

(*The Hasidic Anthology: Tales and Teachings of the Hasidim*, ed. by Louis I. Newman, Schocken, 1963, p. 263)

A Lesson

Rabbi Yehudah ha-Nasi who was responsible for creating one of the first collections of Jewish law, the Mishnah, taught his students: "Be as careful to do an easy מִצְוָה as to do a difficult one. For you cannot know all of the consequences of doing a מִצְוָה." (Avot 2:1) What are some of the small, seemingly unimportant, things people have done for you that have meant much more than they might have imagined? How would you connect Rabbi Yehudah's statement to the above story?

Hands of Service

With the affairs of human beings, knowledge of truth must continually be renewed by ceaseless effort, if it is not to be lost.

It resembles a statue of marble which stands in the desert and is continually threatened with burial by the shifting sand.

The hands of service must ever be at work in order that the marble continue lastingly to shine in the sun.

(Albert Einstein)

How would you relate Albert Einstein's statement to the Jewish duty of doing mitzvot?

Shema: Hear, O Israel

שְׁמַע יִשְׂרָאֵל, יְהֹוָה אֱלֹהֵינוּ, יְהֹוָה אֶחָד.

Hear, O Israel, the Lord is our God, the Lord is One.

בָּרוּךְ שֵׁם כְּבוֹד מַלְכוּתוֹ לְעוֹלָם וָעֶד.

Praised be the name of God, whose glory is for ever and ever.

Commentary

Almost since the beginning of Jewish tradition the שְׁמַע has been considered the most important statement of a Jew's belief in God. It was spoken daily in the prayers at the Temple, and the rabbis included it in the morning and evening services of the synagogue. The שְׁמַע is taken from Deuteronomy 6:4.

Why has the שְׁמַע been considered so important in Jewish tradition? What meaning does it have that Jews throughout the centuries have lovingly repeated its words and have even died with them on their lips?

As God Is One, Humanity Is One

Ancient people believed in many gods. They worshiped stones, animals, stars, and, at times, their kings and queens. Because each people had its own gods, and often its own land, it considered itself separate and unrelated to the other peoples living near it.

With the birth of Judaism, a new idea of God was introduced to the world. Judaism taught that there was one God and that God was the Creator of everything — therefore, the Creator of every human being and all peoples.

This idea meant that no matter what a man or woman's language, or land, or nation was, he or she was related to all people. Since God was the Creator of all people, that meant that all were brothers and sisters.

The prophet Malachi stated the Jewish idea of one God and one interrelated humanity in the form of a question.

> Have we not all one Source?
> Has not one God created us?

When we say the שְׁמַע, we affirm that just as God is one so are all human beings united in one human family.

We Are Witnesses

שְׁמַע יִשְׂרָאֵל, יְהֹוָה אֱלֹהֵינוּ, יְהֹוָה אֶחָד.

Notice that the last letters of the first and last words of the שְׁמַע (the ע and the ד) are enlarged. It is the tradition to print them that way in the Torah and in many prayer books. When the ע and ד are brought together they form the word עֵד (*ayd*) which means witness. The rabbis teach that, when we say the שְׁמַע, we remind ourselves that we are supposed to be witnesses for God.

What does it mean to be a "witness"? A witness gives testimony in a court, that is, he tells the judge and jury what he has seen. The witness

> **Witnesses?**
>
> "You are My witnesses...."
> (Isaiah 43:10)
>
> In the Pesikta deRav Kahana, Rabbi Shimon bar Yochai interpreted the above as follows:
>
> When you are My witnesses, then I am God.
>
> When you are not My witnesses, then I am — as it were — not God.
>
> *What could Rabbi Shimon bar Yochai have meant?*

takes on a very important task because his testimony may determine what will happen to the person or matter on trial.

How can a person be a "witness for God"? In Jewish tradition, we are witnesses for God when we act according to the מִצְוֹת. For example, when we are helpful to a person in need, because we know that we should "love our neighbor as ourself" (Leviticus 19:18), we are showing others the influence of God and the מִצְוֹת in our lives.

Each time we say the שְׁמַע and see the ע and ד, we should be reminded of our ethical responsibilities and of the sacred task we have to be witnesses of God.

A Danger?

What should receive our highest human loyalty? Our race? Sex? Nation? Religion? Family?

That, of course, is a difficult question. Jewish tradition would answer that we owe our highest allegiance to God. In the Ten Commandments we are told: "You shall have no other gods beside Me." (Exodus 20:3)

In ancient times human beings often worshiped a variety of gods. Among the Greeks there were gods for love, wisdom, truth, and mercy. Each person gave his loyalty to whatever god meant the most to him. In modern times people have worshiped political leaders or given their total allegiance to the nation or possessions. Hitler asked for, and received, a worshipful loyalty from his people. To many of them, he became a god.

Jewish tradition has always taught that there was one God, that God was spiritual and not physical, and that human beings could experience God in a whole variety of ways. There are moments when we find God in the beauty and mystery of nature, or in the events and accomplishments of human history. There are other times when we encounter God's power in love and friendship, or when we are moved to reach out and help others.

The God of the universe, Judaism teaches, deserves the highest loyalty because God, alone, is the source of all that we experience in life. Allegiance to God is meant to prevent us from giving our highest loyalties to "other gods" like human beings, a nation, a political party, possessions, or the quest for fame.

The sentence of the שְׁמַע was meant to warn Jews against the danger of worshiping "other gods" (אֱלֹהִים אֲחֵרִים). Students of Jewish tradition point out that this, too, is why the letters ע and ד were enlarged. If they were not, it would be easy to change the meaning of the שְׁמַע.

For example, the ע in the word שְׁמַע could be changed to an א, and the ד in the word אֶחָד could be changed to a ר. Instead of reading שְׁמַע (with the accent on the last syllable): Hear, O Israel, the Lord our God, the Lord is One (אֶחָד), the sentence would read שֶׁמָּא (*shéma*, with the stress on the first syllable): Perhaps, O Israel, the Lord our God is אַחֵר (*acher*), another. In order to make sure that such a distortion would never happen, the letters ע and ד were enlarged.

What does it mean to give (to a human being, a nation, a race, a god of mercy) total loyalty? Why is such allegiance dangerous? Look at Exodus, chapter 32. Why was the building and worship of the golden calf considered by the Torah to be such an evil? Look at I Samuel, chapter 8. Why does Samuel oppose the appointment of a king? What might his opposition have to do with the שְׁמַע and with the commandment: "You shall have no other gods beside Me"?

A Tale of Terror

When the Crusaders reached Xanten, near the Rhine (Germany), in June 1096, the Jewish community was about to welcome the Shabbat. Hearing the Crusaders approach and fearing the worst, Rabbi Moshe ha-Cohen called everyone in the community together.

He told them to have courage. He warned them that death was near.

Together they ate the Shabbat meal and then concluded it with grace. After grace they added the following blessing:

Praised be You, O Lord our God, Ruler of the universe, who has made us holy with Your commandments and commanded us to make Your name sacred in public.

שְׁמַע יִשְׂרָאֵל, יְהוָה אֱלֹהֵינוּ, יְהוָה אֶחָד.

Hear, O Israel, the Lord our God, the Lord is One.

Having concluded the שְׁמַע, they went to their synagogue where they were murdered by the Crusaders. Their act of courage and faith was an act of קִדּוּשׁ הַשֵּׁם.

Kiddush Hashem — קִדּוּשׁ הַשֵּׁם

Kiddush Hashem means "making sacred God's name." How does a person "make sacred God's name"? Jewish tradition teaches that when one acts to bring honor, respect, or credit to the Jewish people or faith, he or she is performing an act of קִדּוּשׁ הַשֵּׁם. To give one's life in a time of persecution, like the followers of Rabbi Moshe ha-Cohen, is to fulfill the highest demand of קִדּוּשׁ הַשֵּׁם.

The Talmud teaches us that קִדּוּשׁ הַשֵּׁם also extends to the Jews' relationship with non-Jews. A Jew should never do anything to a non-Jew which might provoke a false or bad impression of the moral standards of Judaism.

The following story about Rabbi Shimon ben Shetach, who was president of the Sanhedrin during the first century, illustrates this lesson.

One day, the students of Rabbi Shimon ben Shetach joyfully announced to him that they had found a precious stone in the collar of the donkey he had just purchased from an Arab.

Rabbi Shimon said to them: "Return the precious stone to the Arab."

His students were surprised. "Why should it be returned? After all, you bought the donkey. It is yours!"

"I purchased the donkey," said Rabbi Shimon, "not the precious stone. Return it now to the Arab."

When they gave the stone to the Arab and explained to him what had happened and all that Rabbi Shimon had taught them, the Arab exclaimed: "Praised be the God of Shimon ben Shetach!"

(Deuteronomy Rabbah 3:5)

Why was Rabbi Shimon's act considered by

Rabbinic Opinions

Be among the persecuted, not among the persecutors.
(Baba Kamma 93a)

Enough of playing the martyr! Learn to be heroes instead.
(Shetach Zalman)

In time of persecution submit to martyrdom rather than transgress even a seemingly unimportant מִצְוָה.
(Sanhedrin 74a)

Compare and Contrast

Jewish tradition as an act of קִדּוּשׁ הַשֵּׁם? Why did the Arab praise the God of Rabbi Shimon, rather than Rabbi Shimon himself?

READING OR SONG ON THE שְׁמַע THEME

Guardian of Israel

שׁוֹמֵר יִשְׂרָאֵל, שְׁמֹר שְׁאֵרִית יִשְׂרָאֵל,
וְאַל יֹאבַד יִשְׂרָאֵל, הָאוֹמְרִים שְׁמַע יִשְׂרָאֵל.
שׁוֹמֵר גּוֹי אֶחָד, שְׁמֹר שְׁאֵרִית עַם אֶחָד,
וְאַל יֹאבַד גּוֹי אֶחָד,
הַמְיַחֲדִים שִׁמְךָ, יְיָ אֱלֹהֵינוּ, יְיָ אֶחָד.

O Guardian of Israel, preserve the remnant of the people of Israel,
and let not Israel, the people who say "Hear, O Israel," be destroyed.
O Guardian of the one people, preserve the remnant of that one people,
and let not that one people who unify Your name with the words: "The Lord our God, the Lord is one" be destroyed.

Many times in the history of our people, the words of the שְׁמַע were the last words spoken by those who died at the hands of cruel oppressors. The שׁוֹמֵר יִשְׂרָאֵל (*Shomer Yisrael*) is a prayer and song of hope. It asks God to preserve and help Israel, the people who proclaim God's unity. Notice how the poet has incorporated the words of the שְׁמַע into the poem.

Veahavta: You Shall Love the Lord

וְאָהַבְתָּ אֵת יְיָ אֱלֹהֶיךָ בְּכָל לְבָבְךָ וּבְכָל נַפְשְׁךָ וּבְכָל מְאֹדֶךָ. וְהָיוּ הַדְּבָרִים הָאֵלֶּה אֲשֶׁר אָנֹכִי מְצַוְּךָ הַיּוֹם עַל לְבָבֶךָ.

You shall love the Lord, your God, with all your heart, with all your soul, and with all your might. Take to heart these words which I command you this day.

וְשִׁנַּנְתָּם לְבָנֶיךָ וְדִבַּרְתָּ בָּם. בְּשִׁבְתְּךָ בְּבֵיתֶךָ וּבְלֶכְתְּךָ בַדֶּרֶךְ וּבְשָׁכְבְּךָ וּבְקוּמֶךָ. וּקְשַׁרְתָּם לְאוֹת עַל יָדֶךָ. וְהָיוּ לְטֹטָפֹת בֵּין עֵינֶיךָ. וּכְתַבְתָּם עַל מְזֻזוֹת בֵּיתֶךָ וּבִשְׁעָרֶיךָ.

Teach them to your children. Speak of them when you are at home and when you are away, when you lie down and when you arise. Bind them as a sign on your hand and let them serve as symbols between your eyes; inscribe them on the doorposts of your house and on your gates.

לְמַעַן תִּזְכְּרוּ וַעֲשִׂיתֶם אֶת כָּל מִצְוֹתָי וִהְיִיתֶם קְדֹשִׁים לֵאלֹהֵיכֶם. אֲנִי יְיָ אֱלֹהֵיכֶם אֲשֶׁר הוֹצֵאתִי אֶתְכֶם מֵאֶרֶץ מִצְרַיִם לִהְיוֹת לָכֶם לֵאלֹהִים. אֲנִי יְיָ אֱלֹהֵיכֶם.

Remember to do all My commandments, and be holy to your God. I am the Lord, your God, who led you out of Egypt to be your God. I, the Lord, am your God.

Commentary

In the Torah, the sentence of the שְׁמַע is followed by the paragraph which begins with the words: "You shall love the Lord, your God...." This paragraph, Deuteronomy 6:4–9, along with Deuteronomy 11:13–21 and Numbers 15:37–41 make up the section of the service which has, traditionally, been known as the שְׁמַע. The words of the שְׁמַע are placed into the מְזוּזָה (*mezuzah*), which is placed upon the doorpost, and within the תְּפִילִין (*tefilin*), phylacteries, used in morning worship (except on Shabbat and holidays).

The theme of the וְאָהַבְתָּ paragraph is the love of God. What can we mean when we speak of "loving God"? How does a Jew demonstrate such love? An exploration of the וְאָהַבְתָּ paragraph can help us answer these questions.

You Shall Love

What do we mean by "love"? Love is the highest expression of the human spirit, and no explanation will ever fully define its power and meaning. When we consider what love means to each of us, we may think of sharing, giving, respecting, honoring, understanding, appreciating, and being deeply sensitive to the feelings of others.

It has been said that we cannot love another person until we love ourselves. If that is so, then perhaps it is also true that we cannot really love God until we love ourselves. After all, how can we begin to appreciate the complexities, wonders, and order of God's creation until we appreciate how complex and amazing are our bodies and our lives.

How do we achieve self-love? The great talmudic sage, Rabbi Hillel, once said: "If I am not for myself, who will be for me? And if I am only for myself, what am I? And if not now, when?" What do you think he meant by that statement? What does it have to do with self-love and the love of God?

With All Your Heart

We have already seen that the rabbis enjoyed drawing lessons from the way in which words were spelled or written. In the case of the וְאָהַבְתָּ paragraph, they call attention to the word לְבָבְךָ (levavcha), your heart. Usually the word לֵב (lev), heart, is written with one ב. As we can see, it appears with two in the וְאָהַבְתָּ paragraph. Why?

Two Thoughts

How can one love God without loving that which He has made?
(Ludwig Boerne)

Whether a person really loves God can be determined by the love that person shares with others.
(Levi Yitzchak)

Think about these

Each person, the rabbis explain, has two competing powers within him. They are called יֵצֶר הַטּוֹב (yetzer hatov), the power for goodness, and יֵצֶר הָרָע (yetzer hara), the power for evil. Often these powers are at odds with one another. Each ב in the word לְבָבְךָ symbolizes one of these powers.

For example, when we see something we would very much like to possess and we are tempted to take it, we are feeling the יֵצֶר הָרָע. And, when our conscience tells us that it is wrong to steal, that is our יֵצֶר הַטּוֹב speaking within us.

Our task, the rabbis teach, is to let the יֵצֶר הַטּוֹב control and guide the יֵצֶר הָרָע. When we say the words: "You shall love the Lord, your God, with all your heart," we remind ourselves that the love of God is achieved when we use all our powers for goodness for the benefit of all humanity.

With All Your Soul

The sages who interpreted this phrase understood the word נֶפֶשׁ (*nefesh*), soul, to mean a person's life. Many Jews, during Roman oppression and the Middle Ages, died as martyrs because they refused to abandon Judaism or the Jewish people.

To die for one's faith, as we have already seen, is called קִדּוּשׁ הַשֵּׁם, "the making sacred of God's name." The words "with all your soul" recall the bravery of those who gave their נֶפֶשׁ in the name of Jewish dignity and for the cause of human freedom.

When we think about the meaning of the words "with all your soul," we are challenged with a question. Does being a Jew mean so much to us that we could love God with all our soul the way our Jewish ancestors did in the past?

With All Your Might

The rabbis teach that "might" means a person's material possessions — money, property, all that one possesses. What can it mean to love God with your money and property?

The *Zohar*, a book written and studied by Jewish mystics, gives us one answer to think about. "How does one love the Lord? By surrounding oneself with kindness on every side and by doing kind deeds for all without sparing one's strength or one's property."

Take to Heart These Words Which I Command You This Day

By "these words" is meant, not only the שְׁמַע, but the Ten Commandments and all of the מִצְווֹת of the Torah.

Teach Them to Your Children

The love of Judaism comes from a knowledge and experience of Torah. A favorite statement of Jewish tradition is: "The study of Torah equals everything else."

Judaism has always stressed the importance of education. And it has also stressed the teaching role and responsibilities of parents. The father and mother, through their words and example, have the chief influence upon a child's development. In recognition of this, Jewish tradition counsels parents: "Provide your children with a clear, and not confused or stammering, knowledge of the duties and teachings of Torah." (Sifre)

What would you consider the Jewish responsibilities of parents today? You might want to investigate this question by having some students make up a list; some others ask their parents; and, perhaps, some others question the rabbi. Afterwards, compare the different lists and discuss them.

What do you think of the following observation by Rabbi Morris Adler?

> Judaism begins at home.... It begins in homes where Judaism lives in the atmosphere and is integrated in the normal pattern of daily life. It begins in homes where the Jewish words re-echo, where the Jewish book is honored, and the Jewish song is heard. It begins in homes where the child sees and participates in symbols and rites that link him to a people and culture. It begins in homes where the Jewish ceremonial object is visible. It begins in the home where into the deepest layers of a child's developing personality are woven strands of love for and devotion to the life of the Jewish community.
> (*Modern Treasury of Jewish Thoughts*. Sidney Greenberg. Thomas Yosseloff, 1964, pp. 144–145)

Speak of Them

One interpretation of this phrase is: "Make them [the מִצְווֹת] your most important guide and not something to which you pay lip service. Make sure you apply them to all your business dealings." (Sifre)

Another interpretation reminds us that words are easily spoken — especially words of anger, criticism, flattery, and exaggeration.

The chasidic rabbi known as the Koretzer taught that דבר serves as a root for both "speak" and "control." The phrase וְדִבַּרְתָּ בָּם (*vedibarta bum*), and speak of them, teaches us that we must be careful to control the words of our mouth so that we do not speak in anger, falsehood, or flattery.

BIND THEM AS A SIGN ON YOUR HAND, AND LET THEM SERVE AS SYMBOLS BETWEEN YOUR EYES

The command to wear תְּפִילִין is based on four separate portions of Torah: Exodus 13:1–10, 11–16; Deuteronomy 6:4–9, 11:13–21. One box is placed on the weak arm facing the heart (i.e., the left arm if you are right handed) and the other is placed on the center of the forehead.

INSCRIBE THEM ON THE DOORPOSTS OF YOUR HOUSE AND ON YOUR GATES

This phrase was interpreted as the command to place a מְזוּזָה, containing the first two paragraphs of the שְׁמַע, upon the doorposts. According to tradition, the מְזוּזָה is fixed on the right hand doorpost as one enters a synagogue, house, or room.

REMEMBER TO DO ALL MY COMMANDMENTS, AND BE HOLY TO YOUR GOD
(Numbers 15:40)

What can it mean to "be holy" to your God?
The word קְדוֹשִׁים (*kedoshim*), holy, also means different, distinct, special, and sacred. What do these definitions have in common? The word for

a marriage ceremony in Jewish tradition is קִדּוּשִׁין (kiddushin). Can you guess why the two might be related?

In Leviticus 19:2, we find the commandment: קְדֹשִׁים תִּהְיוּ (Kedoshim tiheyu), "You shall be holy."

Look at Chapter 19 of Leviticus and try to figure out what קְדוֹשִׁים means there.

The rabbis interpreted the commandment to "be holy" in the following way: "God says: 'If you observe My מִצְוֹת then you will be holy.'" What do you suppose they meant?

> Holiness is not freely given.
>
> It is the result of devotion, striving, and effort.
>
> When a Jew seeks to fulfill each מִצְוָה with love and care, he is on the way to holiness.

Creating with Kavanah

Themes:
a. Love of God means loving oneself and other human beings.
b. Love of self means learning to let our powers for goodness and truth direct our actions.
c. Love of God for the Jew means living in such a way that we are witness to the highest in our ethical and religious traditions.
d. Love of God means giving of what we possess — sharing generously with others.
e. Love of God means doing all we can to transmit our heritage from one generation to the next.
f. Love of God means controlling our tendency to exaggerate or misuse words.
g. Love of God means seeking to make our lives sacred through the fulfillment of מִצְוֹת.

LOVE OF GOD

וְאָהַבְתָּ אֵת יְהוָה אֱלֹהֶיךָ

We love God when we strive for right over wrong, truth over falsehood, peace instead of quarreling.

בְּכָל לְבָבְךָ

We love with full hearts when we learn to appreciate ourselves — our talents and abilities.

וּבְכָל נַפְשְׁךָ

We love with our souls when we are ready to sacrifice for what we believe.

וּבְכָל מְאֹדֶךָ

We love with our might when we are willing to share what we have with others.

לְמַעַן תִּזְכְּרוּ וַעֲשִׂיתֶם אֶת כָּל מִצְוֹתָי

We love God when the doing of the *mitzvot* leads us to love others and to work for a better world.

Geulah: Redemption

Leader

עֶזְרַת אֲבוֹתֵינוּ אַתָּה הוּא מֵעוֹלָם.

You, O Lord, have been the help of our ancestors throughout history.

Everyone

מִמִּצְרַיִם גְּאַלְתָּנוּ, יְיָ אֱלֹהֵינוּ, וּמִבֵּית עֲבָדִים פְּדִיתָנוּ.

You redeemed us from Egypt and freed us from slavery.

Leader

מֹשֶׁה וּבְנֵי יִשְׂרָאֵל לְךָ עָנוּ שִׁירָה בְּשִׂמְחָה רַבָּה, וְאָמְרוּ כֻלָּם:

When Moses and the children of Israel stood at the Red Sea, they joyously sang this song of praise to you.

Everyone sing

מִי כָמֹכָה בָּאֵלִם יְיָ? מִי כָּמֹכָה נֶאְדָּר בַּקֹּדֶשׁ, נוֹרָא תְהִלֹּת עֹשֵׂה פֶלֶא?

יְיָ יִמְלֹךְ לְעֹלָם וָעֶד.

Who is like You, O Lord, among the mighty? Who is like You, glorious in holiness, awe inspiring, working wonders?

The Lord will rule for ever and ever.

Commentary

This prayer, closing the section of the שְׁמַע, is known as גְּאוּלָה (*Geulah*), Redemption. The word "redemption" means deliver or save. The theme of our prayer is the redemption of Israel from Egyptian slavery.

History, as we have noted before, plays a significant role in Jewish prayer. Jews see God as a power at work in the events of individuals and nations. The first sentence of the Ten Commandments declares:

I am the Lord, your God, who brought you out of the Land of Egypt, out of the house of bondage.

(Exodus 20:2)

In Jewish tradition, the first exodus from oppression became a symbol for freedom from all slaveries and hardships. When Jews recalled the Exodus from Egypt in their prayers, they remembered all the redemptions of their past.

They recalled the bitter oppressions by the Babylonians, the Greeks, the Romans, the Crusaders, and all the other nations who had cruelly persecuted them.

When they sang מִי כָמֹכָה בָּאֵלִם? (*Mi chamochah ba'elim?*), Who is like You among the mighty? they expressed the hope for the day when all men and women would live in freedom, security, and dignity. In II Maccabees, we find a beautiful prayer for גְּאוּלָה, written perhaps by one of those who fought for Jewish freedom during the Maccabean revolt.

> O Lord, gather together our scattered people. Set at liberty those who are in slavery. Look upon those who are despised and let the nations know that You are God.
>
> (II Maccabees 1:27–28)

ALL KINDS OF SLAVERY

There are all kinds of slavery. It is slavery when people are not allowed free speech or when they are denied the right to worship as they wish by oppressive governments. Poverty and horrible living conditions are forms of slavery. And, we can be slaves to bad habits or to fear when it makes us afraid to say what we really feel or think.

Can you think of other examples of slavery? What about the plight of minorities, the condition of women, marriage, the relationship of children to parents? Would you consider these forms of slavery?

Moses Maimonides, the great Jewish medieval philosopher, once wrote: "We naturally like what we have become accustomed to.... This is one of the causes which prevents people from finding the truth." Would you agree with Maimonides? Can you think of illustrations in your life which prove his conclusion?

A chasidic teacher once told his students: "Habit is a thief!" What did he mean? Is habit a form of self-oppression?

There are those who would argue that the pursuit of wealth is a form of slavery. Would you agree? The Mishnah asks the question: "Who is rich?" Then it gives this answer: "He who is happy with his portion." Is that really an answer to the question? How would you answer it?

Two Views on Slavery

The person who lives by a waterfall is hardly disturbed by its roar.

(Judah Moscato)

The real slavery of Israel in Egypt was that they had learned to endure it.

(Rabbi Bunam)

How are these two views related? Is there a connection between them and the following from Yoma 86b: "A sin repeated seems permitted."

EXPRESSING JOY AND HOPE

The Torah informs us that after the children of Israel had crossed the Red Sea and were saved from Pharaoh's army, they sang a song of thanksgiving to God. The words of the מִי כָמֹכָה were a part of that song. The whole song can be found in Exodus 15.

After singing, Miriam took a timbrel, an instrument similar to a tambourine, and led the women in a joyful dance of celebration.

Words are not the only way to pray. Our prayers can be expressed through singing, dancing, playing an instrument, or through the silence of meditation. Why not try some of these forms with the גְּאוּלָה prayer?

Creating with Kavanah

Themes:
a. God works through history toward human freedom.
b. Slavery can be the result of fear, poverty, or habit.
c. Thanksgiving, hope, and the quest for freedom can be expressed in prayer through dance, song, and other creative forms.

Two Readings on the גְּאוּלָה Theme

I. Help Us to Be Free

Slavery is not only a problem of the past. Modern men and women can be slaves.

When we think only of ourselves, we are slaves to selfishness.

When we are hateful to others because of their color or creed, we are slaves to prejudice.

When we always heed what others have, we are slaves to greed.

When we spread lying words about others, we are slaves to falsehood.

When we always have to be right, or the winner, we are slaves to false pride.

When we are afraid to speak out against something we know is wrong, we are slaves to fear.

O Lord our God, help us to be free.

(HJF)

II. Our People Has Suffered

Our people has suffered from cruel hate and oppression.

So teach us not to hate our fellow human beings.

Pharaoh, Haman, Antiochus, and Hitler — all sought to destroy us.

So teach us to treasure our faith and live it proudly.

Even today there are people and nations who preach anti-Semitism and who are slaves to the sickness of prejudice.

צוּר יִשְׂרָאֵל, קוּמָה בְּעֶזְרַת יִשְׂרָאֵל. גּוֹאֲלֵנוּ יְיָ, צְבָאוֹת שְׁמוֹ, קְדוֹשׁ יִשְׂרָאֵל. בָּרוּךְ אַתָּה יְיָ, גָּאַל יִשְׂרָאֵל.

O Rock of Israel, help and redeem the oppressed of Israel wherever they may be. Be praised O God, Redeemer of Israel.

(HJF)

Section Three

עֲמִידָה

THE AMIDAH

Shabbat Morning Amidah

a. Avot *68*
b. Gevurot *72, 73*
c. Kedushah *78*
d. Kedushat Hayom *82*
e. Avodah *87*
f. Hodaah *93*
g. Birkat Shalom *97*
h. Elohai Netzor *101*

On the Amidah

As human beings we have a variety of concerns, feelings, and problems. Some of them we like to share with those we love, others we prefer to keep private. Jewish prayer makes room for both our personal meditations and the concerns we want to share with the community. Perhaps the most beautiful example of the combination of private and community prayer is found in the section of worship known as the עֲמִידָה (Amidah).

The word עֲמִידָה means "standing," and it describes the way in which its prayers are recited. Usually, in a traditional synagogue, the congregation stands and reads the עֲמִידָה in silence. Afterwards, the חַזָּן (chazan), cantor or leader, repeats the prayers. The Talmud informs us that the original reason for the repetition was for those who could not read. The rabbis wanted everyone to feel included in the congregation.

תְּפִלָּה AND שְׁמוֹנֶה־עֶשְׂרֵה

There are two other names by which the עֲמִידָה is known. It is known as the שְׁמוֹנֶה־עֶשְׂרֵה (Shemoneh-esreh), "Eighteen," because it was originally composed of eighteen different blessings. It is also called תְּפִלָּה (Tefilah), "Prayer," because it was considered the heart of Jewish worship.

After the destruction of the Temple (70 C.E.), the Jewish people suffered bitter persecution at the hands of the Romans. During the second century C.E., another prayer was added to the עֲמִידָה. It was called מַכְנִיעַ זֵדִים (Machnia Zedim), "Humbling of the Arrogant." (See page 60.) Since that time, there have been nineteen blessings in the שְׁמוֹנֶה־עֶשְׂרֵה with a personal meditation, אֱלֹהַי נְצוֹר (Elohai Netzor), added later in the fourth century C.E.

Who Wrote the עֲמִידָה?

We are not sure who composed all of the prayers which make up the עֲמִידָה. According to tradition, the עֲמִידָה was written by the rabbis of the Great Assembly and made an official part of Jewish worship by Rabban Gamliel who was the head of the academy at Yavneh in about 100 C.E. For nearly 2,000 years, then, the עֲמִידָה has been recited by Jews in synagogues and in private meditation.

There are two traditional forms of the עֲמִידָה. There is the daily עֲמִידָה and the special Shabbat and holiday עֲמִידָה called תְּפִילַת שֶׁבַע (Tefilat sheva) because it contains seven prayers. The תְּפִילַת שֶׁבַע is composed of the first three prayers of the daily עֲמִידָה, a special prayer for the Shabbat or a holiday called קְדוּשַׁת הַיּוֹם (Kedushat Hayom), and then the last three prayers of the daily עֲמִידָה. See the diagram (at right) for comparison.

We are told that the rabbis instituted the shorter תְּפִילַת שֶׁבַע because they did not think that the middle thirteen prayers of the עֲמִידָה were appropriate to the mood and meaning of the Shabbat and holidays. The middle thirteen prayers, the rabbis thought, reminded one of all of his needs and problems. On the Shabbat and holidays, one should be filled with joy, not the worries or problems of the weekday.

Since *Bechol Levavcha* is meant for use on the Shabbat, you will find the whole Shabbat עֲמִידָה with commentary and additional prayers starting on page 66. On the next few pages is a description of each of the middle thirteen prayers of the daily עֲמִידָה. Having studied them, you may wish to use them, or their themes, in the creation of some of your own עֲמִידָה prayers.

The Daily Amidah		The Shabbat and Holiday Amidah	
שְׁמוֹנֶה־עֶשְׂרֵה		תְּפִילַת שֶׁבַע	
Avot	אָבוֹת	Avot	אָבוֹת
Gevurot	גְּבוּרוֹת	Gevurot	גְּבוּרוֹת
Kedushah	קְדוּשָׁה	Kedushah	קְדוּשָׁה
Daat	דַּעַת		
Teshuvah	תְּשׁוּבָה		
Selichah	סְלִיחָה		
Geulah	גְּאוּלָה		
Refuah	רְפוּאָה	Kedushat Hayom	קְדוּשַׁת הַיּוֹם
Mevarech Hashanim	מְבָרֵךְ הַשָּׁנִים		
Kibbutz Galuyot	קִבּוּץ גָּלֻיּוֹת		
Tzedakah Umishpat	צְדָקָה וּמִשְׁפָּט		
Machnia Zedim	מַכְנִיעַ זֵדִים		
Al Hatzadikim	עַל הַצַּדִּיקִים		
Boneh Yerushalayim	בּוֹנֵה יְרוּשָׁלַיִם		
Keren Yeshuah	קֶרֶן יְשׁוּעָה		
Shomea Tefilah	שׁוֹמֵעַ תְּפִילָה		
Avodah	עֲבוֹדָה	Avodah	עֲבוֹדָה
Hodaah	הוֹדָאָה	Hodaah	הוֹדָאָה
Birkat Shalom	בִּרְכַּת שָׁלוֹם	Birkat Shalom	בִּרְכַּת שָׁלוֹם
*Elohai Netzor	אֱלֹהַי נְצוֹר	*Elohai Netzor	אֱלֹהַי נְצוֹר

* See *Commentary*, p. 101.

The Daily Amidah
The Middle Thirteen Prayers

Daat דַּעַת Knowledge

אַתָּה חוֹנֵן לְאָדָם דַּעַת וּמְלַמֵּד לֶאֱנוֹשׁ בִּינָה. חָנֵּנוּ מֵאִתְּךָ דֵּעָה בִּינָה וְהַשְׂכֵּל. בָּרוּךְ אַתָּה יְיָ חוֹנֵן הַדָּעַת.

O Lord, You give the human being knowledge and teach understanding. May we too be given knowledge, understanding, and good sense. Be praised, O God, Giver of knowledge.

Study and the pursuit of knowledge have always been considered extremely important within Jewish life. Ahad Ha-Am, the modern Jewish essayist, once wrote: "Learning, learning, learning — that is the secret of Jewish survival."

In the complicated modern world we are often overwhelmed by the number of facts and things we must know. Yet, as some philosophers have pointed out, there is a difference between knowing many facts and possessing knowledge. What do you think that difference is? How would you define דַּעַת?

In Kohelet (Ecclesiastes), the biblical philosopher wrote: "He who increases his knowledge increases his sorrow." What did he mean? Would you agree or disagree with him?

On דַּעַת

One loves God only by virtue of knowledge, and the degree of love corresponds to the degree of knowledge.
(Moses Maimonides)

Acquire the habit of saying "I do not know," lest you be led to lie.
(Berachot 4a)

When you do not know, do not be ashamed to admit it.
(Derech Eretz 1:22)

You must learn to know others in order to know yourself.
(Ludwig Boerne)

To know a person you must ride in the same coach with that person.
(Yiddish proverb)

Teshuvah תְּשׁוּבָה Repentance

הֲשִׁיבֵנוּ אָבִינוּ לְתוֹרָתֶךָ. וְקָרְבֵנוּ מַלְכֵּנוּ לַעֲבוֹדָתֶךָ. וְהַחֲזִירֵנוּ בִּתְשׁוּבָה שְׁלֵמָה לְפָנֶיךָ. בָּרוּךְ אַתָּה יְיָ הָרוֹצֶה בִּתְשׁוּבָה.

Help us, O Lord, to return to the practice of Your Torah and to serving You. May we make complete repentance before You. Be praised, O God, who wants us to make repentance.

All of us make mistakes and do things for which we are sorry. תְּשׁוּבָה, repentance, is taken from the Hebrew word שׁוּב (shuv) which means return.

When we have done something wrong, and realize it, our duty is to *return* and seek to correct our mistake. That turning, in Jewish tradition, is called תְּשׁוּבָה.

The rabbis teach that "תְּשׁוּבָה makes a person a new creature" and that תְּשׁוּבָה is great because "it brings healing into the world." (Midrash Tehilim 18a and Yoma 86a) What do you think the rabbis meant by those statements? Compare them with those in the column at the side of this page.

Moses Maimonides writes that "תְּשׁוּבָה means that the sinner forsakes his sins, casts them out of his mind, seeks forgiveness from those he has wronged, and pledges in his heart to sin no more." (Yad, Teshuvah 1180, 2.2) What do you think of this definition of תְּשׁוּבָה? Is it too difficult? How, if you had done something wrong, would you make תְּשׁוּבָה?

On תְּשׁוּבָה

If one says, I will sin again and repent again, that person will have no opportunity to repent.
(Yoma 8:9)

Repentance is a fierce battle with the heart.
(Orot Tzadikim)

The test of repentance is refraining from sin on two occasions when the same temptation returned.
(Yoma 86b)

Great is repentance, for it turns sins into incentives for right conduct.
(Yoma 86b)

Selichah סְלִיחָה *Forgiveness*

סְלַח לָנוּ אָבִינוּ כִּי חָטָאנוּ. מְחַל לָנוּ מַלְכֵּנוּ כִּי פָשָׁעְנוּ. כִּי מוֹחֵל וְסוֹלֵחַ אָתָּה. בָּרוּךְ אַתָּה יְיָ חַנּוּן הַמַּרְבֶּה לִסְלוֹחַ.

Forgive us, O Lord our God, for our sins. Pardon our wrong doings. Be praised, O God, who is gracious to forgive.

Rabbi Eleazar ben Judah taught his students that "the most beautiful thing a person can do is to forgive." And the sage Raba taught that "the person who forgives . . . will be forgiven." (Yoma 23a)

We have already noted that Jewish tradition challenges us to imitate God. Our prayers for סְלִיחָה remind us that God is "gracious to forgive." They challenge us to be forgiving in our relationships with others.

סְלִיחָה is not an easy matter to achieve. It takes courage to admit that we have been wrong or have hurt another person — and then to ask him or her for forgiveness. Nor is it any easier when we have been harmed by another, or angered by someone's insensitivity, to grant forgiveness.

Why do you think סְלִיחָה is so difficult for us to achieve? In what way might this prayer help achieve סְלִיחָה more easily in our behavior with others?

What do you think the rabbis meant by the following statement about סְלִיחָה? "Whoever, instead of forgiving, takes vengeance or bears a grudge acts like one who, having cut one's hand while handling a knife, avenges himself by stabbing the other hand."

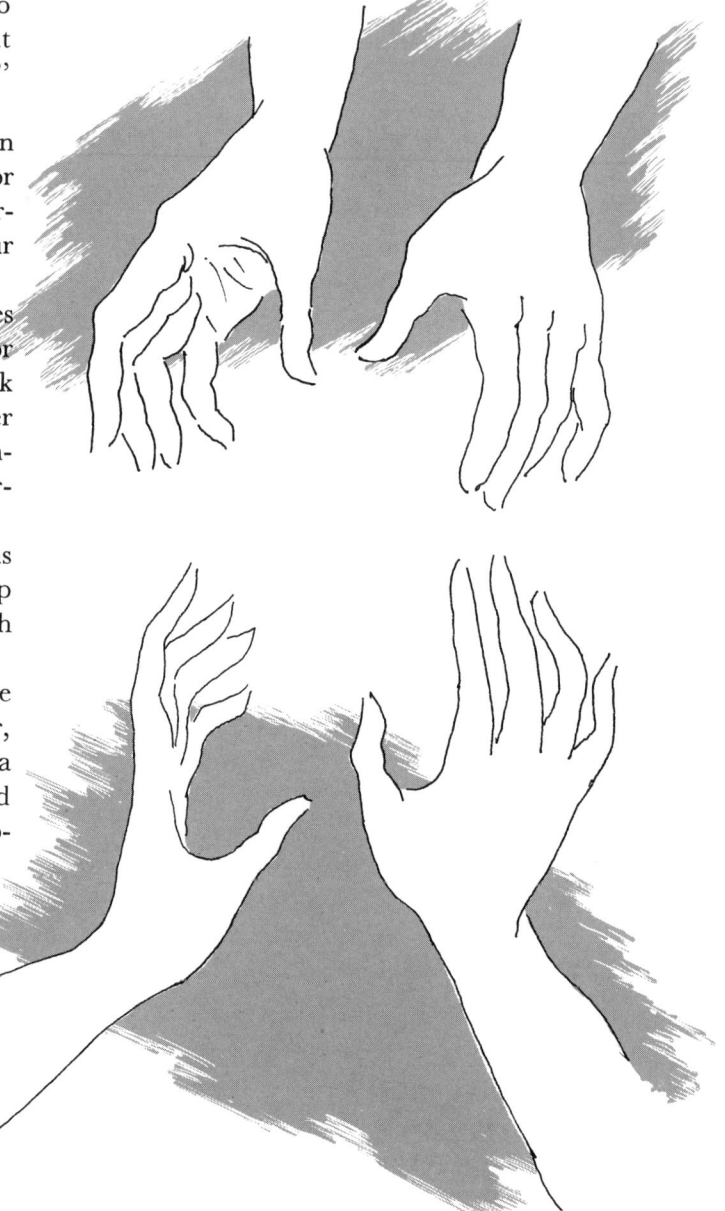

Geulah גְּאוּלָה *Redemption*

רְאֵה נָא בְעָנְיֵנוּ וְרִיבָה רִיבֵנוּ. וּגְאָלֵנוּ מְהֵרָה לְמַעַן שְׁמֶךָ. כִּי גּוֹאֵל חָזָק אָתָּה. בָּרוּךְ אַתָּה יְיָ גּוֹאֵל יִשְׂרָאֵל.

O Lord, look upon our troubles and difficulties, and help us. Be praised, O Lord, Redeemer of Israel.

It is thought that this prayer was written during the time of the Maccabees when Jews were being persecuted by Antiochus.

Notice that the next to the last word is גּוֹאֵל (*Goel*), Redeemer, and that the prayer calls upon God to help us.

Do you think God can help us, in difficult times, with our problems?

In situations of distress, it is natural for us to reach out for help. At times we need courage and determination. At other moments we require renewed strength.

Sometimes that renewal can come from our knowledge of history. For example, knowing that our people has survived storms of hate and persecution may give us courage to endure the difficulties which face us. It may reaffirm our faith in God as a source of גְּאוּלָה and as a power at work in history for goodness, truth, and peace.

Can you think of examples from Jewish history which might provide you with courage in a time of difficulty? Draw up a list, and share your ideas with others in your discussion group. Are there other sources, besides human history, from which we might derive faith or strength in times of distress?

> *After escaping from Egyptian slavery, the Torah tells us that Moses and the Israelites sang:*
>
> Who is like You, O Lord,
>   among the mighty;
> Who is like You,
>   majestic in holiness....
> In Your love You lead
>   the people You redeemed;
> In Your strength You
>   guide them to Your holy
>   abode.
>   (Exodus 15:11–13)

Refuah רְפוּאָה *Healing*

רְפָאֵנוּ יְיָ וְנֵרָפֵא. הוֹשִׁיעֵנוּ וְנִוָּשֵׁעָה. כִּי תְהִלָּתֵנוּ אָתָּה. וְהַעֲלֵה רְפוּאָה שְׁלֵמָה לְכָל מַכּוֹתֵינוּ. כִּי אֵל מֶלֶךְ רוֹפֵא נֶאֱמָן וְרַחֲמָן אָתָּה. בָּרוּךְ אַתָּה יְיָ רוֹפֵא חוֹלֵי עַמּוֹ יִשְׂרָאֵל.

Heal us, O Lord, and we shall be cured. Save us and we shall be saved. For You are worthy of our praise. Grant complete healing to all our sicknesses, for You are a faithful and merciful healer. Be praised, O Lord, who heals the sick of the people Israel.

Sickness and disease frighten all of us. Our prayer for רְפוּאָה, healing, is a natural expression of our human need in times of sickness and pain. Its words speak of God as a power at work in the universe for healing and health. Do you think that makes sense? In what ways might we think of God as a source of healing or health?

Healing of a wound, or overcoming a sickness, is the result of marvelous powers at work in our bodies. Were it not for these healing powers, life would be impossible and filled with constant unbearable tragedy. In what ways might the healing powers in our bodies be a part of God's power to heal?

BIKUR CHOLIM AND HEALING

The sages of the Talmud considered בִּקּוּר חוֹלִים (*bikur cholim*) visiting of the sick, to be a מִצְוָה of great importance. Rabbi Eleazar taught: "Do not forget to visit the sick, for you will be loved for it." (Nedarim 41a) And Rabbi Akiva once observed: "Whoever does not visit the sick is like a murderer!" (Nedarim 40a) What do you think Eleazar and Akiva meant? How might visiting a sick friend, or a loved one, or the aged, be helpful to them? In what ways might it contribute to their cure?

In some Jewish communities there are *Bikur Cholim* groups. Their task is to visit those who are sick and in need of friendship and concern. Your congregation may wish to establish such a group.

FOR JEWS ONLY?

In our prayer God is praised as the Lord "who heals the sick of the people Israel." Is it possible that those who composed this prayer thought that God only took care of the needs of Jews? Why did the prayer not end "who heals the sick of the people Israel *and all human beings*"?

It could be that, since the congregation was Jewish, the concern of the worshiper was turned exclusively to the Jewish people. There are many times when we limit our prayers to our immediate family or to the group in which we find ourselves. Do you think such prayers are selfish or narrow? How would you prefer to end the רְפוּאָה prayer? Can you think of any other reasons why the רְפוּאָה prayer ends with the words "who heals the sick of the people Israel?"

Often, worshipers pause at this place in the עֲמִידָה to offer a special prayer for someone who is suffering from illness.

Whoever visits a sick person helps him to recover.
(Nedarim 40a)

Mevarech Hashanim מְבָרֵךְ הַשָּׁנִים Who Blesses the Years

בָּרֵךְ עָלֵינוּ יְיָ אֱלֹהֵינוּ אֶת הַשָּׁנָה הַזֹּאת וְאֶת כָּל מִינֵי תְבוּאָתָהּ לְטוֹבָה. בָּרוּךְ אַתָּה יְיָ מְבָרֵךְ הַשָּׁנִים.

O Lord, our God, bless this year and all the varieties of its harvest which sustain our lives. Be praised, O God, who blesses the years.

The מְבָרֵךְ הַשָּׁנִים prayer praises God for the bounty of nature. It reminds us that we depend on nature for our survival. Is it really necessary for us to be reminded of such an obvious fact? What might be the connection between this prayer and the blessing said before we eat?

A Tale

The Kobriner Rebbe once turned to his followers and asked: "Do you know where God is?"

When he saw that they could not answer his question, he took a small piece of bread and showed it to them. "God," he said, "is in this piece of bread. Without God's power in all nature, this piece of bread could not exist."

How can one say: "God is in this piece of bread?" What do you suppose the Kobriner Rebbe meant? What does his observation have to do with the מְבָרֵךְ הַשָּׁנִים prayer or with the blessing we say before eating?

Imitating God

We have already noted that Judaism considers it a person's task to imitate God. What does the מְבָרֵךְ הַשָּׁנִים prayer teach us about our task?

In the Torah we read: "If your brother becomes poor, and his means of support fail, you must uphold him. . . . I am the Lord your God. . . ." (Leviticus 25:35–38) Study the whole passage, and discuss it in the light of the מְבָרֵךְ הַשָּׁנִים.

Kibbutz Galuyot קִבּוּץ גָּלִיּוֹת Gathering of Exiles

תְּקַע בְּשׁוֹפָר גָּדוֹל לְחֵרוּתֵנוּ. וְשָׂא נֵס לְקַבֵּץ גָּלֻיּוֹתֵינוּ. וְקַבְּצֵנוּ יַחַד מֵאַרְבַּע כַּנְפוֹת הָאָרֶץ. בָּרוּךְ אַתָּה יְיָ מְקַבֵּץ נִדְחֵי עַמּוֹ יִשְׂרָאֵל.

Blow the shofar for the freedom of our people. Lift up a banner and gather our exiled people from the four corners of the earth. Be praised, O Lord, who gathers the exiled of the people Israel.

An Ancient Idea

The קִבּוּץ גָּלֻיּוֹת prayer voices the hope that someday all who wish will be free to live their lives in the Land of Israel.

The idea of the Jewish people's return to the Land of Israel is nearly as old as the Jewish people itself. Moses led the people out of Egypt so that they could return to the Promised Land. And when the Babylonians destroyed Israel and took thousands of Jews away as captives, the prophets spoke of the day when all of the exiled would be returned to Israel. The words of Isaiah are typical.

> And it shall come to pass in that day,
> That the Lord will set His hand again the second time,
> To recover the remnant of His people . . .
> And will assemble the exiled of Israel,
> And gather together the scattered of Judah
> From the four corners of the earth.
>
> (Isaiah 11:11–12)

What Is Exile

What does it mean to live in גָּלוּת (*galut*), exile? Moses ibn Ezra, the Spanish Jewish poet (1060–1138), defined exile as "a form of imprisonment . . . the refugees are like plants without soil and water." The Zionist leader, Chaim Greenberg, once wrote: "Wherever Jews live as a minority is exile."

What do ibn Ezra and Greenberg mean by exile? What is bad about living in exile? How does living in Israel solve the problems of "exile" for the Jew? Do you believe that there are still some Jews who are living in exile? Are there other people who might be considered exiles? How would you compare their situation to that of the Jewish people?

Someone once remarked: "It is easier to take a Jew out of exile than to take the exile out of the Jew." What do you think he meant? Is it possible for the Jew to live in the Land of Israel and still be in exile?

Tzedakah Umishpat צְדָקָה וּמִשְׁפָּט Righteousness and Justice

מְלוֹךְ עָלֵינוּ אַתָּה יְיָ לְבַדְּךָ בְּחֶסֶד וּבְרַחֲמִים וְצַדְּקֵנוּ בַּמִּשְׁפָּט. בָּרוּךְ אַתָּה יְיָ מֶלֶךְ אוֹהֵב צְדָקָה וּמִשְׁפָּט.

O Lord, our God, rule over us in loving kindness and mercy. May our deeds always be just, and our relationships with others always righteous. Be praised, O God, who loves righteousness and justice.

The Psalmist once asked the question: "O Lord, who shall dwell in Your sanctuary?" By that question he meant: "Who is really the religious person?"

That is a question many of us still ask. How does a religious person's behavior differ from those who are not religious? Is being "religious" only a matter of rituals and ceremonies?

The Psalmist, quoted above, tried to answer his own question. He wrote the following:

> He that walks uprightly and works righteousness
> And speaks truth in his heart;
> That has no slander upon his tongue,
> Nor does evil to his fellow man,
> Nor takes up a reproach against his neighbor;
> In whose eyes an evil person is despised,
> But he honors them that fear the Lord;
> He that keeps his word even if it brings him pain,
> He that does not put out his money on interest,
> Nor take a bribe against the innocent.
>
> (Psalms 15)

How does the author of Psalm 15 define a "religious" person? Would you agree or disagree with his definition? Why? Are there important aspects of being religious which he fails to mention? What part do rituals and prayer play in helping a person become truly religious? What is the relationship of the צְדָקָה וּמִשְׁפָּט prayer to being a "religious" person?

Machnia Zedim מַכְנִיעַ זֵדִים Humbling the Arrogant

וְלַמַּלְשִׁינִים אַל תְּהִי תִקְוָה. וּמַלְכוּת זָדוֹן מְהֵרָה תְעַקֵּר וּתְשַׁבֵּר וּתְמַגֵּר וְתַכְנִיעַ בִּמְהֵרָה בְיָמֵינוּ. בָּרוּךְ אַתָּה יְיָ שֹׁבֵר אוֹיְבִים וּמַכְנִיעַ זֵדִים.

Let there be no hope for those who slander others. May arrogant governments be quickly uprooted, destroyed, and humbled. Be praised, O Lord, who destroys the wicked and humbles the arrogant.

The Jewish people has often suffered from unjust and selfish leaders who blamed Jews for their own mistakes and sometimes tortured them for remaining faithful to their Judaism and to the Jewish people.

The מַכְנִיעַ זֵדִים prayer was written by Shmuel ha-Katan at the request of Rabban Gamliel during the second century C.E. At that time Jews suffered from the brutal persecution of the Romans. Rabbi Shmuel ha-Katan's prayer voices the hope that all evil governments and arrogant leaders — all men and women who are enemies of freedom and human dignity — will be humbled and destroyed.

If you were given the task of composing such a prayer today, what might you write? What are the "enemies of freedom and human dignity" today? What might it mean when we ask God to uproot, destroy, or humble those who are responsible for evil?

SLANDERERS

When Rabbi Shmuel ha-Katan wrote the מַכְנִיעַ זֵדִים prayer, he had in mind, not only those governments who persecuted Jews, but also Jews who had become informers and slanderers of the Jewish community. Why would a Jew become an informer or slanderer of other Jews? Can you think of any other examples where Jews have become informers for anti-Semites? What motivated them?

60

Al Hatzadikim עַל הַצַדִּיקִים For the Righteous

עַל הַצַדִּיקִים יֶהֱמוּ רַחֲמֶיךָ יְיָ אֱלֹהֵינוּ. וְתֵן שָׂכָר טוֹב לְכָל הַבּוֹטְחִים בְּשִׁמְךָ בֶּאֱמֶת. בָּרוּךְ אַתָּה יְיָ מִשְׁעָן וּמִבְטָח לַצַדִּיקִים.

Grant mercy, O Lord our God, to those who are rightous. May all who are faithful to You by pursuing truth be given a good reward. Be praised, O Lord, the strength and support of the righteous.

The word צַדִּיקִים (tzadikim) is the plural of צַדִּיק (tzadik) which means righteous. Who is a צַדִּיק, a "righteous person"?

The Talmud tells us that a צַדִּיק is "good to God and good to people." (Kiddushin 40a) Does being "good to people" necessarily make one "good to God"? What does our relationship to people have to do with our relationship to God? You may wish to arrange a debate on these questions. If you do, be sure to look at Exodus 20–23, and Deuteronomy 22–26. Compare the commandments of Torah with the talmudic statement that a צַדִּיק is one who is "good to God and good to people."

The Talmud also teaches that a צַדִּיק "says little and does much." (Baba Metziah 87a) Would you agree with the Talmud that "saying little and doing much" is an important quality of a צַדִּיק? Why? What other qualities of character would you consider important in making a person a צַדִּיק?

According to the rabbis there are different levels of righteousness. For instance, they claim that Noah, whom the Torah calls righteous, was not a true צַדִּיק. Why? Because when he heard that the world was going to be destroyed, he did not pray for those who were doomed. On the other hand, Abraham is considered by the sages to have been a true צַדִּיק. Why? Because when he heard that the inhabitants of Sodom were about to be destroyed, he argued with God and prayed for the people of Sodom. (*Zohar* I, 82a) What was it about Noah that disqualified him from being a צַדִּיק? Look at Exodus 32:1–14. Would Moses rate as a צַדִּיק. Why?

What personalities, living in our times, would you consider as צַדִּיקִים? You may wish to draw up a list and discuss your opinions with those in your study group.

Statements about the Righteous

The following are some statements from Jewish tradition about the "righteous." Try to understand what they mean and how they might apply to being a צַדִּיק today.

The righteous are superior to angels.
(Sanhedrin 93a)

Righteous persons do not take what is not theirs.
(Sanhedrin 99b)

The righteous protect a city more than sand holds back the sea.
(Baba Batra 7b)

The righteous are called God's friends.
(Seder Eliyahu Rabbah)

When the righteous depart, blessing departs.
(Eliezer Ben Shimon)

The righteous cast out hatred.
(Apocrypha)

Hearing and Seeing

Chasidism teaches that the צַדִּיק is a person who is capable of experiencing God's power in all earthly things. He hears and sees God everywhere. The Koretzer Rebbe taught that the צַדִּיק "is always able to see without eyes and to hear without ears." What do you think the Koretzer meant by that? Can we really see without eyes or hear without ears? Can a blind person see or a deaf person hear? What can a צַדִּיק see and hear without eyes and ears?

We have already noted that the authors of our prayer book often borrowed phrases and ideas from the Hebrew Bible. Look at Psalms 37:39–40, and compare what you find there with the עַל הַצַּדִּיקִים prayer.

Boneh Yerushalayim בּוֹנֵה יְרוּשָׁלַיִם Rebuilding Jerusalem

וְלִירוּשָׁלַיִם עִירְךָ בְּרַחֲמִים תָּשׁוּב. וּבְנֵה אוֹתָהּ בְּקָרוֹב בְּיָמֵינוּ בִּנְיַן עוֹלָם. וְכִסֵּא דָוִד מְהֵרָה לְתוֹכָהּ תָּכִין. בָּרוּךְ אַתָּה יְיָ בּוֹנֵה יְרוּשָׁלָיִם.

Return, O God, to Jerusalem, Your city, in mercy. May it be rebuilt and established in our days as an eternal symbol. May the seat of David be there. Be praised, O Lord, who gives us faith to rebuild Jerusalem.

When King Solomon dedicated the first Temple in Jerusalem, he prayed: "O Lord, hear the prayers... of Your people Israel when they pray toward this place." (I Kings 8:30) Since that time, Jews have always faced toward Jerusalem when they prayed. The rabbis give us the following directions:

> If a Jew is east of Jerusalem, he should turn his face to the west; if in the west, toward the east; if in the south, toward the north; if in the north, toward the south. In this way all of Israel will be turning their hearts toward one place.
>
> (Berachot 30a)

What do the rabbis mean by their explanation: "In this way all of Israel will be turning their hearts toward one place"? What meaning do you think has been added to Jewish history and prayer by all Jews facing toward Jerusalem when they pray? In most synagogues today, the ark is situated so that when the congregation prays it is facing Jerusalem. In the city of Jerusalem, synagogues are built so that worshipers face the place where the Temple once stood. What does this mean to you as a Jew?

Two Jerusalems!

The talmudic sage, Rabbi Yochanan bar Nappaha, once declared:

> The Holy One, blessed be He, said: "I will not enter the heavenly Jerusalem until I can enter the earthly Jerusalem."
>
> (Taanit 5a)

What do you think Rabbi Yochanan bar Nappaha meant?

Perhaps he believed that there were two Jerusalems. That may seem a strange idea at first. But many Jews throughout the centuries have believed it with all their hearts. And there are Jews today who still teach that there are two Jerusalems.

The first is the city where people live and where the modern State of Israel has its busy capital. This is the Jerusalem that devoted Jews have longed to visit throughout the centuries.

The other Jerusalem is what might be called a symbol. It is the perfect city of peace. A city where justice, mercy, love, and goodness are to be found. This is the "heavenly Jerusalem" to which Rabbi Yochanan bar Nappaha referred and, according to tradition, this is the city which the Messiah would establish when he came. This "heavenly Jerusalem" is an ideal and a great human hope.

How are the two Jerusalems interrelated? How might the ideal of the "heavenly Jerusalem" be applied to all cities in the world? How does such an idea relate to the בּוֹנֵה יְרוּשָׁלַיִם prayer?

Remembering Jerusalem

Why do you suppose Jews have remembered Jerusalem in their prayers throughout the centuries? David Ben-Gurion, the first prime minister of the State of Israel, once said: "Jerusalem... has been and will remain forever the capital of the Jewish people." What did he mean? Would you agree with him?

Keren Yeshuah קֶרֶן יְשׁוּעָה The Messianic Hope

אֶת צֶמַח דָּוִד עַבְדְּךָ מְהֵרָה תַצְמִיחַ. וְקַרְנוֹ תָּרוּם בִּישׁוּעָתֶךָ. כִּי לִישׁוּעָתְךָ קִוִּינוּ כָּל הַיּוֹם. בָּרוּךְ אַתָּה יְיָ מַצְמִיחַ קֶרֶן יְשׁוּעָה.

May the Messiah, a descendant of David, come speedily, for we long each day for Your salvation. Be praised, O Lord, who brings forth salvation.

Perhaps one of the most important visions which the prophets of Israel gave to the Jewish people, and to all people, was the hope for a time when human beings would live in justice, peace, and mutual understanding — and war would be no more. That vision is known within Jewish tradition as the "messianic hope." Why? What has the establishment of a day of peace and justice for all have to do with the coming of the Messiah?

Who Is the Messiah?

Our קֶרֶן יְשׁוּעָה prayer begins with the words אֶת צֶמַח דָּוִד (et tzemach David), a descendant of David. For those who composed our prayer, who was the "descendant of David" supposed to be?

In the Book of Isaiah, the prophet tells us:

And there shall come forth a descendant out of the stock of Jesse [David]....
And the spirit of the Lord shall rest upon him,
The spirit of wisdom and understanding,
The spirit of counsel and might,
The spirit of knowledge of the fear of the Lord.
(Isaiah 11)

The prophet Isaiah then goes on to explain how this descendant of David will bring about a new day of peace not only for human beings but for the animal kingdom as well. (Look at Chapter 11 in the Book of Isaiah.) In another place Isaiah proclaims:

[The descendant of David will sit]
Upon the throne of David, and upon his kingdom,
To establish it and uphold it
Through justice and through righteousness.
(Isaiah 9)

In other words, for the prophet Isaiah, the צֶמַח דָּוִד, descendant of David, was to occupy the ancient king's throne. This helps us understand why the descendant of David is called Messiah. In Hebrew, the word for messiah is מָשִׁיחַ (mashiach) which means "the anointed one." In ancient Israel, it was the king who was anointed upon assuming the throne.

The Messiah and a New Day of Peace

The prophet Isaiah, who wrote the words we find in Chapters 9 and 11, lived during the Babylonian exile. He, like many Jews of his day, longed to return to the Land of Israel and to rebuild Jewish national life. His hope was that a new descendant of David would be placed on the throne; that the Temple would be rebuilt; and that Jewish life would see an end to the cruel Babylonian exile. Eventually, his hope became a great vision not only for Jews but for all people. It is expressed with beauty in the following words:

And it shall come to pass in the end of days,
That the mountain of the Lord's house shall be established as the top of the mountains.
And shall be exalted above the hills;
And all nations shall flow unto it.
And many peoples shall go and say:
"Come, let us go up to the mountain of the Lord,

To the house of the God of Jacob;
And He will teach us of His ways,
And we will walk in His paths."
For out of Zion shall go forth the law,
And the word of the Lord from Jerusalem.
And He shall judge between the nations,
And shall decide for many peoples;
And they shall beat their swords into plow-shares,
And their spears into pruning-hooks;
Nation shall not lift up sword against nation,
Neither shall they learn war any more.

(Isaiah 2:2–4)

Often our ideals are not realized. This, however, does not mean that they are either false or unimportant. Isaiah's vision, for instance, has continued to live in the hearts of human beings for centuries. Our קֶרֶן יְשׁוּעָה prayer is an excellent example. It was added to the original *Amidah* as the nineteenth benediction. This was done in about the third century C.E., after the destruction of the Temple and the dispersion of the Jewish people. The קֶרֶן יְשׁוּעָה prayer was an expression of the Jewish people's hope for the re-establishment of a Jewish state and the fulfillment of the messianic vision.

CHRISTIANITY AND THE MESSIAH

The followers of Jesus believed that he was the צֶמַח דָּוִד, descendant of David, and the Messiah. They called him *Christos* which in Greek means "messiah" or "anointed one." The Romans, who put Jesus to death, placed a sign over his head which read: "Jesus, king of the Jews." They were mocking him for claiming to be the Messiah.

Jews rejected Jesus as the Messiah because he did not bring about the realization of the messianic vision. The Christian Church holds that Jesus will return and in the "Second Coming" will bring about the promised messianic times.

THE MESSIAH AND US

What can the קֶרֶן יְשׁוּעָה prayer possibly mean to us? Can we still believe that one human being — Messiah — will be able to bring about Isaiah's vision of a world of justice, human love, and peace?

We are told that Rabbi Eliezer Lippmann constantly asked Rabbi Mendel of Kossov: "Why has the Messiah not come?" One day Rabbi Mendel answered: "He has not come because we are today just the same as we were yesterday." (*Hasidic Anthology*, p. 247) What do you think Rabbi Mendel meant? According to him, what does the coming of the Messiah depend upon?

Another chasidic leader, known as the Stretiner Rebbe, told his students: "Each Jew has within him something of the Messiah. And the Messiah will come when each Jew has developed and perfected the Messiah within him." Are the Stretiner Rebbe and Rabbi Mendel saying the same thing? What can it mean for each Jew to "develop and perfect the Messiah within him"? Could that be a meaning of the קֶרֶן יְשׁוּעָה prayer?

Shomea Tefilah שׁוֹמֵעַ תְּפִילָה Who Hears Prayer

שְׁמַע קוֹלֵנוּ יְיָ אֱלֹהֵינוּ. חוּס וְרַחֵם עָלֵינוּ. וְקַבֵּל בְּרַחֲמִים
וּבְרָצוֹן אֶת תְּפִלָּתֵנוּ. כִּי אֵל שׁוֹמֵעַ תְּפִלּוֹת וְתַחֲנוּנִים אָתָּה.
וּמִלְּפָנֶיךָ מַלְכֵּנוּ רֵיקָם אַל תְּשִׁיבֵנוּ. כִּי אַתָּה שׁוֹמֵעַ תְּפִלַּת
עַמְּךָ יִשְׂרָאֵל בְּרַחֲמִים. בָּרוּךְ אַתָּה יְיָ שׁוֹמֵעַ תְּפִילָה.

Hear our voice, O Lord our God, and be loving and merciful to us. Accept our prayer in mercy and favor, for You hear our prayers. May we not be turned away from Your presence feeling empty. O Hear the prayer of Your people, Israel. Be praised, O Lord, who hears prayer.

This prayer raises an interesting and important question. Does God hear and answer our prayers?

Some Jews believe that God does actually hear and respond to our prayers. They argue that, if God did not hear prayers, then what would be the use of praying? They also hold that the belief that God hears prayer is a matter of faith.

Other Jews have difficulty believing that God hears and answers prayer. They point out that, if God responds to prayer, then why did God not save the sick little child whose parents prayed for it to live?

thinking about whether or not God hears our prayer.

Judaism teaches that each person is created in the image of God and has within him a "spark of the Divine." Some call that spark our conscience. Others refer to it as our נֶפֶשׁ (*nefesh*), soul. When we pray it is possible to say that the "spark of the Divine" within us hears our prayer. In that sense, many Jews believe that God hears prayer. What do you think about such an explanation? Is it one which you could hold for yourself?

ANOTHER WAY

There are no easy or simple answers to such questions. There may, however, be another way of

Does God Answer?

It is one thing to say that "God hears our prayers" but quite another to hold that God answers them. What about the answer? Can we say, in any way, that God answers our prayers?

The answer of Rabbi Morris Adler may be helpful. He wrote:

> Our prayers are answered not when we are given what we ask but when we are challenged to be what we can be.
> (*Modern Treasury of Jewish Thoughts*, pp. 144–145)

What do you think Rabbi Adler means? What is he trying to teach us about prayer and its place in our lives?

Perhaps the deepest meaning and benefit of prayer is that it allows us to think about our lives and all that we experience. It provides us with the opportunity to judge ourselves and to deepen our appreciation of our abilities. It leads us to be more sensitive, aware, and concerned human beings.

Rav Kook, one of the outstanding leaders of Orthodox Jewry in the Land of Israel during the early twentieth century (1864–1935), wrote that "through prayer we lift ourselves to a world of perfection." What did he mean by his statement? Is Rav Kook's observation close to that of Rabbi Adler's? How do you suppose Rav Kook might answer the question: "Does God hear and answer our prayers?"

Once we have an understanding of the traditional עֲמִידָה, *we can create our own. We might begin by making use of some of the middle thirteen prayers. Choose and develop your prayer or prayers on the basis of the commentaries.*

One of the important lessons we have learned from our study of the עֲמִידָה *is that the rabbis developed prayers in response to the needs of their people and times. In creating our own* עֲמִידָה *prayers, we should do the same. Our age and our problems present us with new challenges. In the creation of our* עֲמִידָה *we can use the traditional prayers, and we can develop new ones which will speak of the hopes, joys, doubts, and fears that we feel in our hearts.*

The Shabbat Amidah

Avot

בָּרוּךְ אַתָּה, יְיָ אֱלֹהֵינוּ, וֵאלֹהֵי אֲבוֹתֵינוּ, אֱלֹהֵי אַבְרָהָם, אֱלֹהֵי יִצְחָק, וֵאלֹהֵי יַעֲקֹב. הָאֵל הַגָּדוֹל, הַגִּבּוֹר, וְהַנּוֹרָא. אֵל עֶלְיוֹן.

Be praised, O Lord our God, and God of our fathers, God of Abraham, God of Isaac, and God of Jacob, Great, Mighty, and Exalted.

גּוֹמֵל חֲסָדִים טוֹבִים, וְקֹנֵה הַכֹּל וְזוֹכֵר חַסְדֵי אָבוֹת. וּמֵבִיא גְאֻלָּה לִבְנֵי בְנֵיהֶם. לְמַעַן שְׁמוֹ בְּאַהֲבָה.

You give loving kindness to all, and You are the Source of all that is. You remember the devotion of our ancestors and promise to redeem all of their children for the sake of Your name.

מֶלֶךְ עוֹזֵר וּמוֹשִׁיעַ וּמָגֵן. בָּרוּךְ אַתָּה יְיָ, מָגֵן אַבְרָהָם.

O Lord, our Ruler, Helper, Savior, and Protector. Be praised, O Lord, Shield of Abraham.

Commentary

This is the first prayer of the עֲמִידָה and is called the אָבוֹת because its opening phrase refers to God as אֱלֹהֵי אֲבוֹתֵינוּ (*Elohe avotenu*), God of our fathers. The fathers mentioned here are the patriarchs of Jewish tradition — Abraham, Isaac, and Jacob.

Why is such a formula used? Would it not be sufficient to say simply אֱלֹהֵינוּ (*Elohenu*), our God? Why use such a long introduction mentioning Abraham, Isaac, and Jacob?

An Ancient Formula

Actually, the use of the formula "God of Abraham, God of Isaac, and God of Jacob" is a very ancient one in the Jewish tradition.

In the biblical story of the Exodus, Moses asks God: "What should I say when the people want to know who sent me to take them out of Egyptian slavery?" The Torah tells us that God replied to Moses with the words: "Tell them that the Lord, the God of your fathers, the God of Abraham, the God of Isaac, the God of Jacob sent me to you. And that is My name for all generations." (Exodus 3:15)

The fact that the Torah, at a very early period in Jewish history, designated the phrase: אֱלֹהֵי אֲבֹתֵיכֶם אֱלֹהֵי אַבְרָהָם אֱלֹהֵי יִצְחָק וֵאלֹהֵי יַעֲקֹב God of your fathers, God of Abraham, God of Isaac, and God of Jacob, as the way in which God should be addressed may explain why the formula is used so frequently in Jewish prayer.

What about Today?

We may now understand why the formula was used in the past, but what can it mean for us today? Those who have interpreted the אָבוֹת prayer point out at least three important meanings.

I. Remembering our history

There are those who believe that the phrase "God of our fathers, God of Abraham, God of Isaac, and God of Jacob" is meant to call our attention to the long history of our people.

Certainly, when we say the formula "God of our fathers..." we are immediately reminded that we are a part of a people and heritage that reaches back over 4,000 years. As descendants of Abraham, Isaac, and Jacob, we are related to the Maccabees, the sages of the Talmud, those who suffered in the Crusades, the great chasidic leaders, those who perished in the holocaust, and those who have built the modern State of Israel. In other words when we say אֲבוֹתֵינוּ, God of our fathers, we identify ourselves as a part of the Jewish people.

Have you ever looked at an old family album? What kind of feelings did you have? Would you have experienced different feelings had the album belonged to a friend rather than to your family? Why? How can saying the אָבוֹת prayer be compared to looking into a family album? How do both experiences connect us to our past? How can saying the אָבוֹת prayer help us to identify with our tradition and people in all ages and places?

II. The changing idea of God

The sages of Jewish tradition offer us another interpretation of the phrase Our God and God of our fathers. It is what we might call a "theological" explanation. The word "theological" means the study of what we mean by God. What does the אָבוֹת prayer teach us about God?

Some teachers of Judaism believe that the concept or idea of God has developed and changed over the centuries. They argue that, just as each of us has a different idea of God, so too did Abraham, Isaac, and Jacob. Those who hold this view point out that the formula Our God and God of our fathers, God of Abraham, God of Isaac, and God of Jacob is meant to teach us that, just as Abraham's idea of God was different from Isaac's, and Isaac's different from Jacob's, so too it is permissible, and even natural, for Jews today to have varying ideas of God.

Perhaps an analogy will help us understand this idea better. When two people look at a beautiful picture, each has his own unique conception of what he sees and what the artist meant to portray. The picture which is seen by both is the same picture, but there are two different ideas or views of it.

You need a room, five chairs, some paper, and some pencils. Take a number of objects and place them together in the middle of the room. Place the chairs about six feet away from the collage of objects. Invite five people to be seated. Give them 30 seconds to look and 1 minute to write out what they see. Then compare the varying views. What does this teach us about the different ways people understand God?

You may wish to ask some members of your congregation to write out their ideas about God. Compare and contrast them. How do they differ? How are they alike? What relationship do they have to ideas of God in Jewish tradition? Do you think the idea of God will continue to change? In what ways?

III. TWO KINDS OF FAITH AND PEOPLE

There is still another explanation of our phrase God of our fathers. It comes from the wisdom of Chasidism.

Why, the rabbis ask, do we say Our God and God of our fathers? We do so because there are two kinds of people who believe in God.

One believes because he has taken on the faith of his fathers, and his beliefs are strong because he has the support of tradition. The other person has come to his beliefs on his own, through much thinking and studying.

What are the advantages and disadvantages of each of these beliefs in God?

The advantage of the first is that, no matter what arguments others may bring up against his idea of God, his faith cannot be shaken because it was taken from his fathers and is based on a tradition. But, he has a disadvantage as well. Because he has not arrived at his belief on his own, through study and thinking, he is accepting blindly what others have told him.

The advantage of the second person is that he has come to his belief on his own. His disadvantage is that, because his idea of God is based only upon his own study and thinking, it may easily be contradicted by someone with a good argument.

The Chasidim point out that when we say אֱלֹהֵינוּ, Our God, we realize that every person must reach for his or her own conclusions and idea of God. And, when we say אֱלֹהֵי אֲבוֹתֵינוּ, God of our fathers, we recognize that we can gain many helpful insights from the views of Jews throughout the ages.

Can you name some ideas of God from the past that are helpful to you in formulating your own view? What does the אָבוֹת prayer tell us about God? How do its ideas affect yours?

THE DEVOTION OF OUR ANCESTORS

In the אָבוֹת, we have the statement: "You remember the devotion of our ancestors." What can such a statement mean?

Jewish tradition teaches that the deeds of loving kindness performed by Abraham, Isaac, and Jacob are remembered by God from generation to generation and that they confer merit and benefit upon all the Jewish people. This idea is known as זְכוּת אָבוֹת (zechut avot), the merit of the fathers. The rabbis of the Talmud teach that "זְכוּת אָבוֹת will aid the people of Israel in reaching the messianic age." (Genesis Rabbah 70:8) What did the rabbis mean by that? Did they really think that Jews are somehow given credit or special merit by God for the good deeds of Abraham, Isaac, and Jacob?

In a way, that is precisely what the rabbis believed. They reasoned that, just as the generosity, kindness, or contributions of a father or mother can confer the credit or merit of a respected name upon their children, so too did the good deeds of Abraham, Isaac, and Jacob confer merit upon the Jewish people.

Creating with Kavanah

Themes:

a. Our history and identity as Jews.
b. The idea of God is constantly changing and developing.
c. Each Jew should develop his or her idea of God based on study and tradition.
d. We benefit from the acts of our ancestors and should live so that future Jews will benefit from us.

How do you react to such an idea? What might it teach us about our responsibilities to our families and our people? What are the ways we might earn credit or merit for Jews in the next generation?

Sexist Language

The אָבוֹת prayer raises a difficult question for modern prayer book translators. The word אָבוֹת means "fathers." Yet, what about the important women in Jewish tradition? Are they not as important as Abraham, Isaac, and Jacob? Should we change the ancient prayer to include a mention of the "mothers" of the people of Israel?

In many places in *Bechol Levavcha*, we have translated the word אָבוֹת as "ancestors" instead of "fathers." In *Gates of Prayer*, one version of the אָבוֹת reads: "Lord, You are our God, even as You were the God of Abraham and Sarah, the God of our fathers and mothers, the God of all the ages of Israel.... O God, Shield of Abraham, Sarah's Help, in all generations be our Help, our Shield, our God!"

Compare some translations of prayers from traditional prayer books. Are they male centered? How do the women in your group feel about a prayer which speaks of the "God of our fathers"? If you were composing or translating a prayer book today, what rules would you follow regarding its language? What about descriptions of God? Should a prayer book abandon the use of "He" and "His" and other masculine pronouns? Some people argue that the elimination of masculine references to God would destroy the poetry of the prayer book. Would you agree or disagree? Why?

Prayers on the אָבוֹת Theme

I. God of Our Ancestors

The Lord of the universe is our God, even as He was the God of our ancestors. Our own experience and the historic wisdom of our people unite to teach us of God's redeeming love.

An unbroken chain of tradition links us with the earliest teachers of our faith. May we be reverent in our study of their words and find in them the inspiration to live in obedience to God's will.

Let us learn to enrich the teaching of our heritage with the knowledge of our own time. So shall we, by our lives and our labors, bring nearer to its realization the great hope, inherited from our forefathers, for the redemption of all humanity in a world transformed by liberty, justice, and peace.

(Adapted from *Service of the Heart*)

II. Give Us Jews

O Lord, give us Jews of inspiration! Jews who lead with willing hands and hearts.

    Jews who, like Abraham and Esther, are devoted to their people.

O Lord, give us righteous Jews! Jews who are just and free.

    Jews who work together and respond to their people's needs.

O Lord, give us Jews of courage! Jews of faith and vision.

    Jews who, like our ancestors, dare to do the right.

O Lord give us Jews of truth! Jews who stand up for what they believe.

    Jews who strive after knowledge and seek a future of peace for all.

(HJF)

The Traditional Gevurot

אַתָּה גִּבּוֹר לְעוֹלָם, אֲדֹנָי. מְחַיֵּה מֵתִים אַתָּה, רַב לְהוֹשִׁיעַ.

Eternal is Your power, O Lord. You revive the dead, and You are mighty to save.

מְכַלְכֵּל חַיִּים בְּחֶסֶד, מְחַיֵּה מֵתִים בְּרַחֲמִים רַבִּים, סוֹמֵךְ נוֹפְלִים, וְרוֹפֵא חוֹלִים, וּמַתִּיר אֲסוּרִים, וּמְקַיֵּם אֱמוּנָתוֹ לִישֵׁנֵי עָפָר. מִי כָמוֹךָ, בַּעַל גְּבוּרוֹת, וּמִי דּוֹמֶה לָּךְ, מֶלֶךְ מֵמִית וּמְחַיֶּה, וּמַצְמִיחַ יְשׁוּעָה?

In loving-kindness You sustain the living. With abundant mercy You revive the dead. You uphold the falling, heal the sick, free the captives, and keep faith with those who sleep in the earth. Who is like You, almighty God, and who can be compared to You, the Author of life and death, and the Source of salvation?

וְנֶאֱמָן אַתָּה לְהַחֲיוֹת מֵתִים. בָּרוּךְ אַתָּה יְיָ, מְחַיֵּה הַמֵּתִים.

You are faithful to revive the dead. Be praised, O Lord, who revives the dead.

Commentary

There are two versions of the גְּבוּרוֹת. The *Commentary* will explore their differences.

While the first prayer of the עֲמִידָה, the אָבוֹת, speaks of God at work in history, the גְּבוּרוֹת praises God as the power that sustains all nature.

Compare the two versions of the גְּבוּרוֹת. Their language is similar and different in very important ways. First, let us discuss what the two versions have in common.

Eternal Is Your Power

Some of the most beautiful poetry of the Hebrew Bible is found in the Book of Psalms, סֶפֶר תְּהִלִים (*Sefer Tehilim*). Many of the psalms were composed for use by the people when they worshiped at the Temple in Jerusalem. A favorite subject of the psalmists was nature. They wrote about the wonders of the heavens, the stars, the winds, and the earth with its valleys, mountains, running streams, and the fruits of the fields. Like many great poets throughout the centuries, the psalmists saw God's power at work in nature. Here are some examples of what they wrote:

The heavens declare the glory of God,
And the skies show His handiwork.

(Psalms 19:2)

The Reform Gevurot

אַתָּה גִּבּוֹר לְעוֹלָם, אֲדֹנָי. מְחַיֵּה הַכֹּל אַתָּה. רַב לְהוֹשִׁיעַ.

Eternal is Your might, O Lord. All life is Your gift. Great is Your power to save.

מְכַלְכֵּל חַיִּים בְּחֶסֶד, מְחַיֵּה הַכֹּל בְּרַחֲמִים רַבִּים. סוֹמֵךְ נוֹפְלִים וְרוֹפֵא חוֹלִים וּמַתִּיר אֲסוּרִים. וּמְקַיֵּם אֱמוּנָתוֹ לִישֵׁנֵי עָפָר.

With love You sustain the living, with great compassion give life to all. You send help to the falling and healing to the sick. You bring freedom to the captive and faith with those who sleep in the dust.

מִי כָמוֹךָ בַּעַל גְּבוּרוֹת. וּמִי דּוֹמֶה לָּךְ, מֶלֶךְ מֵמִית וּמְחַיֵּה, וּמַצְמִיחַ יְשׁוּעָה? וְנֶאֱמָן אַתָּה לְהַחֲיוֹת הַכֹּל. בָּרוּךְ אַתָּה יְיָ, מְחַיֵּה הַכֹּל.

Who is like You, Master of might? Who is Your equal, O Lord of life and death, Source of salvation? Blessed is the Lord, the Source of life.

The earth is the Lord's and the fulness thereof;
The world and they that dwell therein.
(Psalms 24:1)

Lord, You have been our dwelling place in all generations.
Before the mountains were brought forth,
Or ever You had formed the earth and the world.
Even from everlasting to everlasting, You are God.
(Psalms 90:1–2)

How great are Your works, O Lord!
In wisdom You have made all of them....
You send forth Your spirit and they are created;
And You renew the face of the earth.
(Psalms 104:24, 30)

Who can express the mighty acts of the Lord,
Or make all His praise to be heard?
(Psalms 106:2)

What do these expressions from the psalmists have in common? How do these psalmists understand God? Open your Bible to Psalm 104. What is God's relationship to nature as described in Psalm 104?

The author of the גְּבוּרוֹת prayer, like the psalmists, saw the wonderful power of God at work in all nature. He called God מְכַלְכֵּל חַיִּים בְּחֶסֶד (*mechalkel chayim bechesed*), the Power "who in loving kindness sustains the living." What do you think he meant by that expression? Which of the psalms quoted above comes close to expressing the same idea? If you were to compose a prayer or poem about God's power in the universe, what are some of the examples you might use? What about those mentioned in the גְּבוּרוֹת prayer?

YOU UPHOLD THE FALLING, HEAL THE SICK, FREE THE CAPTIVES

A sage of Jewish tradition once taught that "God shares in the affliction of the community and of the individual." (Mechilta, Exodus 12:41) What do you believe the sage had in mind? How is it possible to think of God as sharing the pain, or hurt, or problems of a community or an individual?

Perhaps a few analogies will help us. When a child is injured in an accident, his parents and grandparents participate in his or her pain. When a great leader is killed by an assassin's bullet, the pain is not only felt by his family but by all of those who relied upon him for leadership. When one parent is sick, the entire family is affected and may suffer.

What do these examples have in common? What do they teach us about our relationships with others? If each of us is made in "the image of God," and we feel pain or suffer, is it possible to say that God suffers as well?

In Jewish tradition we are taught that God is not only found in the far off heavens or in the realm of nature, but we discover God's presence and power in human life — in each of us.

The phrase "You uphold the falling, heal the sick, free the captives..." is meant to indicate the belief that God, somehow, gives support to those who suffer, healing to those who are ill, and freedom to those who are prisoners. Is this really true? How is it possible to say that God heals the sick or frees the captives?

Some people might respond by saying that the way God helps us in times of trouble is a mystery. It cannot be understood by the human mind any more than we can understand why we were born to live in the twentieth century instead of the fifteenth century. God's ways are not ours, and God is beyond our knowledge. All we can do is feel God's power in our lives and understand small fragments of vast and mighty acts.

What do you think of such an argument? Does it make sense to you? Would you agree or disagree with it?

The Berditschever Rebbe, a leader of Chasidism, offers us another way of looking at God's power at work in our lives. He once explained to his followers that "those who seek God in prayer and in the deeds of their lives will receive in return the strength to serve God further."

In other words, God may help those suffering by inspiring them to find new strength and determination. He may aid the sick by enabling them to discover new hope and courage. And God's influence may be at work in the prisoner who finds within himself the power to stand up to his oppressors and strive for freedom.

What do you think of the Berditschever's statement? How might the doing of charity give "strength" to a person in pain? How might the knowledge that there are powers of healing in the world, and in us, help a person overcome sickness? A prisoner of war, who was captive for over two years, was asked how he had managed to live through his ordeal. He answered: "It was a matter of faith and hope. I had faith that God would not allow me to be forgotten and hope that I would live to be free once again." What did the prisoner mean by "God would not allow me to be forgotten"? How would you relate the Berditschever's and the prisoner's statements to the גְּבוּרוֹת prayer?

WHO REVIVES THE DEAD

We now come to the difference between the two versions of the גְּבוּרוֹת prayer. In the Orthodox and Conservative prayer books, the גְּבוּרוֹת contains the words מְחַיֵּה הַמֵּתִים (mechayeh hametim), who revives the dead, and לְהַחֲיוֹת מֵתִים (lehachayot metim), to revive the dead.

In *Gates of Prayer*, the Reform prayer book, the words מְחַיֵּה הַכֹּל (mechayeh hakol), who sustains all life, are substituted for מְחַיֵּה הַמֵּתִים. In the *Union Prayer Book*, used for many years by Reform Jews, the words נוֹטֵעַ בְּתוֹכֵנוּ חַיֵּי עוֹלָם (notea betochenu chaye olam), who has implanted within us eternal life, were used in place of מְחַיֵּה הַמֵּתִים in the final blessing.

What did those who composed the original גְּבוּרוֹת prayer mean by the words מְחַיֵּה הַמֵּתִים?

What can it mean to praise God for "reviving the dead"? Can those who have died live again?

The concept of the dead coming to life again is called resurrection. There is no mention of resurrection in the Hebrew Bible. Some scholars believe that the idea of life after death became popular among some Jews during the Babylonian exile. Others think that the idea spread among Jews after the coming of Alexander the Great and Greek culture to the Land of Israel.

We do know that the subject of resurrection was a source of disagreement in the Jewish community over 2,000 years ago. The Talmud records that the Sadducees did not believe in resurrection while the Pharisees did. The Sadducees argued that resurrection was not mentioned in the Bible and therefore could not be accepted as a legitimate Jewish belief. The Pharisees, on the other hand, sought to prove that resurrection was mentioned in the Bible and held that belief in life after death was a central teaching of Judaism. Here are two examples of how they sought to prove that resurrection is mentioned in the Bible.

Rabbi Joshua ben Levi said: How can we prove resurrection from the Bible? We can do so from the Bible verse, "Happy are those who dwell in Your house; they shall ever praise You." (Psalms 84:5) Note that the verse does not say "they praised You" but, rather, "they *shall* ever praise You." From this (the future tense) we learn that resurrection is taught in the Bible.

Rabbi Chiyah ben Abba said in Rabbi Yochanan's name: How can we prove resurrection from the Bible? We can do so from the Bible verse, "Your watchmen shall lift up the voice, and with the voice they will sing together." (Isaiah 52:8) Note that the verse does not say "sang together" but, rather, "they *will* sing together." From this (the future tense) we learn that resurrection is taught in the Bible.

(Sanhedrin 91b)

By resurrection the Pharisees meant that, at sometime in the future history of the world, all those who had ever lived would be brought back to life by God. This idea of resurrection became popular and accepted by most Jews. It was included in the גְּבוּרוֹת prayer because it seemed to reflect the greatness of God's power. If God could create life, it seemed logical to assume that God could also revive it after death.

What do you think of the arguments of the Pharisees? Would you agree that they prove that "resurrection" is taught in the Bible?

Who Sustains All Life

When Reform Judaism came into existence, in the early nineteenth century, it rejected the concept of resurrection, or life after death, and substituted the belief in the "immortality of the soul." The Reformers argued that once a person died he was dead and that the body could not be revived. They believed, however, that each person was given a נֶפֶשׁ. The נֶפֶשׁ, they taught, was not physical but spiritual. It was a spark of God, and it was eternal just as God is eternal. Rather than using the phrase מְחַיֵּה הַמֵּתִים, which speaks of reviving the dead, the rabbis of Reform Judaism chose, instead, the phrase נוֹטֵעַ בְּתוֹכֵינוּ חַיֵּי עוֹלָם, who has implanted within us eternal life. In making that change, they meant to call attention to their belief that the נֶפֶשׁ, which God gives to each person, will live on forever.

One of the early leaders of Reform Judaism, Rabbi Abraham Geiger, argued for the change in the following way: "From now on, the hope for an afterlife should not be expressed in terms which suggest a future revival, a resurrection of the body; rather, they must stress the immortality of the human soul. We must eliminate the whole physical pictorialization of the divine household, the detailed description of angelic choirs and holy beasts, which is found especially in the morning prayers."

Within *Gates of Prayer*, Reform rabbis have made another change in the גְּבוּרוֹת prayer. Now, instead of נוֹטֵעַ בְּתוֹכֵינוּ חַיֵּי עוֹלָם, they have chosen the words מְחַיֵּה הַכֹּל, "who sustains all life."

What do you think of these changes by Reform Jews? Does it make more sense to you to speak of a soul which lives forever rather than the resurrection of the dead? Which of the versions do you prefer? If you were composing a new גְּבוּרוֹת prayer, how would you express the idea of immortality?

Some Other Possibilities

> When someone close to us dies, we almost always feel that his death was untimely. He didn't have the chance to do all he could have and should have done, and he wasn't given everything that we think he should have been given. In short, his life was not complete. The Jewish belief in immortality assures us that every life is complete, that death is not the final end.
>
> (Emil L. Fackenheim, *Paths to Jewish Belief*)

> To limit our perspective on human life to the span of our earthly existence would destroy all values. Insofar as the good we do while we live bears fruit after we are gone, we have a share in the world to come. To be sure, we will not be there to enjoy the good achieved, but to ask that we be is to refuse to accept the limitations which God places on individual life. It is as if the acorn were to complain that, in order to give growth to the oak, it must also lose its identity as an acorn.
>
> (Mordecai M. Kaplan, *Questions Jews Ask: Reconstructionist Answers*)

Another Possibility

Some Jews have trouble believing that man has an eternal soul or that there can be any kind of resurrection of the dead. They argue that it is our ideas, and what we have shared with others, that make up our immortality. Rabbi Roland Gittelsohn expresses this thought in his book *Man's Best Hope*. He writes:

> It is my ideas which are important — ideas which have come to me largely from many who died long ago, which are now being filtered through my own mind and which, if they are at all valid, will influence the lives of others after I myself am gone. If this is the truly significant part of me, and if there is every reason to believe that this will endure forever, what more do I need by way of immortality?
>
> In short, my immortality consists of my contribution to the ongoing process of evolution. This is the purpose of my life, hence the only eternally valid meaning in my death. ...When I die, there will be little or much remaining, dependent upon how I shall have conducted myself prior to that moment.

Another way of stating this possibility of immortality is to compare our life to a beautiful flower. After the flower has faded and been thrown away, we still have the memory of it in our minds. That memory can bring us much joy and satisfaction. In this sense, our immortality is in the memory of those who knew us, loved us, and were influenced by us.

Have each person in your study group write an essay on "My Immortality." Include in it a consideration of the ideas of immortality which mean the most to you. Then share your essays in a group discussion.

> **Creating with Kavanah**
>
> **Themes:**
>   a. God's power sustains all life.
>   b. God's power renews life, thereby allowing for growth and evolution.
>   c. God's power is felt in our hearts — it can strengthen the sick and give hope to the needy.
>   d. God's power makes it possible for us to achieve immortality.

Prayers on the גְּבוּרוֹת Theme

I. How Can We Know You?

O Lord, how can we know You? Where can we find You? You are as close to us as our breathing and yet are farther than the most distant star. You are as mysterious as the silences of the night and as familiar to us as the light of the sun.

Your goodness, O Lord, is revealed to us in the realm of nature and in all the experiences of our lives.

When justice burns like a flaming fire within us, or when love makes us willing to sacrifice for others, we feel Your presence. When, with devotion, we proclaim our belief in the triumph of truth and righteousness, we know that our inspiration is from You.

O Lord, our God, Your power fills all the world. And we, with open, searching hearts, behold Your presence.

(Based upon *Union Prayer Book*, adapted by HJF)

II. Who?

Who stretched out the heavens like a curtain?
Who made the clouds?
Who sends the winds like messengers?
Who appoints the moon for seasons?
Who created the depths of the seas?

Who established the earth upon its foundations?
Who sends springs bubbling into valleys?
Who caps the mountains with flakes of snow?
Who causes the grass to shoot forth for cattle?
Who brings forth bread from the earth for man?

How many are Your works, O Lord.
In wisdom You have made them all.
Be praised, O Lord, whose power
Creates and renews the face of the earth.

(Based upon Psalm 104, adapted by HJF)

III. The Creative Flame

God is the oneness
That spans the deeps of space.
   Adonai is the unity of all that is,
   The rhythm of all things.
God is the creative flame
That fires lifeless matter
With living drive and purpose.
   Adonai forms mountains and creates winds,
   Implants in each person the spark of the Divine.
God is in the hope
By which we overcome
Unhappiness, helplessness, and failure.
   Adonai is in the love by which we create
   The beginnings of a new and better world.

(Based upon a poem from the *Reconstructionist Prayer Book*. Mordecai M. Kaplan)

IV. For Being Alive

Beautiful flowers,
Blue and red and yellow and white,
Soft with the dew of the morn.
Freshly cut grass,
Cold and green....
And the rain
As it dribbles off the end of my nose.
As I lift my head to catch glimpses
Of all things —
Powdering snow
On the brown bare limbs sparkling
And on the rocks and earth —
Oh yes, oh yes, oh yes,
Halleluyah.
My eyes are dreaming,
My voice is calling out
To the sheep running in the meadow
And together
We thank God
For being alive.

(Based upon Psalm 148 from *A Contemporary High Holiday Service*. Greenberg and Sugarman)

Kedushah

Leader

נְקַדֵּשׁ אֶת שִׁמְךָ בָּעוֹלָם, כְּשֵׁם שֶׁמַּקְדִּישִׁים אוֹתוֹ בִּשְׁמֵי מָרוֹם.

We sanctify Your name on earth as the heavens declare Your glory.

Everyone sing

קָדוֹשׁ, קָדוֹשׁ, קָדוֹשׁ יְיָ צְבָאוֹת, מְלֹא כָל הָאָרֶץ כְּבוֹדוֹ.

בָּרוּךְ כְּבוֹד יְיָ מִמְּקוֹמוֹ.

יִמְלֹךְ יְיָ לְעוֹלָם, אֱלֹהַיִךְ צִיּוֹן לְדֹר וָדֹר. הַלְלוּיָהּ.

Holy, Holy, Holy is the Lord of all, the whole earth is filled with God's glory.

Praised be the glory of God in all the world.

The Lord will reign for ever, your God, O Zion, from generation to generation. Halleluya!

Leader

לְדוֹר וָדוֹר נַגִּיד גָּדְלֶךָ, וּלְנֵצַח נְצָחִים קְדֻשָּׁתְךָ נַקְדִּישׁ, וְשִׁבְחֲךָ אֱלֹהֵינוּ מִפִּינוּ לֹא יָמוּשׁ לְעוֹלָם וָעֶד.

בָּרוּךְ אַתָּה יְיָ, הָאֵל הַקָּדוֹשׁ.

From generation to generation we declare Your greatness, and throughout all ages we proclaim Your holiness. Your praise shall never cease from our lips.

Be praised, O Lord, the God of holiness.

Commentary

In the Book of Isaiah, we are told of a strange and wonderful vision which the prophet had one day in the Temple of Jerusalem.

Isaiah tells us that he was praying and in the

midst of his prayer he had a vision. In it he was surrounded by angels. They were moving their wings and singing the words:

קָדוֹשׁ קָדוֹשׁ קָדוֹשׁ יְיָ צְבָאוֹת, מְלֹא כָל הָאָרֶץ כְּבוֹדוֹ.

Holy, Holy, Holy is the Lord of all, the whole earth is filled with His glory.

(Isaiah 6:3)

Turn to Chapter 6 of Isaiah and try to figure out what it was that Isaiah saw in his vision. What do you think is the meaning of the angels' words?

MYSTERY?

Isaiah's extraordinary vision, like many of our own experiences and dreams, is hard, if not impossible, to understand. The fact that we may not be able to comprehend something, however, does not necessarily mean that it is without meaning. At times, the experiences we understand the least are the most important. Can you think of any examples in your life which have been very important but difficult, if not impossible, to understand?

What about the deep feelings of love we have for parents or that parents have for their children? What about the excitement or thrill we may experience when we hear beautiful music, or the mystery of our birth and life on earth at this time and not at another? What about the survival of the Jewish people?

Mystery is something which fills our lives. No matter how much we may know, there is still so much that we will never know. It is this feeling of mystery about life that the קְדוּשָׁה section seeks to express.

HOLINESS

The word קְדוּשָׁה is taken from the Hebrew קָדוֹשׁ (kadosh) which means different, unique, special, sacred, unlike anything else. What is the opposite of different or special? As we have already seen on page 45, a marriage ceremony is called קִדּוּשִׁין. What do a man and woman do at a wedding ceremony that makes it קָדוֹשׁ? On Shabbat and on the holidays, when we make the blessing over the wine, we are "making the קִדּוּשׁ (Kiddush)." What makes that moment קָדוֹשׁ?

In Isaiah's vision, the angels express feelings of קְדוּשָׁה about God. Those who composed the קְדוּשָׁה took their words and used them as their own. Perhaps they did so because they expressed the wonder and mystery men and women feel in moments of sensitivity and beauty. Perhaps they used Isaiah's words because they best articulated their idea of God's uniqueness and the wonder of Divine power which fills all the earth.

WE SANCTIFY YOUR NAME

How do we "sanctify" God's name on earth? The Jewish philosopher, Philo, who lived in Alexandria from about 20 B.C.E. to 40 C.E., wrote that "holiness toward God and justice toward human beings usually go together." What do you suppose Philo meant? How is "holiness" connected with "justice" toward our fellow human beings?

Moses Maimonides, in his book סֵפֶר הַמִּצְוֹת (Sefer Hamitzvot) The Book of Commandments, teaches the following:

> When the Torah says: "Be holy" (Leviticus 19:2), it means the same as if it said: "Do my commandments."

Why does Maimonides connect the doing of מִצְוֹת with קְדֻשָׁה? Are Maimonides and Philo saying the same thing?

The Baal Shem Tov, founder of Chasidism, once said to his pupils: "No two persons have the same talents. Each should strive to serve God according to his own abilities. If you imitate another, you may lose yourself. Therefore, always serve God through your own unique capacities."

According to the Baal Shem Tov, how can and should a person sanctify God's name?

What is unique about your own talents? What might the Baal Shem Tov define as קוֹדָשׁ within each person? Why is imitation dangerous? Who, among the people you have known or read about, would you consider to have achieved the expression of what is קוֹדָשׁ within them?

You may wish to have a discussion on how your congregation could help its members express their abilities and capacities.

A PERSON'S DEEDS

The chasidic teacher known as the Sudilkover once remarked: "If a person's action is worthy, its influence makes for holiness." What kind of actions are worthy and make for holiness?

Perhaps an example will help us understand what the Sudilkover Rebbe had in mind. We all know that there are a variety of ways to help others. Suppose, for instance, a friend is having difficulty with a math problem. We can call him stupid and show him our paper. We can quickly tell him what to do and then leave him alone to work it out by himself. We can explain the problem patiently and then stay with him so that if he needs us, or has any further questions, we will be able to offer further assistance.

What are the differences in the kinds of "help" suggested above? What makes one more worthy than the others? Which one would have an "influence making for holiness"? Why? Could it be that the Sudilkover Rebbe had in mind that a person's deeds, actions, and מִצְוֹת are testimonies to God's holiness and influence upon him or her? How, then, can a person achieve "holiness"?

Creating with Kavanah

Themes:

a. The world we live in is filled with mystery and wonder.
b. Men and women experience wonder when trying to understand their lives, abilities, and feelings.
c. Human beings achieve "holiness" through doing the מִצְוֹת.
d. Human beings achieve "holiness" through expressing their unique abilities and talents.

Prayers on the קְדוּשָׁה Theme

I. What Is Holiness?

The Torah commands us: "You shall be holy, for I the Lord, your God, am holy." (Leviticus 19:2) What is holiness?

There is holiness when we strive to be true to ourselves.

There is holiness when we bring friendship into lonely lives.

There is holiness when we reach out to help those who are in want.

There is holiness when we forget petty anger and make up with those we love.

There is holiness when we care for our world and make it a better place to live in.

There is holiness when we praise the Lord who gave us the power to pray.

Holy, Holy, Holy is the Lord.
All life can be filled with God's glory!
(Based upon *Where Can Holiness Be Found*.
Sidney Greenberg)

II. Should We Mark "Holy" between Our Eyes?

We thank You, God, that You let us see a portion of Your goodness in each person.

You gave us the ability to reason, to plan, to teach.

You gave us the heart to love,
The strength to build.

But, in addition to wisdom, understanding, and power,

We need a sense of the sacredness of daily life.
Upon our hands we should mark "Holy."
Between our eyes "Holy."
Upon our gates "Holy."

(Rabbi William Sajowitz)

Kedushat Hayom

אֱלֹהֵינוּ וֵאלֹהֵי אֲבוֹתֵינוּ, רְצֵה בִמְנוּחָתֵנוּ. קַדְּשֵׁנוּ בְּמִצְוֹתֶיךָ, וְתֵן חֶלְקֵנוּ בְּתוֹרָתֶךָ. שַׂבְּעֵנוּ מִטּוּבֶךָ, וְשַׂמְּחֵנוּ בִּישׁוּעָתֶךָ.

וְטַהֵר לִבֵּנוּ לְעָבְדְּךָ בֶּאֱמֶת.

Our God and God of our ancestors, may our Shabbat rest be acceptable to You. Sanctify us through Your commandments, and let us share in the fulfillment of Your Torah. May we be satisfied with the gifts of Your goodness and rejoice in all Your mercies.

Purify our hearts to serve You in truth.

וְהַנְחִילֵנוּ, יְיָ אֱלֹהֵינוּ, בְּאַהֲבָה וּבְרָצוֹן שַׁבַּת קָדְשֶׁךָ, וְיָנוּחוּ בָה יִשְׂרָאֵל מְקַדְּשֵׁי שְׁמֶךָ. בָּרוּךְ אַתָּה יְיָ, מְקַדֵּשׁ הַשַּׁבָּת.

O Lord, our God, let us lovingly preserve Your holy Shabbat as our inheritance. May Israel's celebration of it sanctify Your name. Be praised, O Lord, who sanctifies the Shabbat.

Commentary

On the Shabbat or on a holiday, one special prayer takes the place of the middle thirteen prayers of the daily עֲמִידָה. It is known by the name קְדוּשַׁת הַיּוֹם, the sanctification of the day.

The sages who composed the עֲמִידָה for the Shabbat, and the holidays, excluded all mention of sorrow, suffering, sin, repentance, and any other human problems from the קְדוּשַׁת הַיּוֹם and from the עֲמִידָה. Why? Why not use the Shabbat or the holidays to ask God for help or for forgiveness? Why aren't such requests permitted by Jewish tradition on the Shabbat?

According to the rabbis, nothing should be mentioned in Shabbat worship which might deprive a person of the full enjoyment of the Shabbat or holiday. If one is a mourner, he must stop his mourning on the Shabbat. The Shabbat was to be a day of celebration and joy. The sage, Rabbi Chanina, who lived in Israel in about 350 C.E., taught that "a joyous spirit should be a rule on the Shabbat." (Shabbat 12a–b)

The concept of the Shabbat as a day of celebration and joy is an ancient one in Jewish tradition. It is mentioned by the prophet Isaiah. Here is what he told the people of his times.

> If you will turn away your foot, because of the Shabbat,
> From pursuing your business on My holy day;
> And call the Shabbat a delight,
> And the holy of the Lord honorable;

And will honor it, not doing anything you wish,
Nor pursuing your business, nor speaking about it;
Then shall you delight in the Lord....
(Isaiah 58:13–14)

What do you think Isaiah had in mind when he mentioned "business"? What sort of work should be forbidden on the Shabbat? According to the sages there are 39 categories of "work" which are forbidden on the Shabbat. These include ploughing, reaping, carrying loads, kindling a fire, writing, sewing, and buying or selling. Why might such "work" detract from the joy or celebration of the Shabbat?

How Can We Celebrate the Shabbat?

How can we fulfill Rabbi Chanina's suggestion that "a joyous spirit should be a rule on the Shabbat"? How is it possible for us, and for our families, to develop a Shabbat celebration that brings us happiness? Perhaps some ideas from our tradition will help us formulate some practices of our own.

Our Shabbat Meal

We are told that the sages would do everything possible to make sure that the Shabbat meal was very special. As a matter of fact, Rabbi Chiyya ben Abba, who lived in Israel during the third century C.E., proclaimed that Jews should "sanctify the Shabbat with food, drink, clean garments, and pleasure." (Deuteronomy Rabbah 3.1)

In keeping with Rabbi Chiyya ben Abba's statement, Jews throughout the centuries have sought to make the Shabbat meal a special and beautiful celebration. They would save money each week to purchase the finest foods and wine. And they would set their Shabbat tables with beautiful decorated coverings and with their best dishes.

When it came time for the meal, it was celebrated with the lighting of the Shabbat candles, the singing of the Kiddush, blessings of children by parents, and Shabbat songs. The Shabbat meal was a time of sharing with family and friends. If a stranger happened to be passing through the town, he was invited to join in the Shabbat celebration. In all of these ways a unique atmosphere of joy and happiness was created at the Shabbat meal.

Why do you think that the Shabbat meal became such an important part of the Shabbat celebration of Jews? What do eating and celebrating have to do with one another? How does singing contribute to making an occasion joyful? Are there other holidays, not connected with Jewish tradition, where eating and celebrating go together? What does your family do for the Shabbat meal?

Your congregation or study group may want to set up a Shabbat meal. Prepare the food, invite your families, and have a model Shabbat celebration.

Dressing Up!

Rabbi Chiyya ben Abba mentioned that one can "sanctify the Shabbat with . . . clean garments." Other sages suggest that "a person's Shabbat clothes should not be like his weekday clothes." Some Jews put aside special garments which they wear only on Shabbat and on holidays. Why? In what way do clothes play a part in human celebrations?

What we choose to wear often expresses how

we feel. We call it "dressing up" when we put on special clothing or a costume for a part or important event. What difference do you think it would make to you if you "dressed up" in a special garment (even a costume!) for the Shabbat? How would it help us make the Shabbat different from all other days of the week? (You may wish to refer back to our discussion of the use of the *talit* as a form of "special dress" for prayer.)

SHABBAT REST

The קְדוּשַׁת הַיּוֹם prayer begins with the phrase Our God and God of our fathers, may our Shabbat rest be acceptable to You. What is meant by the word מְנוּחָתֵנוּ (*menuchatenu*), our rest? Is it just physical relaxation or does Jewish tradition have much more in mind?

Rabbi Mordecai Kaplan interprets מְנוּחָתֵנוּ in the following way:

> An artist cannot be continually wielding his brush. He must stop at times in his painting to freshen his vision of the object, the meaning of which he wishes to express on his canvas. Living is also an art....
>
> The Shabbat represents those moments when we pause in our brushwork to renew our vision of the object.

How does Rabbi Kaplan define "Shabbat rest"? Why does he believe it is important for a person to "pause" in the midst of his work? Would you agree with him that "living is an art"?

Our Shabbat rest can and should involve the expression of our spirits — our appreciation of music, art, and literature. It can mean the deepening of our family and friendship relationships through sharing Shabbat experiences and activities. According to Rabbi Shimon ben Lakish, "God lends to each Jew a נְשָׁמָה יְתֵרָה (*neshamah yeterah*), an extra portion of soul, on the eve of the Shabbat and takes it away at the close of the Shabbat." (Betza 16a)

What do you think Rabbi Shimon ben Lakish meant by his observation? What might we do on the Shabbat which would enable us to express our spirits and enlarge our appreciation of the world in which we live?

Statements on Shabbat

The Shabbat... prevents us from reducing our life to the level of a machine.
(Moses Montefiore)

The Jewish tradition, with its love of home life and its devotion to study, has shown how the Shabbat can be made not only a day of respite (rest) from work but a positive factor in human development and well being.
(Leon Roth)

The Shabbat is the day of peace between man and nature.... By not working — by not participating in the process of natural and social change — man is free from the chains of nature and from the chains of time....
(Erich Fromm)

TO SERVE YOU IN TRUTH

One of the most beautiful phrases in the קְדוּשַׁת הַיּוֹם prayer is "Purify our hearts to serve You in truth." The words have been set to a number of melodies, but what do they mean? And how do they relate to our observance of the Shabbat?

As we have already mentioned, the Torah forbids work on the Shabbat. Some of the sages even went so far as to forbid thinking about one's weekday or business responsibilities since that could interfere with the full enjoyment of the Shabbat. We are told, however, that "to plan for a מִצְוָה or for charity is permitted on the Shabbat." (Shabbat 15a) Why do you suppose such planning was permitted?

It might be because both the performance of a מִצְוָה and the celebration of the Shabbat are meant to help a person recognize how precious life is.

When, for instance, we do the מִצְוָה of caring for the sick by helping a member of our family, or a friend who is ill, we may realize how important friendship and the help of others can be. We may even understand how very fortunate we are to enjoy good health. In doing the מִצְוָה,

then, we not only aid another person, but we may also heighten our appreciation of the opportunity we have been given for life.

The commandment in the Torah for the observance of Shabbat is זָכוֹר אֶת יוֹם הַשַׁבָּת לְקַדְּשׁוֹ (*Zachor et yom hashabbat lekadsho*), Remember the Shabbat day to keep it holy. (Exodus 20:8; Deuteronomy 5:12)

What can the Torah mean by asking us to keep a day קָדוֹשׁ? What might be the relationship between the doing of מִצְוֹת on the Shabbat (visiting the sick, helping a friend, planning for charity) and making the day קָדוֹשׁ? What might such activities have to do with the phrase, "Purify our hearts to serve You in truth," in the קְדוּשַׁת הַיּוֹם prayer?

A Complaint

The rabbis loved to teach with legends. One of their favorites was about a complaint which the Torah once brought before God.

> **Creating with Kavanah**
>
> Themes:
> a. The Shabbat is a day of joy and celebration.
> b. Work is forbidden on the Shabbat; we are commanded to rest.
> c. The Shabbat should be celebrated with special meals, dress, and the study of Torah.
> d. The Shabbat is meant to increase our appreciation of life and its opportunities.
> e. One may do מִצְוֹת on the Shabbat (visit the sick, help a friend, and plan for charity).
> f. The Shabbat has contributed to the survival of the Jewish people and Judaism.

The Torah asked: "O Lord, what will happen to me when all the people of Israel are busy at work each day of the week?" God replied: "I am giving them Shabbat, and they will devote themselves to you on that day."

The point of the legend is clear. The Shabbat, in Jewish tradition, was meant for study and the sharing of thoughts. That is why each Shabbat has been assigned a Torah portion for reading and discussion.

Rabbi Leo Baeck, who lived through the Nazi period in a concentration camp helping his fellow Jews, once said: "There is no Judaism without the Shabbat." What do you think he meant by that observation? What is the importance of studying the Torah on each Shabbat? How could such a practice help in preserving the Jewish people?

The Shabbat Has Kept Israel

The Hebrew essayist, Ahad Ha-Am once wrote: "More than Israel has kept the Shabbat, the Shabbat has kept Israel." In what way is Ahad Ha-Am's observation true? How would you relate it to the various areas and ideas discussed in this section of our *Commentary*?

A Shabbat Prayer from Exodus

וְשָׁמְרוּ בְנֵי יִשְׂרָאֵל אֶת הַשַּׁבָּת, לַעֲשׂוֹת אֶת הַשַּׁבָּת לְדֹרֹתָם, בְּרִית עוֹלָם. בֵּינִי וּבֵין בְּנֵי יִשְׂרָאֵל אוֹת הִיא לְעוֹלָם, כִּי שֵׁשֶׁת יָמִים עָשָׂה יְהֹוָה אֶת הַשָּׁמַיִם וְאֶת הָאָרֶץ, וּבַיּוֹם הַשְּׁבִיעִי שָׁבַת וַיִּנָּפַשׁ.

The children of Israel shall keep the Shabbat, to observe the Shabbat throughout their generations, for an everlasting covenant. It is a sign between Me and the children of Israel forever for in six days the Lord made the heavens and the earth, and on the seventh day God rested and was renewed.

One of the best known commandments of Torah regarding the Shabbat is known as וְשָׁמְרוּ (Ve-shamru), and it is recited or sung just before the קְדוּשַׁת הַיּוֹם. It is also the first paragraph of *Kiddush leyom Shabbat* which is recited at the conclusion of the שַׁבָּת morning service. (For the complete קִדּוּשׁ, see page 156.) It calls the Shabbat an אוֹת (*ot*), sign, between God and the Jewish people. What do you think the Torah meant by such a description of the Shabbat? How can a day be a "sign" between God and the Jewish people?

A sage once taught: "To observe the Shabbat is to bear witness to the Creator." (Mechilta) How does this statement help us understand the commandment (Exodus 31:16–17) to observe the Shabbat? What does it mean to "bear witness to the Creator"? What might this have to do with the story of Creation in the first chapters of Genesis?

Prayers on the קְדוּשַׁת הַיּוֹם Theme

I. Remember the Shabbat

Remember to keep the Shabbat and make it a special day.

Shabbat is special when it is the day on which we study Torah.

Shabbat is special when we join with other Jews to celebrate it.

Shabbat is special when we think of the beauty of nature and of our duty to make the world a better place in which to live.

Shabbat is special when we share with others its joys and its song.

Remember to keep the Shabbat and make it a special day.

(HJF)

II. May Each Shabbat . . .

O Lord our God, may each new Shabbat strengthen our love of Torah. Let our actions toward others reflect honor upon our faith and people. Teach us to be more sensitive to the pains and feelings of our friends and family. May we always realize that we are an important link in the chain of our tradition. On this Shabbat, let us rededicate ourselves to being truthful and loving in all that we do. We praise You, O Lord, for the holiness and joy of this Shabbat day. Amen.

(HJF)

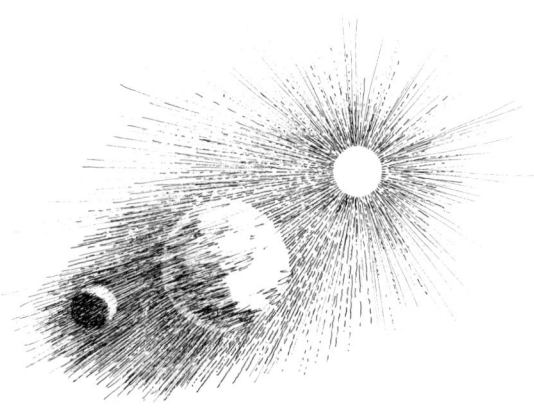

The Traditional Avodah

רְצֵה, יְיָ אֱלֹהֵינוּ, בְּעַמְּךָ יִשְׂרָאֵל וּבִתְפִלָּתָם. וְהָשֵׁב אֶת הָעֲבוֹדָה לִדְבִיר בֵּיתֶךָ, (וְאִשֵּׁי יִשְׂרָאֵל) וּתְפִלָּתָם בְּאַהֲבָה תְקַבֵּל בְּרָצוֹן. וּתְהִי לְרָצוֹן תָּמִיד עֲבוֹדַת יִשְׂרָאֵל עַמֶּךָ.

Be gracious, O Lord our God, to Your people Israel and their prayers. Restore the worship service of Your Temple, and receive in love and favor (the offerings and) the prayers of Israel. O may our worship always be acceptable to You.

וְתֶחֱזֶינָה עֵינֵינוּ בְּשׁוּבְךָ לְצִיּוֹן בְּרַחֲמִים.

בָּרוּךְ אַתָּה יְיָ, הַמַּחֲזִיר שְׁכִינָתוֹ לְצִיּוֹן.

Let our eyes behold Your presence in our midst and in the midst of our people in Zion.

Blessed are You, O Lord, who restores Your presence to Zion.

The Reform Avodah

רְצֵה, יְיָ אֱלֹהֵינוּ, בְּעַמְּךָ יִשְׂרָאֵל, וּתְפִלָּתָם בְּאַהֲבָה תְקַבֵּל. וּתְהִי לְרָצוֹן תָּמִיד עֲבוֹדַת יִשְׂרָאֵל עַמֶּךָ.

Be gracious, O Lord our God, to Your people Israel, and receive our prayers with love. O may our worship always be acceptable to You.

אֵל קָרוֹב לְכָל קֹרְאָיו, פְּנֵה אֶל עֲבָדֶיךָ וְחָנֵּנוּ. שְׁפוֹךְ רוּחֲךָ עָלֵינוּ, וְתֶחֱזֶינָה עֵינֵינוּ בְּשׁוּבְךָ לְצִיּוֹן בְּרַחֲמִים.

בָּרוּךְ אַתָּה יְיָ, הַמַּחֲזִיר שְׁכִינָתוֹ לְצִיּוֹן.

Fill us with the knowledge that You are near to all who seek You in truth. Let our eyes behold Your presence in our midst and in the midst of our people in Zion.

Blessed is the Lord, whose presence gives life to Zion and all Israel.

Commentary

There are two versions of the עֲבוֹדָה. The *Commentary* will explore their differences.

According to the rabbis of the Talmud, the עֲבוֹדָה prayer was said by the priests in the Temple just after they had offered the sacrifices. (Mishnah, Tamid V. 1) We are not absolutely sure what the words of the original עֲבוֹדָה prayer were. The talmudic commentator Rashi (1040–1105) gives us the following version. (Berachot 11b)

The Original Temple עֲבוֹדָה Prayer

רְצֵה יְהֹוָה אֱלֹהֵינוּ עֲבוֹדַת עַמְּךָ יִשְׂרָאֵל, וְאִשֵּׁי יִשְׂרָאֵל וּתְפִלָּתָם תְּקַבֵּל בְּרָצוֹן. בָּרוּךְ הַמְקַבֵּל עֲבוֹדַת עַמּוֹ יִשְׂרָאֵל בְּרָצוֹן.

Be gracious, O Lord our God, with the sacrifices of your people Israel. Accept with favor the offerings of Israel and their prayers. Praised be God who accepts the sacrifices of the people Israel with favor.

In the Jerusalem Talmud, we are told that the final blessing used by the Temple priests was:

בָּרוּךְ אַתָּה יְהֹוָה שֶׁאוֹתְךָ לְבַדְּךָ בְּיִרְאָה נַעֲבוֹד.

Praised be You, O Lord, whom alone we serve in reverence.

Later, in our discussion of the עֲבוֹדָה prayer, we will want to compare and contrast the many changes it has undergone through the ages.

Why Sacrifices?

The word עֲבוֹדָה, when used in the context of worship at the Temple in Jerusalem, meant sacrificial service. When the Temple was destroyed by the Romans in 70 C.E., prayer (תְּפִלָּה) in the synagogue took the place of sacrifices.

If we trace the history of humanity to its most primitive beginnings, we find that sacrifice played a very important part in man's relationship with nature and the Divine. Sacrifices were offered to express thanksgiving or praise. At times they were made as a present to the gods for rain, or sun, or the birth of new life. Sometimes, in preparation for a battle, sacrifices were offered in order to guarantee favor from the gods.

The Jewish people, like many of the ancient peoples about them, used sacrifice as the chief form of their worship. A glance at the final chapters of Exodus, and the Book of Leviticus, will give you an idea of the variety of different sacrifices that ancient Jews offered at the Temple in Jerusalem. There were sin offerings, peace offerings, special Shabbat and holiday offerings, guilt offerings, meal offerings, and so on. All these offerings were ways in which early Jews celebrated life and gave thanks to God. The sin offerings and guilt offerings were means through which a person asked God for forgiveness of his wrong doings. In a sense, sacrifice played the same role for our ancient ancestors as prayer plays in our lives.

The Prophets Speak Out

One of the problems of the sacrificial offerings was that when a man gave his sacrifice he often thought that he had satisfied his obligation to God. As a matter of fact, there were many people who came to believe that they could act unjustly, cheat, lie, and take advantage of the poor so long as they gave their sacrifice at the Temple. Many of these people came to think that all that God wanted from them was sweet-smelling sacrifices and offerings.

The prophets of Israel challenged this idea. They believed that, above all, God wanted justice, righteousness, and the pursuit of truth. For instance, the prophet Micah condemned the people of his day for their corruption and evil behavior, and he questioned their belief that God only wanted sacrifices from them. This is what he told them:

Hear now what the Lord says to you:
. . . That you may know the righteous acts of the Lord.

Wherewith shall I come before the Lord
And bow myself before God on high?
Shall I come before Him with burnt offerings,
With calves of a year old?
Will the Lord be pleased with thousands of rivers of oil?
Shall I give my first-born for my sin,
The fruit of my body for the sin of my soul?
It has been told you, O man, what is good,
And what the Lord requires of you:
Only to do justly, and to love mercy, and to walk humbly with your God.

(Micah 6:6–8)

The prophet Amos joined Micah in condemning those who piously brought their sacrifices to the Temple and then practiced corruption in their dealings with others. Speaking in the name of God, Amos told his people who were gathered at the Temple:

Therefore says the Lord . . . .
I hate, I despise your feasts,
And I will take no delight in your solemn assemblies.
Yea, though you offer me burnt offerings and your meal offerings,
I will not accept them;
Neither will I regard the peace offerings of your fat beasts.
Take away from Me the noise of your songs;
And let Me not hear the melody of your psalteries.
But let justice well up as waters,
And righteousness as a mighty stream.

(Amos 5:21–24)

What are both Micah and Amos saying about sacrifices? Why do they object to them? What do they believe God wants from human beings? What might Micah and Amos criticize in our society today?

Sacrifice Versus Prayer

With the destruction of the Temple by the Romans, the עֲבוֹדָה sacrifices ceased. In their place were the prayers of the synagogue. Actually, we do not know when the synagogue came into existence. It is possible that it developed around the time that Alexander the Great conquered the Middle East. He brought with him the development of cities, and with them most likely came the building of synagogues. By the time the Temple was destroyed in 70 C.E., there were hundreds of synagogues throughout the Land of Israel. In fact there was a synagogue in the Temple itself and over 480 others in the city of Jerusalem. Within these synagogues the practice of תְּפִילָה, prayer, was refined by our people. And, when the Temple fell before the Romans, prayer replaced sacrifice in Jewish life.

TWO OPINIONS

As time went by, two different opinions developed regarding the restoration of the Temple and its sacrifices.

There were those who felt that nothing could replace the old sacrificial ceremonies. Some of these people became אֲבֵלֵי צִיוֹן (*Avelei Tzion*), Mourners of Zion. They refused to eat meat or drink wine. For them there "was no עֲבוֹדָה as precious to God as the עֲבוֹדָה of the Temple."

There were others, however, who felt differently. They taught that "words of learning are more valuable than burnt offerings and peace offerings." (Avot deRabbi Nathan) Others who held similar views taught that "prayer is greater than sacrifices" and that "prayer is dearer to God than all good works and all good sacrifices." (Rabbi Eliezer and Rabbi Abbahu)

These teachers of Judaism may have been troubled by the sacrifices of the Temple and even pleased when they ceased to be a part of Jewish practice. Why might they have been troubled by the sacrifices of the Temple? Why would they have considered prayer superior to sacrifice?

Some of the sages may have realized that, if the Jewish people was to survive, it would have to overcome the loss of the Temple and sacrifices and replace them with the synagogue and prayer. How did the successful replacement of sacrifices with prayer and the Temple with the synagogue enable Judaism to survive?

Changing the עֲבוֹדָה Prayer

We have already noted several times that many of our prayers reflect the feelings and history of our people. The destruction of the Temple was a terrible moment in our national history. For many it may have seemed that Judaism and the Jewish people were destined for death. Yet, for the vast majority of Jews, there was hope that some day the Temple would be rebuilt and that the Jewish people would return to their land.

In order to voice that hope, the rabbis, after the destruction of the Temple, changed the words of the עֲבוֹדָה prayer. In their new version they voiced the yearning that the Temple would be rebuilt and the sacrifices restored. Their version of the עֲבוֹדָה prayer is the Traditional one found on page 87 and in the prayer books of Conservative and Orthodox Jews.

> ### A Question
>
> During the Six Day War, the Israelis regained the old city of Jerusalem. Thousands rushed to the כּוֹתֶל מַעֲרָבִי (*Kotel Maaravi*), Western Wall, and there offered prayers of thanksgiving. The Western Wall is the remaining part of that wall which surrounded the Temple that was destroyed by the Romans in 70 C.E. It has become a national shrine for Jews throughout the world. Why? Why have Jews, religious and non-religious, wept without shame upon seeing and visiting the Western Wall? A popular song about the Wall says: "There are men with hearts of stone, and there are stones with hearts of men." What do those words mean when applied to the Western Wall in Jewish tradition?

The עֲבוֹדָה Prayer and Reform Judaism

The founders of Reform Judaism rejected the hope for rebuilding the Temple and the restoration of sacrifices. They believed that prayer and ethical actions were higher forms of worshiping God than sacrificing animals. Since they were opposed to the reconstruction of the Temple and the reintroduction of sacrifices, they changed the words of the עֲבוֹדָה prayer.

The following is the version they included in the *Union Prayer Book* which was used by Reform Jews until the publication of *Gates of Prayer*.

רְצֵה יְיָ אֱלֹהֵינוּ בְּעַמְּךָ יִשְׂרָאֵל וּתְפִלָּתָם בְּאַהֲבָה תְקַבֵּל וּתְהִי לְרָצוֹן תָּמִיד עֲבֹדַת יִשְׂרָאֵל עַמֶּךָ. בָּרוּךְ אַתָּה יְיָ שֶׁאוֹתְךָ לְבַדְּךָ בְּיִרְאָה נַעֲבוֹד.

Look with favor, O Lord, upon us, and may our service be acceptable to You. Praised be

You, O Lord, whom alone we serve in reverence.

Compare the various versions of the עֲבוֹדָה prayer in the following order: (1) the Temple version used before the destruction; (2) the Traditional version; (3) the version from the *Union Prayer Book*; and (4) the new Reform version in *Gates of Prayer* and *Bechol Levavcha*.

What do you think of the reformers' changes? Would it bother you to pray for the restoration of the Temple and sacrifices? Why do you think the new Reform version is different from that which appeared in the *Union Prayer Book*? If you were writing a new עֲבוֹדָה prayer, what would you include in it?

ACCEPTABLE BEFORE YOU

What makes a person's prayer acceptable before God? Is it his tone of voice, the bowing of his body, the pain or joy out of which he says his prayer?

There are no easy answers to those questions. Jewish tradition, however, offers us some insights to consider.

The rabbis teach that "prayer requires כַּוָּנָה." What is *kavanah*? Maimonides defines it as "the clearing of the mind of all private or selfish thoughts." (Tefilah 4:16) What do you think Maimonides meant? How would "clearing the mind of all selfish thoughts" aid a person in prayer?

Some rabbis have defined כַּוָּנָה as the total involvement and attention of a person in whatever act he or she is engaged. "To pray with כַּוָּנָה means to concentrate completely upon your prayer so that your heart is not divided." (Pesikta Zutarta, Deuteronomy 11:13) Rabbi Ammi had something like this in mind when he said: "A person's prayer is not acceptable unless he puts his heart in his hands." (Taanit 8a) What do you think it means to "put your heart in your hands"? What is a "heart divided"?

A sage once remarked that "prayer without כַּוָּנָה is like a body without a soul." What do you think he meant by that?

INTENTIONS AND MOODS

The talmudic sage Rav, who lived in Babylonia during the third century C.E., once taught his followers that "whoever can pray for his neighbor and does not is called a sinner." (Berachot 12b) Jewish prayer is meant to turn our attention to the needs, problems, and concerns of others, the Jewish community, and the human community. Our prayers are "acceptable" when they express our responsibilities and relationships to others. Rabbi Isaac Luria, a mystic who lived during the sixteenth century, taught that before men or women entered into prayer they should remember the מִצְוָה "Love your neighbor as yourself." (Leviticus 19:18) Why did Rabbi Luria make such a suggestion? What does "Love your neighbor as yourself" have to do with prayer?

Mood also plays a significant role in worship. We are told by the rabbis: "Neither foolishness nor laziness, nor excessive piety, nor overconcern with material things ought to be the mood of worship." What is wrong with each of the things mentioned? How do they hamper prayer?

Rabbi Eliezer commented that "if a person prays according to the exact text of the prayer book and adds nothing from his own mind and heart, his prayer is not proper." (Berachot 28a) Why isn't it? What's wrong with just saying the words? What did he mean by "adding something from his own mind"? How do you add from your mind to the words written in the prayer book?

Another rabbi taught: "Do not pray for the impossible." (Tosefta, Berachot 7a) Why isn't a prayer for the impossible permissible? What is wrong about it? An example from tradition may help explain.

We are told that, if you should be on your way home and see a fire in the distance, do not pray: "O God, please let the fire not be in my house!" What is wrong with that prayer? Why is it not acceptable in Jewish tradition? Could you first say: "Love your neighbor as yourself" and then "O God, please let the fire not be in my house"?

PRAYER, AN ART?

From all this it should be clear that "acceptable" prayer is an art. It requires skill, understanding, and a willingness to express our innermost feelings and selves. Just as an artist cannot be successful unless he gives himself completely to his task, so too our prayers call upon us to be totally open to the world in which we live and involved in the spirit of worship.

PRAYERS ON THE עֲבוֹדָה THEME

I. It Is Not We Alone ..

It is not we alone that pray.
   All things pour out their souls.
The heavens pray —
   The earth prays —
The stars sing out —
   The fragile flower gives praise —
Every creature and every living thing.
   Creation is itself a prayer.
It is the outpouring of longing for God.

(HJF)

II. Accept Our Prayers

O Lord, hear our prayers
   When they are for peace.
O Lord, hear our prayers
   When they are for human cooperation.
O Lord, hear our prayers
   When they are for the freedom of our people.
O Lord, hear our prayers
   When they are for the healing of those who are sick.
O Lord, hear our prayers
   When they remind us to be honest with ourselves and others.
O Lord, hear our prayers
   When we offer them from our hearts.

(HJF)

Creating with Kavanah

Themes:

a. The עֲבוֹדָה prayer was used in the Temple at the time of offering the sacrifices. What sort of sacrifices do we offer today?
b. Prayer and ethical behavior are interrelated in Jewish tradition.
c. The Jewish people expressed the longing for a return to the Land of Israel and a rebuilding of the Temple within their prayers.
d. Reform Jews rejected the idea of rebuilding the Temple and reintroducing sacrifices.
e. Prayer demands כַּוָּנָה — wholehearted attention.
f. Prayer is meant to turn our attention to the needs, problems, and concerns of others — the people of Israel and all peoples.
g. Prayer is an art. It must be practiced and perfected.

Hodaah

מוֹדִים אֲנַחְנוּ לָךְ שָׁאַתָּה הוּא יְיָ, אֱלֹהֵינוּ וֵאלֹהֵי אֲבוֹתֵינוּ, לְעוֹלָם וָעֶד.

We are grateful to You, O Lord, our God and God of our ancestors, for ever and ever.

צוּר חַיֵּינוּ, מָגֵן יִשְׁעֵנוּ, אַתָּה הוּא לְדוֹר וָדוֹר. נוֹדֶה לְךָ וּנְסַפֵּר תְּהִלָּתֶךָ עַל חַיֵּינוּ הַמְּסוּרִים בְּיָדֶךָ, וְעַל נִשְׁמוֹתֵינוּ הַפְּקוּדוֹת לָךְ, וְעַל נִסֶּיךָ שֶׁבְּכָל יוֹם עִמָּנוּ, וְעַל נִפְלְאוֹתֶיךָ וְטוֹבוֹתֶיךָ שֶׁבְּכָל עֵת, עֶרֶב, וָבֹקֶר, וְצָהֳרָיִם.

You are the Rock of our life and the Shield of our help for ever. We give thanks and praise to You for our lives which are in Your hands, and for our souls which are in Your keeping, for Your miracles and wonders that are with us each day, and for all Your goodness which we experience evening, morning, and noon.

הַטּוֹב, כִּי לֹא כָלוּ רַחֲמֶיךָ. וְהַמְרַחֵם, כִּי לֹא תַמּוּ חֲסָדֶיךָ, מֵעוֹלָם קִוִּינוּ לָךְ.

O God of goodness, Your mercies never fail, and Your loving kindness never ceases. Therefore, we put our hope in You.

וְכֹל הַחַיִּים יוֹדוּךָ סֶּלָה, וִיהַלְלוּ אֶת שִׁמְךָ בֶּאֱמֶת, הָאֵל, יְשׁוּעָתֵנוּ וְעֶזְרָתֵנוּ סֶלָה. בָּרוּךְ אַתָּה יְיָ, הַטּוֹב שִׁמְךָ וּלְךָ נָאֶה לְהוֹדוֹת.

Let all that lives give thanks to You. Let all faithfully praise Your name, O God, our salvation and help. Be praised, O Lord, Your name is goodness, and it is pleasant to give thanks to You.

Commentary

The הוֹדָאָה (*Hodaah*) or מוֹדִים (*Modim*) prayer (as it is more commonly known) is the eighteenth of the daily עֲמִידָה and the sixth of the תְּפִילַת שֶׁבַע. Some Jewish scholars believed that the מוֹדִים prayer was recited by the priests in the Jerusalem Temple. After the Temple was destroyed, or perhaps before, it was made a part of the synagogue service.

Thanksgiving

The major theme of the מוֹדִים prayer is הוֹדָאָה, thanksgiving. The word מוֹדִים, we offer thanks, is taken from מוֹדֶה and means grateful, thankful, or appreciative.

The theme of thanksgiving is one of the oldest in the history of prayer. It is likely that the first sacrifices of ancient peoples were given to the gods out of gratitude for new crops, rain, or warm sun.

The psalmists of Israel expressed thanksgiving throughout many of their poems. In Psalm 92, for instance, the poet writes:

> It is good to give thanks to the Lord,
> And to sing praises unto Your name, O Most High;
> To declare Your loving kindness in the morning,
> And Your faithfulness in the night seasons....
> For You, O Lord, have made me glad through Your work;
> I will exult in the works of Your hands.
> (Psalms 92:2–5)

Another example of thanksgiving is found in Psalm 106.

> O give thanks to the Lord, for He is good;
> For His mercy endureth forever.
> Who can express the mighty acts of the Lord,
> Or make all God's praise to be heard?
> Happy are they that keep justice,
> That do righteousness at all times.

Why Give Thanks?

What are the psalmists trying to say in their words of thanksgiving? Why do you suppose parents try to teach their children to say thank you? Is it simply a matter of being polite, or is something more involved?

A Chasid was once asked: "What is stealing?" He thought for a moment and then replied: "A man steals when he enjoys the benefits of the earth without giving thanks to God."

Is that really stealing? What happens inside you when you thank another person, or God, for a favor or gift? When you see a magnificent scene in nature, and you pause and are filled with its beauty and wonder, have you ever felt like giving thanks to God for being alive in that moment? Would the words of the מוֹדִים prayer fit such a moment? What about the expression in Psalm 92?

In Pleasure and Pain

Rabbi Akiva, who died a martyr's death at the hands of the Romans, taught his students the following:

> Be not like those who honor their gods in prosperity and curse them in adversity. In pleasure and pain, give thanks!
> (Mechilta, Exodus 20:20)

What do you think he meant by that? How is it possible to give God thanks in times of pain or sorrow? Helen Keller, who lived her life in blindness and deafness, once wrote: "I have often thought it would be a blessing if each human being were stricken blind and deaf for a few days at some time during his early adult life. Darkness would make him more appreciative of sight; silence would teach him the joys of sound." What is Helen Keller trying to tell us? Would she agree with Rabbi Akiva that a person should give thanks in pleasure or in pain? Why? What are the things singled out in the מוֹדִים prayer for which we give thanks?

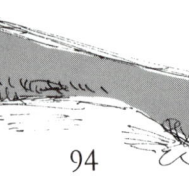

> **Yiddish Proverb**
>
> If a Jew breaks a leg, he thanks God he did not break both legs; if he breaks both, he thanks God he did not break his neck!
>
> *What can the above mean?*

WITHIN US

When we thank another person for a gift, or for helping us, or for sharing with us, more is involved than the expression of courtesy. Something happens within us as well. We not only express our gratefulness, but we become aware of how much we depend upon others for our happiness and our security. When we express our thanksgiving at a beautiful sight or sound, we acknowledge our relationship to all nature and life. Prayers of thanksgiving deepen our awareness and sensitivity to others, to the wonders of life, and to the joys of living.

BEYOND THANKSGIVING

An anonymous author once wrote: "The test of thankfulness is, not what you have to be thankful for, but whether anyone else has reason to be thankful that you are here." What do you think is meant by that observation?

The chasidic leader known as the Alexander Rebbe once remarked: "A Jew who is not always full of joy because he or she is a Jew is ungrateful to the Lord." Would you agree? Why should we be grateful that we are Jews?

> **Creating with Kavanah**
>
> Themes:
> a. Thanksgiving is one of the oldest forms of prayer.
> b. The מוֹדִים expresses our gratefulness for God's work in nature and in our lives.
> c. To give thanks is to open ourselves to the wonders and joys of life.
> d. Thanksgiving can, and should, include both our pains and pleasures.
> e. Thanksgiving should lead us beyond ourselves to מִצְווֹת for others.
> f. Thanksgiving can lead us to a deeper appreciation of what it means to be a Jew.

PRAYERS ON THE הוֹדָאָה THEME

I. *Everything That Lives*

וְכֹל הַחַיִּים יוֹדוּךְ סֶּלָה

Everything that lives thanks You, O God.

The trees with lifted branches,
Flowers with budding blooms.

Birds with chirping melodies,
Animals with howling sounds.

Seas with crashing waves,
Skies with roaring thunder.

And human beings?
How do we thank You?

It has been told you what is good,
And what the Lord requires of you:
To do justly with others,
To be merciful in all your acts,
And to walk humbly with your God.

Be praised, O God of truth. It is pleasant to thank You for the gift of life.

בָּרוּךְ אַתָּה יְיָ, הַטּוֹב שִׁמְךָ, וּלְךָ נָאֶה לְהוֹדוֹת.

(HJF)

II. Co-Workers of God

Behold how good and how pleasant it is for brothers and sisters to live together in peace.

We give thanks, O God, for all that is done for us by our fellow human beings. Some dig far away from the sun that we may be warm. Others serve in distant outposts that we may be secure. And still others search for cures to disease or brave the terrors of unknown skies or waters in order to help and benefit all life. Many blessings have been provided for us.

Let us then, O Lord, be just and generous in our relationships with others. Let us share with others what we are lucky enough to possess. Help us to give to those who are hungry and be friends to those who are lonely.

May we so live that we may be co-workers with You in building a world of cooperation and peace.

(Adapted by HJF, from the *Union Prayer Book*)

Birkat Shalom

שִׂים שָׁלוֹם, טוֹבָה, וּבְרָכָה, חֵן וָחֶסֶד, וְרַחֲמִים עָלֵינוּ וְעַל כָּל יִשְׂרָאֵי שְׁמֶךָ.

Grant peace, goodness, blessing, loving-kindness, and mercy to us and to all who worship You.

בָּרְכֵנוּ אָבִינוּ כֻּלָּנוּ כְּאֶחָד בְּאוֹר פָּנֶיךָ. כִּי בְאוֹר פָּנֶיךָ נָתַתָּ לָּנוּ יְיָ אֱלֹהֵינוּ תּוֹרַת חַיִּים וְאַהֲבַת חֶסֶד וּצְדָקָה וּבְרָכָה וְרַחֲמִים וְחַיִּים וְשָׁלוֹם.

Bless us and unite us, O Lord, in the light of Your presence. For in the light of Your presence, O Lord our God, You have given us a Torah to live by, and the power for loving-kindness, charity, blessing, mercy, life, and peace.

וְטוֹב בְּעֵינֶיךָ לְבָרֵךְ אֶת עַמְּךָ יִשְׂרָאֵל וְאֶת כָּל הָעַמִּים בְּרֹב עֹז וְשָׁלוֹם.

בָּרוּךְ אַתָּה יְיָ, עֹשֵׂה הַשָּׁלוֹם.

May it be Your will to bless Your people Israel and all humanity with great strength and peace.

We praise You, O Lord, Source of peace.

Commentary

The בִּרְכַּת שָׁלוֹם (*Birkat Shalom*), Blessing of Peace, or שִׂים שָׁלוֹם (*Sim Shalom*), as it is popularly known, Grant Us Peace, is the concluding prayer of the daily and Shabbat עֲמִידָה. The talmudic sage Eleazar Ha-kappar, who lived during the second century C.E., taught his students that "שָׁלוֹם is the climax of all blessings." Another teacher, who lived at the same time as Eleazar Ha-kappar, once said: "Our prayers will not help us unless we include a prayer for peace among them."

(Bamidbar Rabbah 11:17)

What do you think those two sages meant by their statements? Why might the שִׂים שָׁלוֹם prayer have been chosen as the last prayer of the עֲמִידָה?

WHAT IS שָׁלוֹם?

The dictionary defines peace as: (1) a state of quiet; (2) freedom from civil disturbance; (3) a state or order within a community provided for by law and custom; (4) freedom from disturbing thoughts and feelings; (5) harmony in personal relations; (6) a state of concord between governments.

The Hebrew word שָׁלוֹם means security, contentment, good health, prosperity, friendship, and peace of mind. How do these definitions match those given for the English word "peace"?

שָׁלוֹם is derived from the Hebrew root שׁלם which means complete, whole, perfect, accomplished, or total. שָׁלוֹם, as understood in Jewish tradition, is the highest human goal. Why? Is the word שָׁלוֹם used as a greeting or as a word of farewell? What is meant when we wish another person שָׁלוֹם?

SEEK PEACE AND PURSUE IT

The theme of peace occupies an important place in Jewish tradition and prayer. In the Book of Psalms, סֵפֶר תְּהִלִּים, we find many statements which remind us to make the pursuit of peace our chief goal. One of the most important of these statements is found in Psalm 34.

> Keep your tongue from evil,
> And your lips from speaking falsehood.
> Turn away from evil and do good.
> Seek peace and pursue it.

We are told that once a group of students were studying the Psalmist's words. They had difficulty understanding the last sentence, so they turned to their teacher and inquired: "Why are we told both to *seek* and to *pursue* peace? Wouldn't it have been enough to say either 'seek peace' or 'pursue peace'?"

The teacher thought a moment and then responded: "The Psalmist reminds us that it is not enough to seek peace in your own place. You must also pursue it everywhere."

What is the difference between "seeking peace in your own place" and "pursuing it everywhere"? Where should one begin in seeking or pursuing peace? How important is it to find inner peace before you go out to make peace in the world? How do you find inner peace? What does the poet of Psalm 34 think is the way to personal "inner" peace? The chasidic leader, Simchah Bunam, once said: "You cannot find peace anywhere save in your own self." What do you suppose he meant by that?

WAR NO MORE!

The prophets of Israel were among the first to dream of the day when all would live in peace. We have already made mention of the messianic days. In them, the prophets believed, humanity would be blessed with peace.

Many of the words and visions of the prophets have become a part of our prayers. In many cases their thoughts about peace express our feelings and aspirations in a beautiful and powerful way. Below are some selections taken from the prophets. As you read them, ask yourself some of the following questions: What does the prophet define as שָׁלוֹם? How is it to be achieved? What needs to be done in our times to help make the prophet's hope for שָׁלוֹם a reality?

> And they shall beat their swords into plowshares
> And their spears into pruning-hooks;
> Nation shall not lift up sword against nation,
> Neither shall they learn war any more.
> (Micah 4:4 and Isaiah 2:4)

98

The work of righteousness will be peace;
And the effect of righteousness, quietness and confidence forever.

(Isaiah 32:17)

Violence shall no longer be heard in your land, Desolation nor destruction within your borders.

(Isaiah 60:18)

All your children shall be taught of the Lord; And great shall be the peace of your children.
(Isaiah 54:13)

These are the things that you should do: Let every man speak the truth with his neighbor; and make peaceful settlements within your gates.

(Zechariah 8:16)

THE TORAH AND שָׁלוֹם

In the שִׂים שָׁלוֹם prayer we find the words: "You have given us a Torah to live by." What is the relationship of the Torah to the pursuit and achievement of peace? As we shall see, further on, when the Torah is returned to the ark we say the words:

It is a tree of life to them that hold fast to it,
And those who uphold it are happy.
Its ways are ways of pleasantness,
And all its paths are peace.

(Proverbs 3:18, 17)

Why is the Torah considered a "tree of life" whose paths are "peace"?

The rabbis taught that all of the מִצְווֹת of Torah have as their chief goal the achievement of שָׁלוֹם. They taught that "the whole Torah exists for the purpose of promoting שָׁלוֹם." (Gittin 59b) How do you think the מִצְווֹת help us achieve שָׁלוֹם?

Rabbi Chanina ben Chama declared that "the students of the wise [who study Torah] increase peace in the world." (Berachot 64a) Dr. Albert Einstein once wrote: "Peace cannot be kept by force. It can only be achieved by understanding." Are Rabbi Chanina and Dr. Einstein saying the same thing?

The chasidic leader, Mendel of Kotzk, once said: "Peace without truth is a false peace." Can there be peace with falsehood or lying? The

> **Creating with Kavanah**
>
> **Themes:**
>
> a. שָׁלוֹם is considered the highest goal of Jewish prayer and life.
> b. שָׁלוֹם must be sought in our personal lives as well as within the world.
> c. The prophets of Israel saw the goal of שָׁלוֹם as a part of their messianic hope.
> d. שָׁלוֹם is to be achieved through the doing of מִצְווֹת and the fulfillment of Torah.
> e. שָׁלוֹם and knowledge go hand in hand with one another.

talmudic sage Rabbi Bar Kappara observed: "For the sake of peace between a husband and a wife, the Torah allows a mistake!" In Genesis 18, Sarah laughs when she is told that she will bear a child in her old age. Then, she denies that she has laughed. Rabbi Bar Kappara understood this to have been allowed because it preserved peace between Abraham and Sarah. (Leviticus Rabbah 9:9) Do you think that, "for the sake of peace," lying or falsehood ought to be allowed in a marriage relationship or in a family? Have the members of your study group discuss this last question with their parents and then report and discuss their findings next time you gather together. You may also wish to invite parents to such a discussion.

ANOTHER PRAYER FOR PEACE

שָׁלוֹם רָב עַל יִשְׂרָאֵל עַמְּךָ תָּשִׂים לְעוֹלָם,
כִּי אַתָּה הוּא מֶלֶךְ אָדוֹן לְכָל הַשָּׁלוֹם, וְטוֹב
בְּעֵינֶיךָ לְבָרֵךְ אֶת עַמְּךָ יִשְׂרָאֵל בְּכָל עֵת וּבְכָל
שָׁעָה בִּשְׁלוֹמֶךָ. בָּרוּךְ אַתָּה, יְיָ, הַמְבָרֵךְ אֶת עַמּוֹ
יִשְׂרָאֵל בַּשָּׁלוֹם.

Grant a full and lasting peace to Israel, Your people. For You are the King and Lord of all peace. May it be good in Your sight to bless

99

Your people Israel at all times and in every hour with Your peace. We praise You, O Lord, who blesses Your people Israel with peace.

This prayer for שָׁלוֹם רָב (*Shalom Rav*), Abundant Peace, is a shorter version of the שִׂים שָׁלוֹם. It is used in the traditional afternoon and evening worship service as a substitute for שִׂים שָׁלוֹם. Some scholars believe that the שָׁלוֹם רָב was written in the eleventh century by Jews who were suffering persecution and death during the Crusades.

The שָׁלוֹם רָב is particularly appropriate for those occasions when we want to express our concern for the safety and welfare of the Jewish people.

PRAYERS ON THE בִּרְכַּת שָׁלוֹם THEME

I

Grant us peace, Your most precious gift, O Eternal Source of peace, and enable the people of Israel to be its messenger unto the peoples of the earth. Bless our country that it may ever be a stronghold of peace and its advocate in the council of nations. May contentment reign within its borders, health and happiness within its homes. Strengthen the bonds of friendship and fellowship among the inhabitants of our land with the inhabitants of all lands. Plant virtue in every soul, and may the love of Your name hallow every home and every heart. Be praised, O Lord, Giver of peace.

(*Union Prayer Book*)

II

O Lord our God, open our eyes to Your truth. Fill our spirits with faith in Your powers for goodness and peace. May we have courage enough to translate our desire to share with others into deeds of loving kindness. Let us take up the task to which generations of Jews were devoted and speed the dawn of the new day when all human beings will be united in justice, cooperation, and peace.

(HJF)

III

Grant peace to our world, goodness and blessing, mercy and compassion, life and love. Inspire us to banish forever hatred, war, and bloodshed. Help us to establish forever one human family doing Your will in love and peace. O God of peace, bless us with peace.

(HJF)

Elohai Netzor

אֱלֹהַי, נְצוֹר לְשׁוֹנִי מֵרָע, וּשְׂפָתַי מִדַּבֵּר מִרְמָה. וְלִמְקַלְלַי נַפְשִׁי תִדּוֹם, וְנַפְשִׁי כֶּעָפָר לַכֹּל תִּהְיֶה.

My God, keep my tongue from evil and my lips from speaking falsehood. Let my soul be silent before those who slander me, and may I be humble before all that lives.

פְּתַח לִבִּי בְּתוֹרָתֶךָ, וּבְמִצְוֹתֶיךָ תִּרְדּוֹף נַפְשִׁי. וְכָל הַחוֹשְׁבִים עָלַי רָעָה, מְהֵרָה הָפֵר עֲצָתָם וְקַלְקֵל מַחֲשַׁבְתָּם. עֲשֵׂה לְמַעַן שְׁמֶךָ, עֲשֵׂה לְמַעַן יְמִינֶךָ, עֲשֵׂה לְמַעַן קְדֻשָּׁתֶךָ, עֲשֵׂה לְמַעַן תּוֹרָתֶךָ. לְמַעַן יֵחָלְצוּן יְדִידֶיךָ, הוֹשִׁיעָה יְמִינְךָ וַעֲנֵנִי.

Open my heart to Your Torah, and let my soul pursue Your commandments. Upset and destroy the plans of those who plot against me. Do it for the sake of Your name, for the sake of Your Torah, that Your beloved may be saved. With Your power save and answer me.

יִהְיוּ לְרָצוֹן אִמְרֵי פִי, וְהֶגְיוֹן לִבִּי לְפָנֶיךָ יְיָ, צוּרִי וְגוֹאֲלִי.

May the words of my mouth, and the meditations of my heart be acceptable before You, O Lord, my Rock and my Redeemer.

עֹשֶׂה שָׁלוֹם בִּמְרוֹמָיו, הוּא יַעֲשֶׂה שָׁלוֹם עָלֵינוּ וְעַל כָּל יִשְׂרָאֵל, וְאִמְרוּ אָמֵן.

May the One who makes peace in the heavens grant peace to us and to all Israel. Amen.

Commentary

The אֱלֹהַי נְצוֹר (*Elohai Netzor*) was composed by Mar ben Rabina who lived in the fourth century C.E. Later it was chosen, because of its popularity, to be placed at the end of the עֲמִידָה. "My God, keep [my tongue from evil]..." is the opening phrase of this prayer. The original prayer most likely concluded with the words "with Your power save and answer me." The sentence "May the words..." is taken from Psalm 19 and was added later to Mar's prayer.

The words "May the One who makes peace . . ." recall the final prayer of the עֲמִידָה, the prayer for שָׁלוֹם.

Personal Prayers

Notice that the אֱלֹהַי נְצוֹר prayer is written in the singular and not plural. All the other prayers we have studied and used addressed God as אֱלֹהֵינוּ (Elohenu), our God. Why does this prayer, at this point in our worship service (just after the עֲמִידָה), address God as אֱלֹהַי, my God?

A part of the answer is found in the rabbis' understanding of prayer. They believed that there should be a balance between the expression of congregational or community needs and those of the individual. So they created a place within the synagogue service for personal prayers. That place came just after the שִׂים שָׁלוֹם prayer of the עֲמִידָה. At that time, according to tradition, the individual could express whatever might be on his heart or mind.

Mar's prayer was one of many written for this place in our service. Below you will find a brief selection of some others.

I

May it be Your will, O Lord our God, to cause love and cooperation, peace and friendship to abide in our midst; to enlarge the number of our students; to prosper our goal with happy ends and the fulfillment of our hopes. May we be among those who have a portion in the world to come. Strengthen us with good friends and with the use of our powers for goodness in this life so that reverence for Your Name will always be the longing of our heart.

(Rabbi Elazar)

II

May it be Your will, O Lord our God, that we may return to You in perfect repentance so that we may not be ashamed to meet our ancestors in the world to come.

(Rabbi Zera)

III

May it be Your will, O Lord our God, to place us in light and not in darkness. . . . Lord of the universe! You know that it is our desire to do as You wish, but what stands in the way? It is the power of evil in us and the persecution of nations. May it be Your will to deliver us from both so that we may again perform Your laws with a perfect heart.

(Rabbi Alexander)

IV

May it be Your will, O Lord our God, and God of our fathers, that no one hate nor envy us and that neither hatred nor envy of any person find a place in our hearts. May Your Torah be our chief task, and may we love You with a whole heart. Keep us from what You hate and near to what You love, and be merciful to us for the sake of Your name.

(Rabbi Pedat and Rabbi Chiyya)

What do these personal prayers have in common? How are they similar in style and theme to the אֱלֹהַי נְצוֹר? How are they different? What do you think Rabbi Zera meant by his request that we may not be ashamed to meet our ancestors in the world to come? What is living a life so that our ancestors will not be ashamed of us? What does that mean to you as a Jew?

Rabbi Alexander indicates that there are two things which keep a person from the pursuit of goodness. They are the power of "evil in us (יֵצֶר הָרָע) and the persecution of nations." How do each of these prevent us from doing good and pursuing justice or peace? Do you think that there are other things which keep us from the ethical life? What are they?

We have already noted that one of the important purposes of Jewish prayer is "judging oneself." How do these personal prayers, and the אֱלֹהַי נְצוֹר prayer, lead us to "judging ourselves"? How, and with what, do they challenge us?

The chasidic leader known as the Lizensker used to offer the following prayer:

> O Lord! Guard us from selfish motives and from pride when we do Your מִצְווֹת. Guard us from anger and sadness, from tale bearing and from other evil traits. May no jealousy of our friends enter our heart and no jealousy of us enter the hearts of others. Grant us the ability to appreciate only the virtues of our fellow human beings.

What are the concerns voiced by the Lizensker rabbi? Are any of them "problems" which you face or things which you are sometimes guilty of? How is the Lizensker's prayer a prayer for self-improvement?

Perhaps one of the best ways to prepare for the writing of your own אֱלֹהַי נְצוֹר *prayer is to make a list of those things which you wish to improve about yourself and life and those things which need improving for the sake of the world and humanity.*

Once you have made up such a list, compare it with those things mentioned in the prayers quoted above. Then, write your own personal meditation.

Keep My Tongue from Evil

What is meant by Mar's statement: "Keep my tongue from evil . . ."? An insight into an answer may be found in the Bratzlaver Rebbe's comment on the talmudic command: "Judge not your neighbor until you stand in his place." (Avot 2:5) The Bratzlaver explained that a person "should never talk against another, since no person can possibly know when he will stand in another's position." What did the Bratzlaver mean by his interpretation? Does this mean that we should not evaluate the actions or words of others?

What is the danger of words? The poet Heinrich Heine once observed: "When the arrow has left the bow-string, it no longer belongs to the archer and, when the word has left the lips, it is no longer controlled by the speaker." What do you think he meant by that? Would you agree with Heine? Rabbi Shimon bar Yochai taught that "verbal wrong is worse than monetary wrong." (Baba Metzia 58b) Is that true? How do Heine and Shimon bar Yochai's observations compare with one another?

Let My Soul Be Silent before Those Who Slander Me

Does this mean that Mar believed that a person should "turn the other cheek" or let others say whatever they wanted without answering back in self-defense? Does Judaism teach that people should sit silently by while others curse or oppress them?

In one place the rabbis of the Talmud teach the following:

> Whoever does not persecute them that persecute him, whoever takes an offense in silence, whoever does good because of evil, whoever is cheerful under sufferings — is a lover of God.

(Shabbat 88b)

How does such an expression compare with Mar's אֱלֹהַי נְצוֹר prayer? Would you agree that whoever is cheerful under sufferings is a lover of God? What is the strength and power in keeping silent before those who would persecute or say nasty things about us? Can you give examples of those who have used silence in the face of oppression and nonviolence in the face of brutality in the twentieth century? How successful were they?

Two Sides to the Issue

There are those who would argue that "silence in the face of slander" or the use of nonviolence when you are attacked is wrong and even foolish. Tragically, Jews have been the recipients of hate and hostility for over 2,000 years. We have suffered at the brutal hands of the Romans, the Crusaders, and the Cossacks. During the Second World War, Hitler sought to eliminate the Jewish people from the face of the earth. Most recently, the Jews of Russia have endured bitter persecution, and Arab armies have sought to destroy the State of Israel. What do you think is the best way to meet and deal with such hostility?

According to the Talmud: "If someone comes to kill you, you should go ahead and kill him." (Berachot 58a) In another place we are told: "Whoever defends Israel is exalted by God." (Pesikta deRav Kahana) What kind of action should one take in "self-defense"? Is speaking out or taking violent action against those who slander Jews or other minorities justified?

One American Jewish organization suggests that "the best defense against hostile attitudes directed toward Jews is a firm identification with Judaism, coupled with full participation in the broad community life of America." Would you agree with that position? How does it compare with the thought expressed in the אֱלֹהַי נְצוֹר or with the statement: "Whoever defends Israel is exalted by God"?

Within Jewish literature there are several suggestions about how one should treat an enemy. In Proverbs we are told: "If your enemy is hungry, give him bread to eat." (25:21) In another place we are told: "If your enemy meets you with evil, meet him with wisdom." (Apocrypha) Within the Talmud we are counseled: "Who is a hero? The person who turns an enemy into a friend." (Avot deRabbi Nathan 23)

How do these suggestions about treating an enemy compare with the others already mentioned in this section? Are they more or less realistic? Which do you prefer?

Perhaps another position, between those who advocate answering violence with violence and those who believe in nonviolence, might be found in Hillel's famous statement: "If I am not for myself, who will be for me? If I am only for myself, what am I? And, if not now, when?" (Avot 2:4) What do you think he meant by that? Does Hillel offer us a third alternative? What is it?

Arrange a debate among two or four people in your study group on the question: How should we treat an enemy? A Jewish question and answer! Those participating should try to answer the question by taking examples from Jewish history and experience. Some excellent examples may be found in the history of the Maccabees, the Jews of Massada, during Hitler's time, the building of the State of Israel, or the Jews of Russia.

> **The prayer just after the עֲמִידָה is a personal one. It ought to express, in our own way, our feelings, hopes, and desires. As we have seen, it was also used as a moment of self-judgment.**

Section Four

קְרִיאַת הַתּוֹרָה

THE READING OF TORAH

Keriat Hatorah

a. At the Ark   *112*
b. Taking the Torah from the Ark   *116*
c. Aliyah and Torah Service   *120*
d. Haftarah Blessings   *124*
e. The New Month   *130*
f. Returning the Torah to the Ark   *135*

קְרִיאַת הַתּוֹרָה — Keriat Hatorah

When and where did the custom of the reading of Torah originate? Why is the Torah divided into sections or weekly portions? What is a פָּרָשָׁה (*parashah*)? These are some of the questions with which we wish to deal in this section.

In Deuteronomy 31, we are told that Moses wrote the Torah and then "delivered it to the priests, the sons of Levi, that carried the ark of the covenant of the Lord, and to all of the elders of Israel." Moses commanded them to read the Torah to the people of Israel every seven years, on the Sabbatical year, during the festival of Sukot. Why did Moses want the people to hear the Torah?

The Book of Deuteronomy answers our question with these words of Moses:

> Assemble the people, the men and the women and the little ones, and the stranger that is within your gates, that they may hear, and learn, and fear the Lord your God, and observe to do all the words of this Torah and that their children, who have not known, may hear and learn to fear the Lord your God. . . .
>
> (Deuteronomy 31:12–13)

What, according to the above passage from Deuteronomy, is the purpose of hearing the Torah? How did the *reading* of Torah play a part in transmitting Jewish tradition from one generation to the next?

Ezra the Scribe

About the year 421 B.C.E., many Jews, under the leadership of Ezra and Nehemiah, returned from Babylonia to the Land of Israel. Their hope was to rebuild their land and to reestablish their nation. The Babylonians, who had taken them into exile in 586 B.C.E., had been defeated by the Persians who were led by Cyrus. The Jewish people, who had vowed never to forget Jerusalem, or "the Land," applied to Cyrus for the opportunity to return to their land. In response to their plea, the Persian leader issued the following declaration:

> All the kingdoms of the earth, the Lord, the God of the heavens, has given to me, and He has charged me to build Him a house in Jerusalem, which is in Judah. Whoever there is among you of all His people — may his God be with him — let him go up to Jeru-

salem, which is in Judah, and build the house of the Lord, the God of Israel, He is the God who is in Jerusalem. And whoever is left, in any place where he lives, let the men of his place help him with silver, and with gold, and with goods, and with beasts, beside the freewill offering for the house of God which is in Jerusalem.

(Ezra 1:2–4)

With those words, and that proclamation, Cyrus made it possible for Jews to return to the Land of Israel and to begin the long process of rebuilding the Temple. We are also told that the Persian leader gave the Jews all of the precious "vessels" which the Babylonians had removed from the Temple, so that they could restore them to their proper place. In all, the Book of Ezra reports that over 5,400 vessels were returned to the Jewish people.

Upon their return to the Land of Israel, the Jews prepared themselves for the celebration of Rosh Hashanah and the holidays which were to follow. We are informed that on Rosh Hashanah the people gathered and asked Ezra the Scribe to read the Torah to them. The Book of Nehemiah gives us the following description:

> And Ezra the priest brought the Torah before the congregation, both men and women, and all that could hear with understanding, upon the first day of the seventh month. . . .
>
> Also Jeshua, and Bani, and Sherebiah, Jamin, Akkub, Shabbethai, Hodiah, Maaseiah, Kelita, Azariah, Jozabad, Hanan, Pelaiah, even the Levites caused the people to understand the Torah. And the people stood in their place. And they read in the book, in the Torah of God, distinctly; and they gave the sense, and caused them to understand the reading.
>
> (Nehemiah 8:2, 7–8)

The Book of Nehemiah also tells us that the Torah was read on the second day of Rosh Hashanah and on each day of Sukot.

Torah and the Shabbat

It is likely that, from the time of Ezra to the development of the synagogue, the Torah was read on festivals and celebrations. It was, however, with the birth of the synagogue, sometime after 300 B.C.E., that the reading of the Torah became a regular practice within Jewish life.

It was the rabbis and the people of the synagogue who made קְרִיאַת הַתּוֹרָה a part of their prayer experience on the Shabbat and other holidays. As a matter of fact, they believed that the study of Torah within the synagogue was so important that they introduced the reading of it at their services on Mondays and Thursdays as well as on the Shabbat.

Rabbi Meir, who lived in the second century C.E., told his students: "Take time off from your business and engage in Torah." (Avot 6:1) Moses Maimonides wrote that "every Jew, rich or poor, or even a beggar, healthy or not, young or old is obliged to study Torah." (*Yad Hachazakah*) A sage, who may have lived during the period in which the synagogue was developing and the Torah reading was being accepted as a regular part of its worship, once put forth the question: "Why is Israel called God's people"? He answered his own question by saying: "Because of the Torah." (Tanchuma Vaera 9a)

In light of these statements, why do you think the rabbis, and those who developed the synagogue, were anxious to make the reading of Torah as a regular part of their worship services?

We know that after Alexander the Great conquered the Middle East (in about 333 B.C.E.) he introduced the culture and way of life of Hellenism. Many Jews began to forsake their Judaism for the attractive Greek way of life. The rabbis and Jewish leaders of that period worried

---

Different Because of Torah

If not for the Torah, Israel would not at all differ from the nations of the world!

(Sifra 112c)

about the growing assimilation in their midst. Do you think that might explain why they introduced the tradition of reading and studying the Torah in the synagogue? How might such a custom have helped to prevent assimilation? Look at the quotation in "Different Because of Torah" on the previous page. Would you agree with the statement? How does the Torah still play a part in making us different "from the nations of the world"?

The Weekly Torah Portion

Where did the custom of reading a פָּרָשָׁה or weekly Torah portion, originate? We don't know!

We do know that by the time of Rabban Gamliel (80–120 C.E.), under whose leadership many of the prayers of the synagogue were arranged, the custom of reading the Torah was accepted practice. Rabban Gamliel lived in the first century C.E. Rabbi Meir, who lived in the century just after Gamliel, ruled that the Torah should be read consecutively so that ultimately those studying it would cover the entire text. (Megillah 31b) Sometime during the latter part of the second century C.E., assigned פָּרָשִׁיוֹת (*parashiyot*), weekly Torah portions, were drawn up by the rabbis.

Those who were responsible for developing the Torah portions and order of readings in the Land of Israel divided the Torah into 154 sections. This meant that the Torah was read from the first chapter in Genesis to the last chapter in Deuteronomy once every three years. This triennial cycle became the accepted custom in the Land of Israel.

The Jews of Babylonia, however, developed another division of the Torah. They chose to divide it into 54 sections and to complete its reading and study once each year. On each Simchat Torah they would finish reading Deuteronomy and immediately begin reading Genesis. In this way the cycle of Torah readings and study never ended. As the Babylonian Jewish community grew in size and importance, and as the Jewish community of Israel dwindled in size, the Babylonian custom of reading the entire Torah in one year became the dominant practice of Jews throughout the world. If you look in your Bible at the Five Books of Moses, or the Torah, you will notice that it is divided into the 54 weekly sections suggested by the sages of Babylonian Jewry.

Why do you think that in the Land of Israel the rabbis thought it sufficient to read the entire Torah over a period of three years but in Babylonia they chose a yearly cycle? What might have been some of the factors that influenced their decision? Rabbi Israel Goldman, commenting in 1938 on Jewish survival told an audience: "The learned Jew is the complete Jew.... The Jew who knows Jewish culture is the Jew who knows himself. To know oneself is to have integrity." What does Rabbi Goldman's observation have to do with a regular reading of the Torah? How does a knowledge of Torah strengthen Jewish survival?

Talmud Torah

The Torah has been called "the map of the world" by devoted Jews. The talmudic rabbis taught that the study of Torah "promotes peace in heaven and on earth." (Sanhedrin 99b) In another place they suggest that "the existence of the world depends upon three things: upon Torah, upon worship, and upon deeds of loving kindness." (Avot 1:2) The great sage Hillel taught that "the more Torah, the more life." (Avot 2:8)

Why?

Why did Jewish tradition consider the study of Torah so important?

One answer may be found in the Mishnah of Rabbi Yehudah ha-Nasi. He taught: "These are the things for which a person enjoys the fruits in this world and the principal in the world to come: the honoring of parents, the practice of charity, and making peace between neighbors. But the study of Torah is more important than all of them." (Peah 1:1) What do you think Rabbi Judah meant by the statement "the study of Torah is more important than all of them"? How could he consider the study of Torah more important than doing charity or making peace? Would you agree with him?

Another well-known teacher, Isaac ben Samuel, who lived in Babylonia during the fourth century C.E. taught that the "study of Torah is superior to honoring parents." (Megillah 16b) How could he teach such a lesson when one of the Ten Commandments is "Honor your father and mother"?

There are no simple answers to these questions. Perhaps, however, if we try to understand what the Torah has meant to the Jewish people throughout the ages, we will begin to comprehend its importance, not only to the past, but in our lives as well.

A Tree of Life!

The chasidic leader known as the Gerer Rebbe once related the following parable. A man fell from a boat into the sea. The captain of the boat threw him a rope and shouted: "Take hold of this rope, and do not let go. If you do, you will lose your life."

"What is the meaning of the parable" his students asked. The Gerer replied: "When we return the Torah to the ark, we say: 'It is a tree of life to those who hold fast to it.' If you let the Torah go, you will lose your life."

What do you think the Gerer Rebbe meant by the explanation to his parable? How is the Torah a "life line"?

The rabbis of the Talmud comment: "If it were not for the Torah, Israel would not be different from the nations of the world." (Sifra 112c) What does this comment have to do with the Gerer Rebbe's parable? How is the Torah a "tree of life" for the Jewish people? Would you agree that without the Torah "Israel would not be different from the nations of the world"?

A Torah-Person!

The Baal Shem Tov once said to his followers: "The object of the whole Torah is that a person should become a Torah!" How is that possible? What is a "Torah-person?"

In the Talmud, we find a fascinating definition of a Torah-person. We are told that he or she possesses 48 qualities. They are as follows:

1 a listening ear, **2** studying aloud, **3** developing an ability to grasp ideas, **4** developing an ability to understand issues, **5** respect for one's teachers, **6** reverence for God, **7** humility, **8** cheerfulness, **9** helping one's teachers, **10** associating with one's fellow students, **11** a disciplined approach to one's studies, **12** knowledgeable in Bible and Talmud, **13** fair in business practices, **14** courteous manners, **15** avoiding of extremes in pleasures, **16** avoiding of extremes in sleep, **17** avoiding of extremes in conversation, **18** avoiding of extremes in laughter, **19** patient, **20** sensitive, **21** faith in teachers, **22** knowing how to accept troubles and suffering, **23** knowing when to keep silent and when to speak, **24** appreciating one's self, **25** care with words, **26** not needing to claim credit for good deeds, **27** being beloved, **28** loving God, **29** loving one's fellow human beings, **30** loving justice, **31** loving righteousness, **32** appreciating criticism, **33** shunning honors, **34** not being boastful, **35** not delighting in giving decisions, **36** sharing burdens with

> **Torah**
>
> With the Torah freedom came into the world.
> (Genesis Rabbah)
>
> Why is Israel God's people? Because of the Torah!
> (Tanchuma)
>
> Do not make the Torah a crown to magnify yourself or a spade with which to dig.
> (Avot)
>
> Approach the Torah with joy and also with trembling.
> (Yoma)
>
> *What might these quotes have to do with becoming a Torah-person?*

Two Torahs?

In Jewish tradition, Torah is more than just the Five Books of Moses (Genesis, Exodus, Leviticus, Numbers, and Deuteronomy). By "Torah" is meant all of Jewish teaching throughout the ages. The rabbis taught that two Torahs had been given to Moses on Mount Sinai. One was the תּוֹרָה שֶׁבִּכְתָב (*Torah shebichtav*), the written Torah, or the *Tanach* (see page 124), and the other they called the תּוֹרָה שֶׁבְּעַל פֶּה (*Torah shebe'al peh*), the oral Torah. The oral Torah contained, according to the sages, all of the interpretations of the written Torah to be discovered and taught throughout the ages.

The teachers of Judaism have always realized that changes in society require changes and adjustments in the application of Torah. One example will help us understand. The Torah tells us: "You may not make a fire on Shabbat." (Exodus 35:3) That law seems clear enough. But, what about our modern times and the use of electric lights? Is the use of an electric light the same as making a "fire"? In other words, with the invention of electricity, the Torah must be applied to a new situation. The Baal Shem Tov taught: "The Torah is eternal, but its explanation and interpretation are to be made by the leaders of Judaism in accordance with the age in which they are living."

It has often been observed that ideas which are written down or printed seem more permanent and more difficult to change than ideas or suggestions which are shared by word of mouth. Why do you think this is so? What might have been the reason the rabbis taught that an oral Torah had been given on Mount Sinai? In the United States we have a constitution. It might be considered as our "written Torah." Do we have an "oral Torah"?

Actually, in the course of history, the oral Torah also became a written document. After about two hundred years of teaching the interpretations by word of mouth from one generation to the next, it was decided to organize the laws. This was done first by Rabbi Akiva and then, finally, by Rabbi Yehudah ha-Nasi in about 200 C.E. Rabbi Yehudah's collection became known as the Mishnah. Then there was another three hundred-year period when the interpretations of the Mishnah were passed on

other human beings, **37** judging others fairly, **38** leading others to truth, **39** leading others to peace, **40** calm in the midst of learning, **41** knowing how to ask questions, **42** knowing how to answer questions, **43** knowing how to add to what he or she hears, **44** learning in order to teach, **45** learning in order to practice, **46** adding to his or her teachers' knowledge, **47** knowing how to listen to the lessons of a teacher, **48** always repeating a matter honestly in the name of whoever said it. (Avot 6:6)

If you were to list all of those characteristics of a "good person," which of the 48 qualities, listed above, would you select? Which of them do you feel are the most important, and why?

Divide your study group into three groups. Have two groups draw up what they feel are the characteristics of a modern Torah-person. Each list ought to be rated with the most important qualities on the top and the less important toward the bottom. Have the third group make a list of the 48 qualities in the order they believe most important to least important. Then compare and contrast the lists. Each group should be ready to defend its presentation.

orally. Finally, in about the sixth century C.E., that oral tradition, known as Gemara, was also put down in writing. Together the Mishnah and Gemara form what is known as the Talmud.

The vast books of the Talmud, however, were not considered to contain the whole oral Torah. Rabbis and students of Jewish tradition have continued the process of interpretation to this very day. Why? How does the process of continued interpretation help to keep Judaism alive and vital? What would happen if Jews stopped interpreting their tradition?

Rabbi Levi Yitzchak was once asked by his students: "Why does each book of the Talmud begin with page two and not with page one?" He replied: "To remind us that no matter how much we study and learn, we have not yet come to the first page." What do you think Levi Yitzchak meant? How might his statement relate to the interpretation of Torah within Judaism?

A Life-Giving Medicine!

Rabbi Yehudah bar Chiyya, who lived in the Land of Israel during the third century C.E., once observed: "A drug may be beneficial to one and not to another. The Torah, however, is a life-giving medicine for all Israel." (Eruvin 54a)

The sages of Jewish tradition believed that the Torah contained the knowledge and directions for the best possible way of life. For them, the Torah was a "map" or a "prescription" of the ethical ways in which a human being ought to live. Yosef Albo, a medieval Jewish philosopher, commented: "The purpose of the Torah is to guide human beings to obtain spiritual happiness." And other rabbis taught: "Each מִצְוָה is a branch of the Torah, and the person who honors the Torah by performing מִצְוֹת will receive honor." In another place we are taught: "Through Torah, man becomes God's partner in creation." (Maalot Hatorah)

Is it possible for the modern Jew to still consider the Torah "a life-giving medicine"? In what ways? How can the Torah, written and oral, help us obtain "spiritual happiness"?

Look at Exodus 21:33–37; 22:24–26; 23:1–9; Leviticus 19:9–18 and ask: How can these be applied to modern society? How can they help us achieve spiritual happiness? How in the doing of these מִצְוֹת *are we partners of God? You may wish to divide up into groups for this project and then report your findings. You may also wish to develop your own talmudic commentary on the meaning of these Torah quotations. If you do, remember that the Talmud records both majority and minority opinions.*

At the Ark

Leader

אֵין כָּמוֹךָ בָאֱלֹהִים, אֲדֹנָי, וְאֵין כְּמַעֲשֶׂיךָ.

There are no gods that can compare to You, O Lord, and there are no works like Yours.

Everyone

יְיָ עֹז לְעַמּוֹ יִתֵּן, יְיָ יְבָרֵךְ אֶת עַמּוֹ בַשָּׁלוֹם.

The Lord will give strength to His people. The Lord will bless His people with peace.

(Ark is opened)

Leader

וַיְהִי בִּנְסֹעַ הָאָרֹן וַיֹּאמֶר מֹשֶׁה: קוּמָה יְיָ.

And when the Ark was about to be moved, Moses would say: Rise up, O Lord.

Everyone sing

כִּי מִצִּיּוֹן תֵּצֵא תוֹרָה, וּדְבַר יְיָ מִירוּשָׁלָיִם.

For out of Zion will go forth the Torah and the word of the Lord from Jerusalem.

בָּרוּךְ שֶׁנָּתַן תּוֹרָה לְעַמּוֹ יִשְׂרָאֵל בִּקְדֻשָּׁתוֹ.

Praised be the One who, in holiness, has given the Torah to His people Israel.

(Special prayer if desired)

Commentary

The Torah service is the dramatic center of the Shabbat worship service. In taking the Torah from the ark, and then reading it, Jews relive the giving of the Torah on Mount Sinai, the carrying of it across the wilderness, and the study of it in synagogues for over 2,000 years. In order to help celebrate such a special moment, those who composed the prayer book selected special sentences from the Bible and from the tradition. They then wove them together as poetry expressing the special significance of Torah to the Jewish people and the joy of taking it from the ark and studying it.

There Are No Gods

The אֵין כָּמוֹךָ (*En Kamocha*) is taken from Psalm 86, verse 8. In that psalm the poet goes on to say: "All nations which You have created, O Lord, will come and bow themselves before You.... For You are great and do wonderful things — You are God alone!"

Why would the authors of the Torah service begin it with the words of Psalm 86? What is so special about the declaration of the אֵין כָּמוֹךָ? Why did the poet's declaration: "There are no gods that can compare to You, O Lord" seem so appropriate?

Perhaps the authors of the Torah service wanted to remind those who were about to take the Torah from the ark of the time when the Torah was first given to the people of Israel. That, according to tradition, took place on Mount Sinai with the giving of the Ten Commandments. The first two commandments read as follows:

> I am the Lord, your God, who brought you out of the land of Egypt, out of the house of bondage.
> You shall have no other gods before Me.
> (Exodus 20:2–3)

Do you see a connection between the אֵין כָּמוֹךָ prayer and the first two commandments? Jews believe that God's power can be seen not only in the wonderful works of nature but in human history as well. How do both the אֵין כָּמוֹךָ prayer and the first two commandments express the Jewish idea that God is to be found in human history and in nature?

No Gods That Can Compare to You

The second commandment forbids idolatry. After the words: "You shall have no other gods before Me" is the following:

> You shall not make for yourself a graven image, nor any likeness of any thing that is in the heavens above, or that is on the earth beneath, or that is in the water under the earth; you shall not bow down to them nor serve them.
> (Exodus 20:4–5)

The אֵין כָּמוֹךָ reminds us of the commandment which forbids idolatry. It declares: "There are no gods that can compare to You." Why did ancient Jews deplore idolatry? Why did some Jews, even though their laws forbid it, build and worship idols? What is so attractive and dangerous about idol worship?

The prophet Isaiah tells about a carpenter who cuts down a tree. He chops it in two, and with one half he "makes the figure of a man," and with the other, he builds a fire to warm himself and cook his food. Then he sets up the image he has made, bows down to it, and prays: "Save me, for you are my god." Having given us this description of idolatry, Isaiah comments about those who worship idols:

> They do not know, neither do they understand;
> For their eyes are blinded so that they cannot see,
> And their hearts, that they cannot understand.
> They are incapable of saying to themselves:
> "I have burned the one half of it for fire,
> And have baked bread on the coals. . . .
> How, then, can I make an idol with the other half
> And bow down to the stock of a tree?"
> Such a man strives after ashes,
> He has been turned aside by a deceived heart.
> (Isaiah 44:18ff.)

According to Isaiah, why do people worship idols? What does he find foolish and wrong about idol worship? What does idol worship do to the worshiper?

Does idol worship still exist in modern times? Psychologist Dr. Erich Fromm has written: "Words can become idols, and machines. . . . Science and the opinions of one's neighbors can become idols, and God has become an idol for many." (*Psychoanalysis and Religion*) The medieval Jewish philosopher, Bachya, observed in his times: "People make their bellies, their fine clothes, and their homes their gods." (*Chovot Halevavot*) What do you think Fromm and Bachya meant by their statements? How do people make the things they mention idols? What is the danger when "science" or "religion" become idols? The well-known Zionist leader, Shemarya Levin, once remarked: "Every idol demands sacrifices." What do you suppose he meant? How do the modern idols, mentioned by Fromm, demand "sacrifices" from human beings?

The chasidic leader, Rabbi Mendel of Kotzk, once warned his followers: "The Torah prohibits us from making idols out of the מִצְוֹת." How can a מִצְוָה become an idol?

Divide your study group into small research groups. The task is to find objects of which modern people have made idols. Take your evidence from newspapers, magazines (watch out for the ads!), radio and television (watch out for the commercials!), and any other areas where you can find good examples. Don't overlook your school classroom, the sports field, and your house. After you have compiled your evidence, make a list indicating the idol, the evidence, why you think people today worship the idol, and whether you feel it is dangerous for people to have such an idol. Then, share the results with the members of your study group.

THE LORD WILL GIVE STRENGTH TO HIS PEOPLE
THE LORD WILL BLESS HIS PEOPLE WITH PEACE

Those words are taken from Psalm 29, verse 11, and they are used not only in the Torah service but in many other places in Jewish worship as well. In the Torah service, however, they have a special meaning, for they apply to the Torah and to its role in the life of the Jew.

The teachers of Jewish tradition believed that the Torah was a source of strength for the Jewish people and that its purpose was to help people achieve peace. "Without the Torah," the rabbis teach, "a person stumbles and does not know which path to take; with the Torah, however, a person walks like one who has a lantern in the dark. He can find his way." (Exodus Rabbah 36:3) What do you suppose the rabbis meant by that analogy?

Can you think of examples where the Torah helps men decide between right and wrong or between justice and injustice? (Some good examples may be found in Deuteronomy 16:18–20; 19:15–19; 20:19–20; 22:1–3.) How do these examples fulfill Rabbi Joseph's observation that "the whole Torah exists only for the sake of peace"? (Gittin 59b)

MOSES WOULD SAY

Just as the ark is opened, the congregation says: "And when the ark was about to be moved, Moses would say: 'Rise up, O Lord.'"

While the Jewish people were in the desert their מִשְׁכָּן (*Mishkan*), Sanctuary, and its ark were portable. Each time the camp moved, the Sanctuary was taken down and the ark was carried by the people. As a matter of fact, the ark was given the honor of being placed ahead of the people so that they could follow it.

The words: "And when the ark was about to be moved . . ." remind us of the honor given by our ancestors to the ark and to the Torah. Together with the words taken from Isaiah 2:3: "For out of Zion will go forth the Torah . . ." — they help us celebrate the importance of Torah to our people in the past and to our hopes for the future.

What are those hopes? Look at Isaiah 2:1–4. There the prophet expresses the hope for a messianic time. What does he envision, and how does the Torah help us achieve his hopes? In what ways might the State of Israel help the Torah "go forth . . . from Jerusalem"?

Who Has Given the Torah to His People Israel

The בָּרוּךְ שֶׁנָּתַן (*Baruch Shenatan*), thanks God for giving the Torah to the people of Israel.

In some congregations this praise is followed by a prayer found in the *Zohar*, a book containing all sorts of fascinating and complicated interpretations of the Torah. Some believe it was written by Rabbi Shimon bar Yochai who lived in the second century C.E. Most likely, however, it was written in Spain during the thirteenth century and attributed to Rabbi Shimon.

In one place, the *Zohar* teaches: "The Torah is a garment for God's presence." In another it says: "If one is far from Torah, he is far from God." How can the Torah be "a garment for God"? If we are known by what we say and do, how is the Torah also known by what it "says" and "does" in the lives of those who cherish it?

Just after the בָּרוּךְ שֶׁנָּתַן, we have a place for private devotion. In it a person can use the words of the *Zohar*, found on this page, or compose some expression of his or her own. The theme of this special prayer is the meaning of the Torah to the people of Israel and to us as individuals.

Prayer from the Zohar

אֲנָא אֵמַר תֻּשְׁבְּחָן. יְהֵא רַעֲוָא קֳדָמָךְ, דְּתִפְתַּח לִבִּי בְּאוֹרַיְתָא. וְתַשְׁלִים מִשְׁאֲלִין דְּלִבִּי, וְלִבָּא דְכָל עַמָּךְ יִשְׂרָאֵל, לְטָב וּלְחַיִּין וְלִשְׁלָם. אָמֵן.

May it be Your will, O Lord, to open my heart to Your Torah and to fulfill the wishes of my heart and the hearts of all Your people Israel for good, for life, and for peace.

The Torah and Israel

Rabbi Yehoshua ben Chanania said:

The people of Israel cannot exist without devotion to the Torah!
(Mechilta 17:8)

115

Taking the Torah from the Ark

(Leader removes Torah from Ark)

Everyone

שְׁמַע יִשְׂרָאֵל, יְהוָֹה אֱלֹהֵינוּ, יְהוָֹה אֶחָד.

Hear O Israel, the Lord our God, the Lord is One!

אֶחָד אֱלֹהֵינוּ, גָּדוֹל אֲדוֹנֵינוּ, קָדוֹשׁ שְׁמוֹ.

Our God is One, great is our Lord, holy is God's name.

Leader

גַּדְּלוּ לַייָ אִתִּי, וּנְרוֹמְמָה שְׁמוֹ יַחְדָּו.

Magnify the Lord with me, and let us praise God's name together.

(Torah is taken to reading desk while everyone sings)

לְךָ, יְיָ, הַגְּדֻלָּה וְהַגְּבוּרָה וְהַתִּפְאֶרֶת וְהַנֵּצַח וְהַהוֹד כִּי כֹל בַּשָּׁמַיִם וּבָאָרֶץ. לְךָ, יְיָ, הַמַּמְלָכָה וְהַמִּתְנַשֵּׂא לְכֹל לְרֹאשׁ. רוֹמְמוּ יְיָ אֱלֹהֵינוּ, וְהִשְׁתַּחֲווּ לַהֲדֹם רַגְלָיו, קָדוֹשׁ הוּא. רוֹמְמוּ יְיָ אֱלֹהֵינוּ וְהִשְׁתַּחֲווּ לְהַר קָדְשׁוֹ, כִּי קָדוֹשׁ יְיָ אֱלֹהֵינוּ.

Yours, O Lord, is the greatness, and the power, and the glory, and the victory, and the majesty; for all that is in the heaven and earth is Yours. Yours, O Lord, is the kingdom and the rulership of all. Praise the Lord, our God, and worship in His Temple. Holy is God. Praise the Lord, our God, worship at His holy mountain, for the Lord our God, is holy.

Commentary

The drama of the Torah service now turns to taking the Torah from the ark. Notice, however, that nothing is said here about the importance or significance of Torah. Indeed, the word Torah is not even mentioned. Why not? Wouldn't it be logical for us to say something about how much the Torah means to us as we take it out of the ark?

Notice, also, that the words spoken here are very few. The שְׁמַע and the אֶחָד אֱלֹהֵינוּ (*Echad Elohenu*) both say the same thing. The גַּדְּלוּ (*Gadlu*) is taken from Psalm 34, verse 4. It is simply a call to the congregation to magnify and praise God. But how is that to be done? We are not told, we are just challenged.

Is "Doing" the Essential Thing?

The fact that there is no mention of Torah, and nothing said about its importance, when we take it from the ark may provide a significant lesson. Let's see if we can understand why the authors of the Torah service omitted the mention of Torah, or its meaning, at this point.

Rabbi Elazar ben Azarya served as the vice president and president of the Sanhedrin at Yavneh during the Roman persecutions from 80 to 135 C.E. He was a man of wisdom, political insight, and action. Together with Rabbi Akiva, he represented the Jewish people in Rome before the leaders of the Roman empire.

One of Rabbi Elazar's best known teachings is the following:

To what is he to be compared whose wisdom exceeds his deeds? To a tree whose branches are many, but whose roots are few. What happens to such a tree when a strong wind comes along? It is plucked up and overturned on its face!

To what is he to be compared whose deeds exceed his wisdom? To a tree whose branches are few, but whose roots are many. What happens to such a tree when a strong wind comes along? Even if all the winds of the world blow upon it, it can not be uprooted from its place!
(Avot 3:22)

What is the meaning of Rabbi Elazar's observation? What is the difference between the two men he describes? Rabbi Elazar's traveling companion, Rabbi Akiva, taught: "Everything depends upon deeds." (Avot 3:15) What do you think he meant? What is the relationship of his statement to Rabbi Elazar's?

A Debate

The issue of what is more important, knowledge or deeds, is a very old one. We have already seen that Judaism emphasizes the study of Torah. The rabbis taught that תַּלְמוּד תּוֹרָה כְּנֶגֶד כֻּלָּם (talmud Torah keneged kulam), the study of Torah comes before everything. On the other hand, they also taught that "the pursuit of knowledge is not essential, but rather the doing of it." (Avot 1:17) In one place Shammai teaches his pupils: "Say little and do much" (Avot 1:15), and in another Abbahu tells his students: "Study must precede practice." (Kiddushin 40b)

Who are we to follow here? Who is right? Which is more important — study or practice?

About 120 C.E., the leaders of the Jewish people in the Land of Israel met in the town of Lod. At their meeting, they debated several issues. One of them was the question: "Which is more important — study or practice?" Rabbi Tarfon said "Practice." Rabbi Akiva said "Study." Have two groups prepare and reenact each side of the debate, and then vote on which your study group believes to be the most important. Your reasons for favoring one over the other ought to be based on examples taken from the past and from the present. Note the quotes in the box dealing with both sides of the issue.

Why We Say Nothing

We have still not answered the question asked earlier in this section: "Why is nothing said about the Torah when we take it from the ark"?

Perhaps what the authors of this part of our service wanted to teach us is that the very act of taking the Torah from the ark speaks for itself. It is the tradition to lift the Torah from the ark, to hold it high above the head when the congregation says the שְׁמַע and recites the אֶחָד אֱלֹהֵינוּ. Then the leader challenges everyone with the words of Psalm 34: "Magnify the Lord with me, and let us praise God's Name together." That challenge is to "live the Torah" — to incorporate its teachings into one's practice and deeds.

Practice

Practice makes the artist.
  (Rabbi Hanau)

It is in the deed that God is revealed in life.
  (Rabbi Leo Baeck)

True wisdom can only be obtained through practice.
  (Moses Maimonides)

My deeds are both my witnesses and my judges.
  (Moses ibn Ezra)

We can judge people faithful or unfaithful only by their deeds.
  (Baruch Spinoza)

Study

Do not neglect the knowledge of the wise.
  (Ben Sira)

Study from love, and honor will follow.
  (Bachya)

Study strengthens our good powers for victory over our evil ones.
  (Bratzlaver Rebbe)

The ignorant person cannot be religious.
  (Hillel)

Learning! Learning! Learning! That is the secret of Jewish survival.
  (Ahad Ha-Am)

How Do We "Magnify the Lord"?

Look at Psalm 34. Notice that it is written in the form of an acrostic. It begins with א (alef), the first letter of the Hebrew alphabet and ends with ת (taf), the last letter. The first words of the psalm are:

I will bless the Lord at all times;
God's praise shall continually be in my mouth.

Those first lines provide us with a clue as to why the author may have used the acrostic form and the 22 letters of the Hebrew alphabet. Perhaps he wished to suggest that, just as one can praise God using every letter of the alphabet, so also one can serve God with every human ability and deed.

The poet who wrote Psalm 34 not only voiced the challenge "Magnify the Lord with me . . ." but he tried to describe how human beings should "magnify the Lord." Notice, especially, verses 12–16. How, according to the Psalmist, does a person express "fear of the Lord"?

Yours, O Lord, Is the Greatness

Just before his death, King David called his people together and announced that his son, Solomon, would become king of Israel. At the same time, he told the people that, during his reign, Solomon would build a Temple in Jerusalem. David's announcement was made in the form of a prayer found in I Chronicles 29:10–19. That prayer includes the words: "Yours, O Lord, is the greatness. . . ." They are usually sung while the Torah is being taken to the reading desk. Look at the whole prayer in Chronicles. Why do you think a part of it was chosen for this particular place in our Torah service. Could it be that those who placed the words: "Yours, O Lord, is the greatness . . ." wished to teach that, just as David handed tradition to his son, Solomon, each generation of parents has the task of handing that tradition to its children? How is a Bar or Bat Mitzvah ceremony the fulfillment of such a task?

The Aliyah

(Blessings before reading of Torah)

בָּרְכוּ אֶת יְיָ הַמְבֹרָךְ.

Praise the Lord to whom all praise is due.

בָּרוּךְ יְיָ הַמְבֹרָךְ לְעוֹלָם וָעֶד.

Praised be the Lord to whom all praise is due for ever and ever.

בָּרוּךְ אַתָּה, יְיָ אֱלֹהֵינוּ, מֶלֶךְ הָעוֹלָם, אֲשֶׁר בָּחַר בָּנוּ מִכָּל הָעַמִּים וְנָתַן לָנוּ אֶת תּוֹרָתוֹ. בָּרוּךְ אַתָּה יְיָ, נוֹתֵן הַתּוֹרָה.

Be praised, O Lord our God, Ruler of the universe, who has chosen us from among all people and has given us the Torah.

Be praised, O Lord, who gives the Torah.

(Blessings after reading of Torah)

בָּרוּךְ אַתָּה, יְיָ אֱלֹהֵינוּ, מֶלֶךְ הָעוֹלָם, אֲשֶׁר נָתַן לָנוּ תּוֹרַת אֱמֶת וְחַיֵּי עוֹלָם נָטַע בְּתוֹכֵנוּ. בָּרוּךְ אַתָּה יְיָ, נוֹתֵן הַתּוֹרָה.

Be praised, O Lord our God, Ruler of the universe, who has given us a Torah of truth and has implanted within us eternal life.

Be praised, O Lord, who gives the Torah.

Commentary

Among many ancient peoples, it was the priests who were the privileged, educated class. They were charged with the responsibility of knowing and preserving the tribal traditions. Often, their knowledge was kept a secret from others and passed on only to members of their families.

Among Jews, however, even though there were priests, the Torah was considered the possession of all the people. When Ezra read and taught the Torah, he did so "before the congregation, both men and women, all that could hear. . . ." Jewish tradition revolutionized and democratized religion. In Judaism the Torah was open to everyone, and each Jew became responsible for both knowing Torah and living according to its מִצְוֹת.

The reading of the Torah in the ancient synagogue demonstrated the democratic spirit of Jewish tradition. From biblical times the Jewish people had been divided between כֹּהֲנִים (*Kohanim*), priests, לְוִיִּים (*Leviim*), Levites, and יִשְׂרְאֵלִים (*Yisre'elim*), Israelites. The synagogue gave ceremonial honor to these divisions during the Torah service. When it came time to read from the

Torah, first the כֹּהֵן (*Kohen*) was called, afterwards a לֵוִי (*Levi*) and, then, a יִשְׂרָאֵל (*Yisrael*). Once called to the Torah there was no difference between what each person did. Each would read his designated portion.

What Is an Aliyah?

The privilege of being "called up" to read from the Torah is known as עֲלִיָּה (*aliyah*). Why?

Remember the passage sung while the Torah is being placed on the reading desk? Its words are: "Praise the Lord, our God, worship at His holy mountain...." In Psalms 24:3 the poet asks:

Who shall ascend to the mountain of the Lord?
And who shall stand in His holy place?

For the Jew, in biblical times, the "mountain of the Lord" was Mt. Zion, in Jerusalem, where the Temple stood. It was from there that the Torah was to go forth to all nations. In order to visit Mt. Zion, or Jerusalem, one must "go up" or "ascend," for it is located on one of the highest places in the Land of Israel. In biblical times, "going up" to Jerusalem for a festival was called עֲלִיָּה לְרֶגֶל (*aliyah leregel*). In our own times, the word used for immigration to Israel is עֲלִיָּה.

Now, how did the word עֲלִיָּה come to be associated with being called up to read from the Torah? Perhaps because the Torah was associated with Jerusalem, the reading of it became a substitute for "going up" to the holy city. It follows that the reader became known as an עוֹלֶה (*oleh*) because he "goes up" to the pulpit to read the Torah. Whatever the explanation, over the course of years the word עֲלִיָּה came to designate the privilege of reading from the Torah.

The בַּעַל קוֹרֵא — Baal Kore

From about 300 B.C.E., the language of Aramaic began to replace Hebrew as the spoken language of the people. Gradually, over the years, many

Jews lost the art of reading from the Torah or even of being able to understand all of the Hebrew of the Torah. As one might imagine, this posed a serious problem for the future of Judaism.

In order to solve the problem, the rabbis created the position of בַּעַל קוֹרֵא, the trained reader of the Torah. In this way they could be sure that the text would be read correctly. Their solution, however, brought with it another problem. It removed the privilege of reading the Torah from most Jews. In order to solve that problem, the rabbis assigned the blessings before and after the reading of Torah to the עוֹלֶה. This meant that any Jew, whether he could read from the Torah or not, could be called upon for an עֲלִיָּה. In this way, the rabbis preserved the democracy of the synagogue.

Translating the Torah

As we have already discovered, the introduction of Aramaic as the spoken language of the people meant that many were unable to understand the Hebrew of the Torah. Again, in order to preserve the democratic nature of Jewish knowledge, the rabbis introduced the position of מְתוּרְגְּמָן (*meturgeman*), translator, into the synagogue. They also developed and accepted an Aramaic translation of the Torah which was used by the translator. That translation is known as *Targum Onkelos*. It is interesting to note that the Jews of Egypt, who spoke Greek, developed a translation of the Torah in Greek.

And Caused Them to Understand the Reading

When Ezra and his fellow priests read the Torah to the people of Israel, we are told that "they gave the sense and caused them to understand the reading." What, exactly, does it mean to "give the sense" or "cause" someone to understand the Torah?

The sages of Jewish tradition believed that Ezra sought to "interpret" the Torah and provide the people with its application in their lives. The task of "interpreting Torah" required knowledge and skill. In the ancient synagogue, the interpretation of Torah was called a דְּרָשָׁה (*derashah*). The word דְּרָשָׁה is derived from the root דרש which means to search or to investigate and to explain. Today, we call the דְּרָשָׁה a sermon.

Creating the Sermon

In the ancient synagogue, as in most modern ones, the דְּרָשָׁה was delivered just after the reading of the Haftarah. (For discussion of Haftarah, see pp. 124–129.)

The rabbis developed the sermon to explain the Torah and inspire Jews toward its fulfillment. In order to make their points clear, the sages used stories, analogies, legends, and incidents from their own experiences. Most of their sermons were organized in the following way.

a. The first section called attention to the story, or theme, or subject of the Torah or Haftarah they wished to interpret.

b. Then the rabbis would ask questions about the section which seemed challenging.

c. Having asked the questions, they tried to answer them and apply their answers to the lives of those who were listening.

d. The conclusion of the sermon would include a summary and a statement meant to inspire the listeners to "take to heart" the message of the Torah or Haftarah interpretation.

This outline of the דְּרָשָׁה ought to be helpful to you when you are called upon to write a sermon for your congregation. Remember that your task is to help others appreciate and understand the Torah or Haftarah text.

Contributions

The practice of reading from Torah and Haftarah, as well as delivering the sermon, were borrowed by Christianity and Islam. In both the church and the mosque, Scripture is read and interpreted. In the church, Scripture includes the Hebrew Bible and the New Testament. In the mosque, Scripture is the Koran which Moslems believe was dictated to Muhammad by the angel Gabriel. The Hebrew word for biblical verse, קְרָא (*kera*), and the word Koran both come from the same root.

THE BLESSINGS BEFORE AND AFTER THE READING OF TORAH

Who wrote the blessings which come before and after the reading of Torah? We do not know! We really do not even know when they were composed. In the Book of Nehemiah, we are told that when Ezra read from the Torah he "blessed the Lord, the great God. And all the people answered 'Amen, Amen' with the lifting up of their hands. . . ." (Nehemiah 8:6)

It seems that by the end of the first century C.E., the custom of saying blessings before and after the reading of Torah was accepted. The blessings we recite today are those most likely used by Jews since that time.

WHO HAS GIVEN US THE TORAH WHO GIVES THE TORAH

Notice that, in both the blessings before and after the reading of Torah, the author has used the words נָתַן (natan), gave, and נוֹתֵן (noten), gives. Why do you suppose Jews utilize both past and present tenses when thanking God for the Torah?

A sage known by the strange name of Ben Bag Bag once taught: "Turn the Torah, and turn it over again, for everything is in it!" (Avot 5:25) What might Ben Bag Bag's statement have to do with the use of past (נָתַן) and present (נוֹתֵן) in the blessings for the reading of Torah?

Is Torah still in the process of being given today? In what ways? Remember the quote from the Baal Shem Tov? He said: "The Torah is eternal, but its explanation is to be made by the spiritual leaders of Judaism . . . in accordance with the age." How are new "explanations" a modern giving of Torah?

The Art of the Sermon

Before delivering a sermon, review and revise it carefully. God revised the Torah four times before giving it to Israel.
(Exodus Rabbah)

A sermon is becoming to one who practices it.
(Elazar ben Azarya)

The Haftarah Blessings

(Blessings before Haftarah reading)

בָּרוּךְ אַתָּה, יְיָ אֱלֹהֵינוּ, מֶלֶךְ הָעוֹלָם, אֲשֶׁר בָּחַר בִּנְבִיאִים טוֹבִים, וְרָצָה בְדִבְרֵיהֶם הַנֶּאֱמָרִים בֶּאֱמֶת. בָּרוּךְ אַתָּה יְיָ, הַבּוֹחֵר בַּתּוֹרָה, וּבְמֹשֶׁה עַבְדּוֹ, וּבְיִשְׂרָאֵל עַמּוֹ, וּבִנְבִיאֵי הָאֱמֶת וָצֶדֶק.

Praised be You, O Lord our God, Ruler of the universe, who has chosen good prophets and has been pleased with their faithful and truthful words. Praised be You, O Lord, who has singled out the Torah, Moses as Your servant, Israel as Your people, and prophets of truth and righteousness.

(Haftarah is read)

Commentary

Among Moslems, Jews have historically been known as "the people of the Book." They were given that name because of their devotion to their Bible. While the Torah occupies a special place, not only in the ark, but in the history of the Jewish people, the rest of the Hebrew Bible was also considered holy. The "Prophets" of Israel were believed to have spoken "in the name of the Lord," and the "Writings" (such as Psalms, Proverbs, or the Book of Job) were all considered sacred.

When Jews refer to the Hebrew Bible they call it תַּנַ״ךְ (Tanach). That name is made up of the three first letters taken from the titles of the three sections of the Hebrew Bible.

Torah	ת = תּוֹרָה	Taf
Prophets (Neviim)	נ = נְבִיאִים	Nun
Writings (Ketuvim)	ך = כְּתוּבִים	Chaf (the final Chaf)

The תּוֹרָה section, as we have indicated, includes the Five Books of Moses. נְבִיאִים begins with the Book of Joshua and concludes with the Book of Malachi. כְּתוּבִים begins with Psalms and ends with the final book of the Hebrew Bible, II Chronicles.

What Is the הַפְטָרָה — Haftarah?

The word הַפְטָרָה means conclusion or dismissal. Why would a reading from the Bible be given such a name? We are not sure.

It could be that it was the custom in the ancient synagogue to follow the reading of the Torah with a reading from the Prophets and then dismiss or conclude the worship service. We do know that such a custom did exist in some synagogues, and this may explain how the reading selected from the Prophets came to be known as the הַפְטָרָה.

Selecting the Haftarah

By the second century C.E., the practice of reading a selection from the Prophets was well established. The blessings, both before and after the reading, had been written and were used throughout the Jewish world. The selection of the specific הַפְטָרָה reading, however, was left to those in charge of each local synagogue.

How did they make their selection of an appropriate הַפְטָרָה for each Shabbat? Interestingly enough, the New Testament gives us a good description.

> [Jesus] came to Nazareth where he had been brought up and, as was his custom, he went to the synagogue on the Shabbat day. While there, he was called upon to read, and the Book of Isaiah was given to him. . . .
>
> (Luke 4:16–17)

It seems clear from this description of Jesus at the synagogue in Nazareth that it was the custom to call upon a member of the congregation to come forward to read from the הַפְטָרָה. We are not sure whether the selection of a passage from Isaiah was made by the leaders of the synagogue or by Jesus. The description in Luke, however, does indicate that, after he had completed the reading, Jesus went on to deliver a sermon based upon it.

There are those who believe that by the time of Jesus it had become the custom to select a הַפְטָרָה reading which would have some connection with the Torah portion. This, too, is entirely possible. Later, by the seventh century C.E., a full cycle of הַפְטָרָה readings had been developed. All of these were selected by the rabbis because they complemented or developed the subject found in the Torah portion. For example, when the first chapters of Genesis are read, the הַפְטָרָה is taken from Isaiah, chapter 42. The theme of the first chapters of Genesis is the creation of the world by God. The chapter of Isaiah which is read as the הַפְטָרָה includes the words:

> Thus says the Lord,
> He that created the heavens and stretched them forth,
> He that spread forth the earth and that which comes out of it,
> He that gives breath to the people upon it,
> And spirit to them that walk therein.
>
> (Isaiah 42:5)

The Hebrew Bible

Torah תּוֹרָה
  Genesis
  Exodus
  Leviticus
  Numbers
  Deuteronomy

Prophets נְבִיאִים
  Joshua
  Judges
  I Samuel
  II Samuel
  I Kings
  II Kings
  Isaiah
  Jeremiah
  Ezekiel
  Hosea
  Joel
  Amos
  Obadiah
  Jonah
  Micah
  Nahum
  Habakkuk
  Zephaniah
  Haggai
  Zechariah
  Malachi

Writings כְּתוּבִים
  Psalms
  Proverbs
  Job
  Song of Songs
  Ruth
  Lamentations
  Ecclesiastes
  Esther
  Daniel
  Ezra
  Nehemiah
  I Chronicles
  II Chronicles

You may wish to compare the order of the Hebrew Bible with the order of the Christian Bible. What is the difference, and why do you think Christians have arranged the books of the Hebrew Bible in a different order?

As is indicated on page 125, the selection of the הַפְטָרָה was done on the basis of its having something in common with the Torah portion. Below are some Torah portions and their הַפְטָרָה selections. Divide them up, and have two or three groups examine them. Try to figure out the relationship of the הַפְטָרָה to the Torah selection. Then share your results.

1. *Genesis 6:9—11:22 and Isaiah 54.*
2. *Exodus 6:2—9:35 and Ezekiel 28.*
3. *Exodus 13:17—17:16 and Judges 5.*
4. *Exodus 21:1—24:18 and Jeremiah 34.*
5. *Numbers 22:1—25:9 and Micah 6.*
6. *Deuteronomy 3:23—7:11 and Isaiah 40.*
7. *Deuteronomy 33:1—34:12 and Joshua 1.*

The Maccabees and the הַפְטָרָה

Some Jewish scholars trace the beginning of the custom of reading a הַפְטָרָה to the time of the Maccabees. Just before the revolt led by Mattathias and his sons, Antiochus Epiphanes decreed that there should be no public reading of the Torah. Some Jews responded to this form of persecution by substituting a reading from the Prophets for the Torah portion. After the successful uprising and defeat of the Greek-Syrians, the custom of the הַפְטָרָה reading was continued.

Do you think that substituting the הַפְטָרָה reading for the Torah portion was a good way to handle Antiochus Epiphanes' decree? What would be your reaction if a modern government prohibited the reading of Torah in the synagogue? What might be some of your reactions if your government began to force Jews to close some of their synagogues? What do you believe would be the most effective response to such anti-Semitism? How have Jews in the past reacted to such persecution?

What do you think of the three following statements and responses to anti-Semitism? How do they differ? Which, if any, would you agree with?

I

Anti-Semitism is a mad passion, akin to the the lowest perversities of diseased human nature. It is the will to hate.

(Leo Tolstoy)

II

Anti-Semitism is not to be overcome by getting people to forget us but to know us.

(Meyer Levin)

III

For the Jews, the moral is to answer anti-Semitism with more Semitism . . . greater devotion to the great ideals which Judaism proclaimed to the world.

(Israel Abrahams)

Blessings Before Haftarah Reading

The blessings before the reading of the הַפְטָרָה praise God for the "faithful and truthful" words of the prophets. They also thank God for the Torah and for those who have passed the Torah from generation to generation. We are not sure when the blessings before the reading of the הַפְטָרָה were written. It is likely that they were composed sometime during the second to the seventh century C.E.

Study the blessings before the reading of the הַפְטָרָה. Notice that their themes are God's choosing "good prophets," the "truthfulness" of their messages, and the faithful passing on of the tradition from generation to generation.

On the basis of these themes, what would you include, today, if you were challenged to write a new הַפְטָרָה prayer? Take up the challenge and write one!

Blessings After Haftarah Reading

The blessings after the reading of the הַפְטָרָה are divided into four sections. We might expect that their theme would have to do with the importance of the prophets or their message. That is not what we find. The first section voices praise for the truthfulness and fulfillment of God's words. The second section asks for mercy upon Zion and the people of Israel. The third section voices the hope for the coming of Elijah and the messianic kingdom. And the fourth thanks God for the Torah, the prophets, worship, and the Shabbat day.

The Haftarah Blessings

(Blessings after Haftarah reading)

I

בָּרוּךְ אַתָּה, יְיָ אֱלֹהֵינוּ, מֶלֶךְ הָעוֹלָם, צוּר כָּל הָעוֹלָמִים, צַדִּיק בְּכָל הַדּוֹרוֹת, הָאֵל הַנֶּאֱמָן, הָאוֹמֵר וְעוֹשֶׂה, הַמְדַבֵּר וּמְקַיֵּם שֶׁכָּל דְּבָרָיו אֱמֶת וָצֶדֶק.

Be praised, O Lord our God, Ruler of the universe, Creator of all worlds, righteous in all generations, the faithful God who says and does, who speaks and fulfills for all of the Lord's words are truthful and just.

נֶאֱמָן אַתָּה הוּא, יְיָ אֱלֹהֵינוּ, וְנֶאֱמָנִים דְּבָרֶיךָ, וְדָבָר אֶחָד מִדְּבָרֶיךָ, אָחוֹר לֹא יָשׁוּב רֵיקָם, כִּי אֵל מֶלֶךְ נֶאֱמָן וְרַחֲמָן אָתָּה. בָּרוּךְ אַתָּה יְיָ, הָאֵל הַנֶּאֱמָן בְּכָל דְּבָרָיו.

You are faithful, O Lord, our God, and all of Your words are to be trusted. Not one of Your words is empty, for You are a faithful and merciful God. Be praised, O Lord, the God whose words can be trusted.

II

רַחֵם עַל צִיּוֹן, כִּי הִיא בֵּית חַיֵּינוּ, וְלַעֲלוּבַת נֶפֶשׁ תּוֹשִׁיעַ בִּמְהֵרָה בְיָמֵינוּ. בָּרוּךְ אַתָּה יְיָ, מְשַׂמֵּחַ צִיּוֹן בְּבָנֶיהָ.

Have mercy upon Zion, for it is the source of our life. Save the oppressed of soul speedily in our days. Be praised, O Lord, who makes Zion rejoice in her children.

Commentary

Why is it that these four sections, which make up the blessings after the reading of the הַפְטָרָה, do not include, save for the phrase וְעַל הַנְּבִיאִים (ve'al haneviim), [and] for the prophets, mention of the prophets or the meaning of their message? Are they really appropriate as blessings after the reading of the הַפְטָרָה? How were they chosen? By whom? And when?

ORIGINS OF THE FINAL הַפְטָרָה BLESSINGS

If you reread the הַפְטָרָה blessings, you will note that we have studied their themes before. Look back at the *Amidah* sections on בּוֹנֵה יְרוּשָׁלַיִם, Rebuilding Jerusalem; קֶרֶן יְשׁוּעָה, the Messianic Hope; קְדֻשַּׁת הַיּוֹם, the Sanctification of the Day.

What we seem to have here in the final bless-

III

שַׂמְּחֵנוּ, יְיָ אֱלֹהֵינוּ, בְּאֵלִיָּהוּ הַנָּבִיא עַבְדֶּךָ, וּבְמַלְכוּת בֵּית דָּוִד מְשִׁיחֶךָ. בִּמְהֵרָה יָבֹא, וְיָגֵל לִבֵּנוּ. עַל כִּסְאוֹ לֹא יֵשֵׁב זָר, וְלֹא יִנְחֲלוּ עוֹד אֲחֵרִים אֶת כְּבוֹדוֹ, כִּי בְשֵׁם קָדְשְׁךָ נִשְׁבַּעְתָּ לּוֹ, שֶׁלֹּא יִכְבֶּה נֵרוֹ לְעוֹלָם וָעֶד. בָּרוּךְ אַתָּה יְיָ, מָגֵן דָּוִד.

Make us happy, O Lord our God, with the coming of Your servant, Elijah the prophet, and with the establishment of the kingdom of the house of David, Your messiah. May he soon come and bring joy to our hearts. May no stranger sit on his throne, nor others assume for themselves his glory. For You have promised by Your holy name that his light would never go out. Be praised, O Lord, the Shield of David.

IV

עַל הַתּוֹרָה, וְעַל הָעֲבוֹדָה, וְעַל הַנְּבִיאִים, וְעַל יוֹם הַשַּׁבָּת הַזֶּה, שֶׁנָּתַתָּ לָּנוּ, יְיָ אֱלֹהֵינוּ, לִקְדֻשָּׁה וְלִמְנוּחָה, לְכָבוֹד וּלְתִפְאָרֶת. עַל הַכֹּל, יְיָ אֱלֹהֵינוּ, אֲנַחְנוּ מוֹדִים לָךְ, וּמְבָרְכִים אוֹתָךְ. יִתְבָּרַךְ שִׁמְךָ בְּפִי כָּל חַי תָּמִיד לְעוֹלָם וָעֶד. בָּרוּךְ אַתָּה יְיָ, מְקַדֵּשׁ הַשַּׁבָּת.

For the Torah, for worship, for the prophets, and for this Shabbat day which You have given to us, O Lord our God, for holiness and rest, for honor and for glory — for all of these, O Lord our God, we thank You and praise You. May Your name be praised continually in the mouth of all that lives. Be praised, O Lord, who sanctifies the Shabbat.

ings of the הַפְטָרָה is an abbreviated עֲמִידָה! How is this possible? Why would the rabbis have concluded the הַפְטָרָה with such a group of prayers?

Some scholars believe that the four sections which make up the final הַפְטָרָה blessings were written sometime before the first century C.E. Like the rest of the prayers of the עֲמִידָה they were in existence when the rabbis, under the leadership of Rabbi Gamliel II, head of the Academy at Yavneh, chose those which would be included in the עֲמִידָה. We know that there were several prayers which were not chosen. These, however, remained in the possession of Jewish scholars, and some of them were later included in different sections of the prayer book. A good example of this is the שָׁלוֹם רָב prayer. The rabbis chose the שִׂים שָׁלוֹם for the concluding prayer of the עֲמִידָה rather than the שָׁלוֹם רָב. Later, as we have already seen, (see page 100), the שָׁלוֹם רָב was added to the prayer book.

Jewish scholars believe that the four sections of the final הַפְטָרָה blessings were once a version

Abbreviated Final Haftarah Blessings

(Recited after the Haftarah reading)

בָּרוּךְ אַתָּה, יְיָ אֱלֹהֵינוּ, מֶלֶךְ הָעוֹלָם, צוּר כָּל הָעוֹלָמִים, צַדִּיק בְּכָל הַדּוֹרוֹת, הָאֵל הַנֶּאֱמָן הָאוֹמֵר וְעוֹשֶׂה, הַמְדַבֵּר וּמְקַיֵּם, שֶׁכָּל דְּבָרָיו אֱמֶת וָצֶדֶק.

Be praised, O Lord our God, Ruler of the universe, Rock of all creation, righteous one of all generations, the faithful God whose word is deed, whose every command is just and true.

עַל הַתּוֹרָה, וְעַל הָעֲבוֹדָה, וְעַל הַנְּבִיאִים, וְעַל יוֹם הַשַּׁבָּת הַזֶּה, שֶׁנָּתַתָּ לָנוּ, יְיָ אֱלֹהֵינוּ, לִקְדֻשָּׁה וְלִמְנוּחָה, לְכָבוֹד וּלְתִפְאָרֶת, עַל הַכֹּל, יְיָ אֱלֹהֵינוּ, אֲנַחְנוּ מוֹדִים לָךְ, וּמְבָרְכִים אוֹתָךְ.

For the Torah, for the privilege of worship, for the prophets, and for this Shabbat day that You, O Lord our God, have given us for holiness and rest, for honor and glory, we thank and bless You.

יִתְבָּרַךְ שִׁמְךָ בְּפִי כָּל חַי תָּמִיד לְעוֹלָם וָעֶד.

May Your name be blessed for ever by every living being.

בָּרוּךְ אַתָּה יְיָ מְקַדֵּשׁ הַשַּׁבָּת.

Blessed is the Lord for the Shabbat and its holiness.

of an עֲמִידָה. After the עֲמִידָה was formulated at Yavneh, the blessings were preserved. When the tradition of concluding the worship service with the הַפְטָרָה developed, it is likely that the abbreviated version of the עֲמִידָה was reintroduced as a final set of prayers for the worship service. In other words, the four sections were not thought of as a blessing for the reading of the Haftarah but, rather, as concluding prayers for the whole worship service. This would explain why there is practically no mention of the prophets or of the Haftarah in the four sections.

What would be an appropriate prayer after the reading of the הַפְטָרָה? What themes would you include in such a prayer? Would you retain any of the older sections?

Here you will find an abbreviated version of the blessings after the reading of the הַפְטָרָה from the Reform prayer book, *Gates of Prayer*. How does this version differ from the traditional one? *Gates of Prayer* includes both the traditional version and this abbreviated one.

The New Month (Traditional version)

I

יְהִי רָצוֹן מִלְּפָנֶיךָ יְיָ, אֱלֹהֵינוּ וֵאלֹהֵי אֲבוֹתֵינוּ, שֶׁתְּחַדֵּשׁ עָלֵינוּ אֶת הַחֹדֶשׁ הַזֶּה לְטוֹבָה וְלִבְרָכָה. וְתִתֶּן לָנוּ חַיִּים אֲרֻכִּים, חַיִּים שֶׁל שָׁלוֹם, חַיִּים שֶׁל טוֹבָה, חַיִּים שֶׁל בְּרָכָה, חַיִּים שֶׁל פַּרְנָסָה, חַיִּים שֶׁל חִלּוּץ עֲצָמוֹת, חַיִּים שֶׁיֵּשׁ בָּהֶם יִרְאַת שָׁמַיִם וְיִרְאַת חֵטְא, חַיִּים שֶׁאֵין בָּהֶם בּוּשָׁה וּכְלִמָּה, חַיִּים שֶׁל עֹשֶׁר וְכָבוֹד, חַיִּים שֶׁתְּהִי בָנוּ אַהֲבַת תּוֹרָה וְיִרְאַת שָׁמַיִם, חַיִּים שֶׁיִּמָּלְאוּ מִשְׁאֲלוֹת לִבֵּנוּ לְטוֹבָה, אָמֵן סֶלָה.

May it be Your will, O Lord, our God and God of our ancestors, to renew us with goodness and blessing in the new month ahead. Grant us life — a life of length of days, a life of peace, a life of goodness, a life of blessing, a life of sustenance, a life of strength, a life of reverence for God, fear of sin, without shame or disgrace, a life of riches and honor, a life marked by our love of Torah, a life in which the wishes of our hearts may be fulfilled for good. Amen. Selah.

II

מִי שֶׁעָשָׂה נִסִּים לַאֲבוֹתֵינוּ וְגָאַל אוֹתָם מֵעַבְדוּת לְחֵרוּת, הוּא יִגְאַל אוֹתָנוּ בְּקָרוֹב, וִיקַבֵּץ נִדָּחֵינוּ מֵאַרְבַּע כַּנְפוֹת הָאָרֶץ, חֲבֵרִים כָּל יִשְׂרָאֵל, וְנֹאמַר אָמֵן.

רֹאשׁ חֹדֶשׁ ... יִהְיֶה בַּיּוֹם ... הַבָּא עָלֵינוּ וְעַל כָּל יִשְׂרָאֵל לְטוֹבָה.

May He who has done wonderful things for our ancestors, who redeemed them from slavery to freedom, soon redeem us and gather our scattered people from the four corners of the earth. Israel is one united people! And let us say: Amen.

The new month of _____ will begin on _____.
May it bring goodness to us and to all of Israel.

III

יְחַדְּשֵׁהוּ, הַקָּדוֹשׁ בָּרוּךְ הוּא, עָלֵינוּ וְעַל כָּל עַמּוֹ, בֵּית יִשְׂרָאֵל, לְחַיִּים וּלְשָׁלוֹם, לְשָׂשׂוֹן וּלְשִׂמְחָה, לִישׁוּעָה וּלְנֶחָמָה, וְנֹאמַר: אָמֵן.

May the Holy One renew in the new month, life and peace, rejoicing and happiness, salvation and consolation for us, and for all of the people of the house of Israel. And let us say: Amen.

The New Month (Reform version)

According to our calendar, the month of _____ begins _____.

יְהִי רָצוֹן מִלְּפָנֶיךָ יְיָ, אֱלֹהֵינוּ וֵאלֹהֵי אֲבוֹתֵינוּ, שֶׁתְּחַדֵּשׁ עָלֵינוּ אֶת הַחֹדֶשׁ הַזֶּה לְטוֹבָה וְלִבְרָכָה. וְתִתֶּן לָנוּ חַיִּים אֲרֻכִּים, חַיִּים שֶׁל שָׁלוֹם, חַיִּים שֶׁל טוֹבָה, חַיִּים שֶׁל בְּרָכָה, חַיִּים שֶׁתְּהִי בָנוּ אַהֲבַת תּוֹרָה וְיִרְאַת שָׁמַיִם, חַיִּים שֶׁיִּמָּלְאוּ מִשְׁאֲלוֹת לִבֵּנוּ לְטוֹבָה.

O Lord our God, let the coming month bring us renewed goodness and blessing.

May we have long life, a life of peace, prosperity, and health, a life full of blessing, a life exalted by love of Your Torah and devotion to Your service, a life in which our heart's desires are fulfilled for good.

מִי שֶׁעָשָׂה נִסִּים לַאֲבוֹתֵינוּ וְגָאַל אוֹתָם מֵעַבְדוּת לְחֵרוּת, הוּא יִגְאַל אוֹתָנוּ בְּקָרוֹב, חֲבֵרִים כָּל יִשְׂרָאֵל, וְנֹאמַר. אָמֵן.

O wondrous God who in ancient days led our people from bondage to freedom, redeem us now out of our exile from one another, making all Israel one united people. Amen.

רֹאשׁ חֹדֶשׁ ... יִהְיֶה בְּיוֹם ... הַבָּא עָלֵינוּ וְעַל כָּל יִשְׂרָאֵל לְטוֹבָה.

יְחַדְּשֵׁהוּ, הַקָּדוֹשׁ בָּרוּךְ הוּא, עָלֵינוּ וְעַל כָּל עַמּוֹ, בֵּית יִשְׂרָאֵל, לְחַיִּים וּלְשָׁלוֹם, לְשָׂשׂוֹן וּלְשִׂמְחָה, לִישׁוּעָה וּלְנֶחָמָה, וְנֹאמַר: אָמֵן.

God of holiness, let the new month bring for us, and for the whole House of Israel, life and peace, joy and happiness, deliverance and comfort, and let us say: Amen.

Commentary

One of the most ancient celebrations among Jews is the observance of רֹאשׁ חֹדֶשׁ (*Rosh Chodesh*), the New Month. It was celebrated even before the Temple came into existence. During Temple times, special sacrifices were brought to the sanctuary and offered by the priests. (Numbers

28:11ff.) It was the task of the High Court, or Sanhedrin, which sat in the Hall of Hewn Stone in the Temple, to determine the time of the new month and then to announce it to the Jewish community.

Determining the New Month

The Jewish calendar consists of 12 months with a little more than 29½ days in each. Each month begins at the time of a new moon, and an entire year contains about 354⅓ days. That is 11 less than the solar calendar years of 365¼ days. As a result, every few years, an extra month is added to the Jewish calendar to make up a leap year and to keep the adjustment of months to the seasons accurate. The extra month is known as אֲדָר שֵׁנִי (*Adar sheni*), Adar II.

What are the origins of the Jewish calendar?

In the Torah, only four names of months are mentioned. They are Aviv, Ziv, Etanim, and Bul. The rest of the months are designated by numbers. For example, when the Torah calls upon the Israelites to observe the Passover, it says: "In the first month, on the fourteenth day of the month at dusk, is the Lord's Passover." (Leviticus 23:5)

The names of the months of the Jewish calendar were taken by Jews in Babylonian exile from the Babylonian calendar. When Jews returned to the Land of Israel, they continued to use the Babylonian names. The months and their lengths are as follows:

Nisan	30 days	נִיסָן
Iyar	29 days	אִייָר
Sivan	30 days	סִיוָן
Tamuz	29 days	תַּמּוּז
Av	30 days	אָב
Elul	29 days	אֱלוּל
Tishri	30 days	תִּשְׁרֵי
Cheshvan	29 days	חֶשְׁוָן
Kislev	30 days	כִּסְלֵו
Tevet	29 days	טֵבֵת
Shevat	30 days	שְׁבָט
Adar	29 days	אֲדָר

(In a leap year, Adar I has 30 days and Adar II has 29 days.)

The Talmud gives us a good description of how ראש חֹדֶשׁ the New Month, was determined and announced during the time of the Temple. Witnesses would watch for the appearance of the new moon and, when they saw it, they would report it to the Sanhedrin. The Sanhedrin would examine the testimony of the witnesses and then announce ראש חֹדֶשׁ. A fire signal would then be lit on a special mountain top and from there to Babylonia signal fires would be kindled to carry the announcement of ראש חֹדֶשׁ to all Jewish communities. When enemies of the Jews ruined this method by lighting fires early, the Jewish community developed a system of messengers whose task it was to carry the news of ראש חֹדֶשׁ

Why Two Days for Some Holidays?

You may have wondered why Orthodox and Conservative Jews celebrate an extra day of Rosh Hashanah and add one extra day to the celebration of Sukot, Pesach, and Shavuot. In the biblical tradition, Rosh Hashanah is celebrated for one day, Sukot and Pesach are celebrated for seven days. Why did Jews, living outside the Land of Israel, add an extra day to their observance of these holidays?

Problems with the calendar explain the addition of the extra days. Since there were often problems with both the accuracy of lighting fires and the arrival of messengers, those who lived outside the Land of Israel decided to celebrate their holidays for two days so that, if they hap-

132

pened to be a day late, they would still be observing at the proper time.

When, in the middle of the fourth century C.E., Hillel II, the head of Jewry living in Israel, developed and published scientific rules for determining the calendar, the use of signals and messengers was stopped. By then, however, the celebration of extra days had become a tradition for Jews living outside the Land of Israel. To this day, Jews in Israel celebrate according to the biblical tradition. Reform Jews did away with the extra days in the middle of the nineteenth century. Orthodox and Conservative Jews living outside of Israel still continue the practice of observing the extra days.

Do you think it is still valid for Jews, living outside of the Land of Israel, to observe extra days of the festivals and Rosh Hashanah? Should there be a difference between Jews who live in Israel and Jews who live outside the land? Why?

Look at the Zodiac. Compare the symbols of the months with those of the Jewish months. What are the similarities and differences?

Notice which Jewish holidays fall into which months. Do you notice any relationship between the meaning of the holiday or holidays and the symbol of the month?

Prayers for Announcing the New Month

As we have already indicated, the practice of announcing רֹאשׁ חֹדֶשׁ was an ancient one. Even with the development of Hillel II's rules of calculation, it was still necessary to inform the people of the beginning of רֹאשׁ חֹדֶשׁ. This was done in the synagogue on the Shabbat preceding the first day of the month. The announcement was made in the form of a simple statement: "The new month of _____ will begin on _____. May it bring goodness to us and to all of Israel."

About two hundred years ago, the other prayers which we have included in *Bechol Levavcha* were added to the announcement. The first paragraph: "May it be Your will . . ." is based upon an ancient prayer written by the sage Rav, the founder of Sura, the most important academy of Jewish learning in Babylonia. Rav wrote his prayer in the third century C.E. as a personal expression to be recited after the עֲמִידָה. His original prayer did not include the words: ". . . to renew us with goodness and blessing in the new month ahead."

Read Rav's prayer without the addition above. What is its theme? What are the things which Rav considered important for a "fulfilled life"? Would you agree with him? If you could ask for twelve things meant to give you a happy, fulfilled life — what would they be?

Have each person in your study group make up a list of the twelve things he or she believes would bring joy and happiness for a lifetime. Each list should go from the most important to the least important. And each person should try to develop some reasons why one thing is more important than another. Then discuss the three most important on everyone's list. Put each list on the board. Don't forget the last three on your lists. What makes them the least important for achieving happiness in life? Compare your lists with that of Rav. Also ask yourselves why the author of our רֹאשׁ חֹדֶשׁ *ceremony thought that Rav's prayer was appropriate.*

Israel Is One United People

What does the second prayer: "May He who has done wonderful things . . ." mean to express? Does it remind you of a prayer in the עֲמִידָה? Which one and why?

The prayer contains the phrase: חֲבֵרִים כָּל יִשְׂרָאֵל (*chaverim kol Yisrael*), Israel is one united people. What does that statement have to do with the theme of the prayer? Of what does it remind us? During the bitter persecutions of Jews in Russia from 1870 through the 1880s, Rabbi Israel Kagan wrote: "All Jews constitute one soul and one body." What do you think he meant? What does Rabbi Kagan's statement mean when read together with the prayer which says: "Israel is one united people"? In what ways are Jews still "one soul and one body"? What about the Jews of Israel and the Jews of the United States? What about our relationship to Jews in Russia?

The modern philosopher, Martin Buber, once wrote: "We have been held together and upheld by common remembering." Would you agree? Is there more that holds us together as Jews? What are the elements which "unite" us as a people?

As the Moon Goes ... So Israel

The modern scholar, Abraham Millgram, has written the following about the "May He who has done wonderful things ..." prayer.

The monthly reappearance of the moon became the symbol of Israel's restoration. As the moon emerges from its total eclipse into brightness, so will Israel be redeemed from its exile and brought back to the land of its fathers.

(*Jewish Worship*, p. 265)

What does Rabbi Millgram mean? What is Israel's eclipse? What is meant by "Israel's restoration"? The second book of Maccabees (1:27) contains a prayer which defines redemption or restoration. It reads:

Gather our dispersion, free those in bondage, look upon them that are despised, and let the nations know that You are God!

Does that description seem to say what our prayer says? How does it compare with Rabbi Millgram's idea?

Realizing now what has been added to the announcement of the new moon, what would you include and exclude? What themes do you feel are important? Create your own "new moon announcement" and prayers using some of the old along with some of your own ideas. Compare the Traditional prayer for the new moon with the Reform version (pp. 130–131) and in Gates of Prayer. What have Reform Jews changed, and why?

Returning the Torah to the Ark

(Torah is lifted before the congregation)

Leader

וְזֹאת הַתּוֹרָה אֲשֶׁר שָׂם מֹשֶׁה לִפְנֵי בְּנֵי יִשְׂרָאֵל, עַל פִּי יְיָ בְּיַד מֹשֶׁה.

This is the Torah which Moses placed before the children of Israel, in accordance with the Lord's command through Moses.

(The following is sung or read while Torah is wrapped)

Everyone

עֵץ חַיִּים הִיא לַמַּחֲזִיקִים בָּהּ, וְתֹמְכֶיהָ מְאֻשָּׁר. דְּרָכֶיהָ דַרְכֵי נֹעַם, וְכָל נְתִיבוֹתֶיהָ שָׁלוֹם. הֲשִׁיבֵנוּ יְיָ אֵלֶיךָ, וְנָשׁוּבָה. חַדֵּשׁ יָמֵינוּ כְּקֶדֶם.

It is a tree of life to those who hold fast to it, and its supporters are happy. Its ways are ways of happiness, and all its paths are peace. Return us to You, O Lord, and let us return. Renew our days as of old.

(Reader holds Torah and says)

יְהַלְלוּ אֶת שֵׁם יְיָ כִּי נִשְׂגָּב שְׁמוֹ לְבַדּוֹ.

Let us praise the name of the Lord for God alone is worthy of praise.

(Everyone sings while Torah is placed in Ark)

הוֹדוֹ עַל אֶרֶץ וְשָׁמָיִם וַיָּרֶם קֶרֶן לְעַמּוֹ תְּהִלָּה לְכָל חֲסִידָיו לִבְנֵי יִשְׂרָאֵל עַם קְרֹבוֹ הַלְלוּיָהּ.

God's glory is above the earth and heaven. God has raised the honor of His people, the glory of all faithful followers, the people Israel, who are near to Him. Praise the Lord.

(At this point, a sermon may be given)

Commentary

We are told that, when Ezra first read the Torah to the people of Israel, he "opened the book in the sight of all ... and, when he opened it, all the people stood up." (Nehemiah 8:5) For cen-

136

turies, now, it has been the custom, after the Torah is read, to lift it up so that the entire congregation could see it. The honor of "lifting the Torah" is called הַגְבָּהָה (hagbahah), lifting. The person given the honor of הַגְבָּהָה holds the Torah so that the members of the congregation can see at least three columns of the Torah text. As he lifts the Torah, the congregation stands, and everyone says: "This is the Torah which Moses placed before the children of Israel, in accordance with the Lord's command through Moses."

THIS IS THE TORAH

The words for the statement: "This is the Torah..." are taken from Deuteronomy 4:44. The whole statement reads:

> This is the Torah which Moses set before the children of Israel; these are the testimonies, and the statutes, and the ordinances, which Moses spoke unto the children of Israel, when they came forth out of Egypt....

The words "... in accordance with the Lord's command through Moses" are taken from Numbers 9:23.

Why do you think the sages, who composed the Torah service, combined both statements? Why are they said by the entire congregation, rather than just by the one who holds up the Torah? What do they have to do with the "action" of holding up the Torah? Look at the statements about the relationship of the Jewish people to Torah. What do these statements have to do with the declaration from Numbers 9:23?

HONOR FOR THE TORAH

Actually some of the decorations for the Torah once had a practical purpose. For instance, the breastplate was first used in order to mark which Torah should be read at which time. On some holidays, more than one Torah section is read. Rather than having to roll the Torah from one place to the next, two Torahs would be used. The first breastplates were markers indicating when the Torah should be read. Later, artists were invited to create the beautiful ornamental

---

Israel's Relationship to Torah

As soon as they received the Torah, the Jews became a whole nation.
(Pesikta Kahana)

Why is Israel called God's people? Because of the Torah.
(Tanchuma)

The soul of every Jew stood at Sinai to accept its share in Torah.
(Abdimi ben Chama)

---

breastplates now used. Some of them still have a place where the Torah reader can mark the holiday for which the Torah is ready to be read.

The יָד (yad), hand or Torah pointer, also has a very practical use. It was developed in about the sixteenth century, in Germany, as an aid to the person reading from the Torah.

The רִמּוֹנִים (rimonim), Torah crowns, are purely decorative and symbolic. They are meant to serve the same purpose as the crown worn by a king or queen. The Torah crowns (or crown) symbolize the devotion, commitment, and love the Jew has for Torah.

Usually, while the congregation is singing the עֵץ חַיִּים (etz chaim), a tree of life, the Torah is rolled, tied, covered, and, then, its breastplate crowns are placed upon it.

The rolling of the Torah is called גְּלִילָה (gelilah).

The acts of הַגְבָּהָה and גְּלִילָה the congregation rising as the Torah is lifted, the use of beautiful ornaments for the Torah — all confirm the Jew's appreciation of Torah. That appreciation is also spoken or sung in the words: "It is a tree of life...." (Proverbs 3) How do these words about Torah relate to what we have already learned about the Jew's relationship to it?

The famous Rabbi Akiva who was arrested and put to death by the Romans for teaching Judaism was once approached by a fellow teacher, Pappos ben Judah. The Talmud records their conversation:

Rabbi Pappos ben Judah said to Akiva: "Are you not afraid of what the Romans will do if they catch you teaching and studying Torah?" Akiva replied: "I will tell you a parable. The matter may be compared to a fox who was walking along the bank of a stream. He saw some fish gathering together to move from one place to another. He said to them: "What are you fleeing from?" They answered: "From the nets of fishermen." So the fox said: "Why don't you come up here on dry land, and we will dwell together?" "O fox," they replied, "you are the cleverest of animals, but you are a fool! If we are afraid to be in a place vital for our survival, how much more dangerous would it be for us to go to a place which is certain death for us?"

"So it is with us," Rabbi Akiva said to Rabbi Pappos ben Judah, "it is better for the Jew to stay in an atmosphere vital for our survival, and face Roman threats, than to abandon our Torah, for it is our "tree of life" and the "length of our days."

(Berachot 61b)

Would you agree with Rabbi Akiva's argument? How does his view of Torah as "vital for our survival" compare with the Gerer Rebbe's point of view (see page 109)? Is Akiva's position realistic or unrealistic?

Section Five

סִיוּם הָעֲבוֹדָה

CONCLUSION OF THE SERVICE

Siyum Haavodah

a. The Aleynu *140*
b. The Kaddish *145*
c. Adon Olam *151*
d. En Kelohenu *153*
e. Yigdal *154*
f. Kiddush for Shabbat Day *156*

The Aleynu

I

עָלֵינוּ לְשַׁבֵּחַ לַאֲדוֹן הַכֹּל, לָתֵת גְּדֻלָּה לְיוֹצֵר בְּרֵאשִׁית,
שֶׁלֹּא עָשָׂנוּ כְּגוֹיֵי הָאֲרָצוֹת, וְלֹא שָׂמָנוּ כְּמִשְׁפְּחוֹת הָאֲדָמָה.
שֶׁלֹּא שָׂם חֶלְקֵנוּ כָּהֶם וְגוֹרָלֵנוּ כְּכָל הֲמוֹנָם.
וַאֲנַחְנוּ כּוֹרְעִים וּמִשְׁתַּחֲוִים וּמוֹדִים
לִפְנֵי מֶלֶךְ מַלְכֵי הַמְּלָכִים, הַקָּדוֹשׁ בָּרוּךְ הוּא.

It is our duty to praise the Lord of all, to praise the Creator of the universe, for God has not made us like the nations of other lands, nor like other families of the earth. The Lord has not made our portion like theirs, nor our lot like all others.

We bend the knee, bow, and give thanks before God, the Source of all life.

II

שֶׁהוּא נוֹטֶה שָׁמַיִם וְיוֹסֵד אָרֶץ, וּמוֹשַׁב יְקָרוֹ בַּשָּׁמַיִם
מִמַּעַל, וּשְׁכִינַת עֻזּוֹ בְּגָבְהֵי מְרוֹמִים. הוּא אֱלֹהֵינוּ, אֵין
עוֹד. אֱמֶת מַלְכֵּנוּ, אֶפֶס זוּלָתוֹ, כַּכָּתוּב בְּתוֹרָתוֹ: וְיָדַעְתָּ
הַיּוֹם וַהֲשֵׁבֹתָ אֶל לְבָבֶךָ, כִּי יְיָ הוּא הָאֱלֹהִים בַּשָּׁמַיִם
מִמַּעַל וְעַל הָאָרֶץ מִתָּחַת. אֵין עוֹד.

For God stretched out the heavens and laid the foundations of earth. God's glory is in the heavens above, and God's mighty power is in the height of heights. We worship the Lord alone, there is none else. Truly God is supreme, there is none other. As it is written in the Torah: And you shall know this day, and reflect upon it, that the Lord is God in the heavens above and upon the earth beneath. There is none else.

(For other versions for parts one and two on the Aleynu see *Commentary*)

III

עַל כֵּן נְקַוֶּה לְךָ, יְיָ אֱלֹהֵינוּ, לִרְאוֹת מְהֵרָה בְּתִפְאֶרֶת עֻזֶּךָ, לְהַעֲבִיר גִּלּוּלִים מִן הָאָרֶץ, וְהָאֱלִילִים כָּרוֹת יִכָּרֵתוּן. לְתַקֵּן עוֹלָם בְּמַלְכוּת שַׁדַּי, וְכָל בְּנֵי בָשָׂר יִקְרְאוּ בִשְׁמֶךָ, לְהַפְנוֹת אֵלֶיךָ כָּל רִשְׁעֵי אָרֶץ.

Therefore, we put our hope in You, O Lord our God, that we may soon see the glory of Your power — when all evil will be removed from the earth — when false gods will be completely destroyed — when the world will be perfected under God's rule and all human beings will call upon Your name — and when the wicked of the earth will turn and worship you.

יַכִּירוּ וְיֵדְעוּ כָּל יוֹשְׁבֵי תֵבֵל, כִּי לְךָ תִּכְרַע כָּל בֶּרֶךְ תִּשָּׁבַע כָּל לָשׁוֹן. לְפָנֶיךָ, יְיָ אֱלֹהֵינוּ, יִכְרְעוּ וְיִפֹּלוּ, וְלִכְבוֹד שִׁמְךָ יְקָר יִתֵּנוּ, וִיקַבְּלוּ כֻלָּם אֶת עוֹל מַלְכוּתֶךָ, וְתִמְלֹךְ עֲלֵיהֶם מְהֵרָה לְעוֹלָם וָעֶד, כִּי הַמַּלְכוּת שֶׁלְּךָ הִיא, וּלְעוֹלְמֵי עַד תִּמְלֹךְ בְּכָבוֹד, כַּכָּתוּב בְּתוֹרָתֶךָ: יְיָ יִמְלֹךְ לְעוֹלָם וָעֶד. וְנֶאֱמַר: וְהָיָה יְיָ לְמֶלֶךְ עַל כָּל הָאָרֶץ, בַּיּוֹם הַהוּא יִהְיֶה יְיָ אֶחָד וּשְׁמוֹ אֶחָד.

May all the inhabitants of earth know that to You every knee must bend and every tongue swear allegiance. Before You, O Lord our God, let all bow, worship, and give honor. And let all of them accept the yoke of Your kingdom, and rule over them for ever. For Yours is the Kingdom, and You will rule for ever and ever. As it is written in Your Torah: The Lord will rule in all the earth. On that day the Lord will be one and God's name will be one.

Commentary

The עָלֵינוּ (*Aleynu*) marks the actual conclusion of the worship service. However, it was not always considered as the final prayer. As we have already seen, the Shabbat service, at one time, may have concluded with the final blessings after the הַפְטָרָה reading.

What, then, are the origins of the עָלֵינוּ prayer? How and when did it become the final prayer of the Shabbat service?

A Fascinating History

Seldom do we come across a poem or prayer which is ancient, has brought persecution and death upon those who used it, and has become a symbol of a people's courage and bravery. The עָלֵינוּ is one of those rare pieces of literature.

We are not sure when the עָלֵינוּ was first written, and we are not sure who its author was. However, most Jewish scholars agree that it was composed around the time of the Maccabees. It is likely that when the author wrote: "... when all evil will be removed from the earth — when false gods will be completely destroyed . . ." he had in mind the idol worship of the Greek-Syrians and their attempt to force Jews into abandoning their worship of one God.

The author of the עָלֵינוּ also sought to express the uniqueness of the Jewish people. The prayer declares: "For God has not made us like the nations of other lands, nor like other families of the earth. The Lord has not made our portion like theirs, nor our lot like all others." In other words, the prayer expresses the thought that Jews are different from all other peoples of the earth!

When the sage, Rav, who headed the Academy of Sura in Babylonia during the third century C.E., composed the Rosh Hashanah prayers, he included the עָלֵינוּ in the Shofar service. This was most likely done because it voiced the hope for the day when "all inhabitants of the earth" would worship God and be united in justice and peace.

About the thirteenth century, the עָלֵינוּ was introduced into the Shabbat and daily services as a final prayer. Apparently, there were many Jews who thought that it was appropriate and beautiful as a conclusion to their worship. For them it was a hope that soon the "messianic days" would come when God would rule over the whole earth.

PERSECUTION AND DEATH

What was meant to be a prayer of hope, however, became a prayer of controversy. If we look at the original prayer carefully, we can see why it might have been misunderstood. The first paragraph of the עָלֵינוּ prayer originally read as follows:

It is our duty to praise the Lord of all, to praise the Creator of the universe, for He has not made us like the nations of other lands, nor like other families of the earth. He has not made our portion like theirs, nor our lot like all others. <u>For they bow down to vanity and emptiness and pray to a god that cannot save.</u>

We bend the knee, bow, and give thanks before the King of kings, the Holy One, blessed be He.

The words underlined were a part of the original prayer. They were based upon two sentences found in the Book of Isaiah (30:7 and 45:20). Look at those sentences in the Book of Isaiah and see if you can figure out what the prophet meant by them and why the author of the עָלֵינוּ used them for his prayer.

Not long after the עָלֵינוּ had been introduced into the daily and Shabbat worship, Christians and Jewish converts to Christianity accused Jews of slandering the beliefs of Christianity in their worship. Those who made the accusation claimed that the words "For they bow down to vanity and emptiness and pray to a god that cannot save" were meant as a deliberate slur, by Jews, of Christianity.

During the Crusades, and most of the Middle Ages, the words of the עָלֵינוּ were held up as evidence of Jewish prejudice and slander against Christians. When Jews tried to explain that the words being used against them had been written by the prophet Isaiah, over seven hundred years before the birth of Jesus, their arguments were dismissed as untruth and trickery. During the Inquisition, in Spain, Jews suffered death and torture at the hands of church leaders who accused them of reciting the עָלֵינוּ prayer and thereby slandering the beliefs of Christians. In many cases, it is reported that Jews went to their deaths with the עָלֵינוּ on their lips.

What is your opinion of the accusations of Church leaders? Why would a convert to Christianity from Judaism accuse his abandoned faith and people of such slander? What do you think about the older (full) version of the עָלֵינוּ prayer?

In about the year 1400, a convert to Christianity from Judaism sought to prove that the עָלֵינוּ prayer was a deliberate slander and attack upon Christianity. What was his proof? He pointed to the word "emptiness" in the sentence "For they bow down to vanity and emptiness." He claimed that the word וָרִיק (varik) had a numerical value of 316 (ו = 6, ר = 200, י = 10, ק = 100) and that Jesus' name in Hebrew, יֵשׁוּ (Yeshu), also had the numerical value of 316 (י = 10, שׁ = 300, ו = 6). In this way he claimed that Jews were really saying: "For they [Christians] bow down to vanity and (וָרִיק) emptiness [which is Jesus]." What do you think about such an argument? How would you attempt to answer it? The words "vanity and emptiness" are found in Isaiah 30:7. That verse reads: "Egypt's help will be vanity and emptiness." What do you suppose Isaiah meant by his statement?

Changing the עָלֵינוּ Prayer

At the beginning of the eighteenth century, the Prussian government censored the Jewish prayer book and issued a decree forbidding Jews to include the words: "For they bow down to vanity and emptiness and pray to a god that cannot save" in the עָלֵינוּ prayer or anywhere within their worship. From that time on the עָלֵינוּ prayer has not included those words.

Should Jews have given in to the Prussian authorities and government and changed their prayer book? If you were printing a new prayer book today, would you include the controversial words? Why? One of the freedoms guaranteed by the United States Constitution is "free exercise of religion." What is this?

We Put Our Hope in You

The second section of the עָלֵינוּ prayer declares that God is the power responsible for the heavens and the earth and that there is none else. This Jewish idea of God is found throughout the Torah and the rest of תַּנַ"ךְ. The words of עָלֵינוּ, however, are very close to those expressed by the prophet Isaiah. Look, for instance, at Isaiah 40:12–20, 42:5–8, 43:10–11, 44:6–8, 45:4–8, 45:18—46:13.

Compare these quotes from the prophet Isaiah with the second section of the עָלֵינוּ prayer. What do they teach us about the Jewish idea of God? Why was Isaiah so opposed to idol worship? If you were to write a prayer about the "greatness of God" or the "power of God," what passages or thoughts from Isaiah would you include?

The third section of the עָלֵינוּ prayer expresses the hope for the kingdom of God, or the messianic days. What are the things mentioned in the prayer which were believed would lead to the coming of an age of justice and peace? How does this section compare with the hope for the "messianic days" voiced by Isaiah (2:1–21)?

On That Day

Judaism was the first religion to teach the idea that there is one God over all nations and human beings. And it was the first faith to put forward the hope that all human beings would, one day, be united. The prophet Malachi put this teaching of Judaism into the form of a question. He asked: "Have we not all one Source? Has not one God created all of us? Why, then, do we deal treacherously every man against his neighbor?" (Malachi 2:10)

The hope that some day all human beings would live together in peace was also expressed by the prophet Zechariah. He said:

And it shall come to pass in that day
That living waters shall go out from Jerusalem:
Half of them toward the eastern sea,
And half of them toward the western sea;
In summer and in winter shall it be.
And the Lord shall be King over all the earth;
On that day the Lord will be one and His name will be one.

(Zechariah 14:8–9)

The authors of the עָלֵינוּ prayer chose these last words of Zechariah as the conclusion of the עָלֵינוּ prayer. For them, Zechariah's words represented the highest hope for humanity. Would you agree with them? Were both Malachi and Zechariah saying the same thing?

Would human beings need to share the same religion in order to fulfill Zechariah's or Malachi's hope? Does the עָלֵינוּ prayer say that all people must have the same religion in order for God's name to be one?

Moses Maimonides describes the "messianic days" as follows: "In the Messiah's days there will be no hunger, nor war, nor jealousy, nor strife; there will be plenty for all, and the world's chief occupation will be to know the Lord." (*Yad Hachazakah*) How does Maimonides' statement compare to the עָלֵינוּ prayer? Does he seem to believe that all human beings will have to share the same religion in the days of the Messiah?

Prayers on the עָלֵינוּ Theme

I

May the time not be distant, O God, when Your name shall be worshiped in all the earth, when unbelief shall disappear and error be no more. Fervently we pray that the day may come when all shall turn to You in love, when corruption and evil shall give way to integrity and goodness, when superstition shall no longer enslave the mind nor idolatry blind the eye, when all who dwell on earth shall know that You alone are God. O may all, created in Your image, become one in spirit and one in friendship, forever united in Your service. Then shall Your kingdom be established on earth and the word of Your prophet be fulfilled: "The Lord shall reign for ever and ever."

(*Gates of Prayer*)

Creating with Kavanah

Themes:

a. The uniqueness of the Jewish people and its beliefs.
b. God as the Creator of all that is — the heavens, the earth, all life.
c. The hope for the day when all human beings will live in peace and harmony.
d. The hope for the day when all human beings will worship God as a united family.

Before you begin to create your own עָלֵינוּ prayer, make a list of those things you believe necessary for "peace and harmony" among human beings. You may, then, wish to create your prayer of hope using several of the ideas you have included on your list.

II

O Lord, our God, we face the future with hope. Despite the suffering of our people, Israel, we have faith in the possibilities of a world without injustice and hate, without poverty and war.

May we, the people of Israel, accept the responsibilities of Your covenant. Grant us strength to share the struggles of others, and determination to pursue the blessings of peace. May we strive to create the day when every human being will rejoice in a world of cooperation and love.

(HJF)

The Kaddish

יִתְגַּדַּל וְיִתְקַדַּשׁ שְׁמֵהּ רַבָּא בְּעָלְמָא דִּי בְרָא כִרְעוּתֵהּ. וְיַמְלִיךְ מַלְכוּתֵהּ בְּחַיֵּיכוֹן וּבְיוֹמֵיכוֹן וּבְחַיֵּי דְכָל בֵּית יִשְׂרָאֵל, בַּעֲגָלָא וּבִזְמַן קָרִיב, וְאִמְרוּ אָמֵן.

May God's great name be magnified and made holy in the world created according to His will. May God soon establish His kingdom during your life and days and during the lifetime of the whole house of Israel. And let us say, Amen.

יְהֵא שְׁמֵהּ רַבָּא מְבָרַךְ לְעָלַם וּלְעָלְמֵי עָלְמַיָּא.

May God's great name be blessed now and forever.

יִתְבָּרַךְ, וְיִשְׁתַּבַּח, וְיִתְפָּאַר, וְיִתְרֹמַם, וְיִתְנַשֵּׂא, וְיִתְהַדָּר, וְיִתְעַלֶּה, וְיִתְהַלָּל שְׁמֵהּ דְּקֻדְשָׁא, בְּרִיךְ הוּא. לְעֵלָּא מִן כָּל בִּרְכָתָא וְשִׁירָתָא, תֻּשְׁבְּחָתָא וְנֶחֱמָתָא דַּאֲמִירָן בְּעָלְמָא, וְאִמְרוּ אָמֵן.

May the name of the Holy One be blessed, praised, glorified, exalted, extolled, honored, magnified, and celebrated, even though God is above and beyond all the blessings, songs, praises, and consolations that are spoken in the world. And let us say, Amen.

יְהֵא שְׁלָמָא רַבָּא מִן שְׁמַיָּא וְחַיִּים עָלֵינוּ וְעַל כָּל יִשְׂרָאֵל, וְאִמְרוּ אָמֵן.

May there be great peace from heaven and life for us and all Israel. And let us say, Amen.

עֹשֶׂה שָׁלוֹם בִּמְרוֹמָיו, הוּא יַעֲשֶׂה שָׁלוֹם עָלֵינוּ וְעַל כָּל יִשְׂרָאֵל, וְאִמְרוּ אָמֵן.

May the One who makes peace in the heavens make peace for us and for all of Israel. And let us say, Amen.

Commentary

The קַדִּישׁ (Kaddish) may be the best known and most often recited prayer in all of Jewish tradition. Why? What are its origins? What is its meaning? Why has it become so important a prayer within Judaism?

Origins of the קַדִּישׁ

As with many prayers within Judaism, we are not sure who wrote the קַדִּישׁ or when it was written. It may be that it began as a brief, one sentence prayer and, over the ages, gathered additions and increased in size.

Some scholars believe that the original קַדִּישׁ prayer is to be found in either the Book of Daniel (2:20) or in Psalms (113:2). Those sentences read as follows:

לֶהֱוֵא שְׁמֵהּ דִּי אֱלָהָא מְבָרַךְ מִן עָלְמָא וְעַד עָלְמָא.

Blessed be the name of God forever and ever.
(Daniel 2:20)

יְהִי שֵׁם יְהֹוָה מְבֹרָךְ מֵעַתָּה וְעַד עוֹלָם.

May the name of the Lord be blessed now and forever.
(Psalms 113:2)

Compare the two quotes above with the second paragraph of the קַדִּישׁ prayer. What are the similarities and differences?

One of the differences is that of language. The sentence from the Book of Daniel and the קַדִּישׁ prayer are both written in Aramaic rather than Hebrew. The sentence from Psalm 113 is in Hebrew. Aramaic was spoken by Jews from the time of the Babylonian exile (586 B.C.E.) until about the fifth century of the Common Era. According to the Talmud, when a teacher finished his lesson or when the rabbi finished his sermon in the synagogue, they would dismiss their listeners with the words: "May His great name be blessed now and forever." (Berachot 3a, 21b)

That sentence of dismissal formed the kernel of what became the קַדִּישׁ prayer. Gradually, over the course of centuries, there developed five different versions of the קַדִּישׁ.

The Half Kaddish

The half Kaddish, חֲצִי קַדִּישׁ (chatzi Kaddish), is the most frequently recited version of the קַדִּישׁ prayer. It is made up of the first three paragraphs found on page 145. It is recited by the reader and congregation at the end of each section of the prayer service, at the end of the פְּסוּקֵי דְזִמְרָה and at the end of the Torah service.

The Full Kaddish

The full Kaddish, קַדִּישׁ שָׁלֵם (Kaddish shalem), is recited after the עֲמִידָה by the reader and congregation. It is also known as קַדִּישׁ תִּתְקַבֵּל (Kaddish titkabel) because of its petition for acceptance of the prayer. Just after the third paragraph, it contains this additional sentence:

תִּתְקַבֵּל צְלוֹתְהוֹן וּבָעוּתְהוֹן דְּכָל יִשְׂרָאֵל קֳדָם אֲבוּהוֹן דִּי בִשְׁמַיָּא, וְאִמְרוּ אָמֵן.

May the prayers and supplications of all Israel be acceptable to their God who is in heaven. And let us say, Amen.

The Mourners' Kaddish

The mourners' Kaddish, קַדִּישׁ יָתוֹם (Kaddish yatom), is recited, by those who have lost a parent, at the conclusion of every service for eleven months. The version of the קַדִּישׁ found on page 145 is the קַדִּישׁ יָתוֹם.

Why did the קַדִּישׁ become a prayer for mourners? There are several possible answers to our question. We know, for instance, that it was the custom during talmudic times for mourners to devote time to the study of Torah during their days of mourning. At the conclusion of each study session, the קַדִּישׁ was recited. This may have been the beginning of the custom.

Another explanation is found in a legend about Rabbi Akiva. It is said that he once came upon a man carrying a heavy load of wood and wandering about in a cemetery. He asked him: "What are you doing here? Are you a man or a demon?" The man replied: "I am dead, but I have been condemned to carry wood in the cemetery." "What did you do?" asked Akiva, "Why have you been condemned to such a fate?" The man answered: "I was a tax collector who favored the rich and oppressed the poor." Akiva then inquired: "Is there no way that you can be saved from such a terrible fate?" The man replied: "If my son will recite the קָדִישׁ, I will be saved from this punishment in Gehenom and will rest in Heaven." It is said that Akiva then went to find the son, taught him the קָדִישׁ prayer, and that the man finally came to rest in Heaven.

What is the point or lesson of this legend? How might it have inspired Jews to recite the קָדִישׁ for their parents? It is reported that there were many Jews who strongly disagreed with the idea that the קָדִישׁ prayer would save a parent from Gehenom. Rabbi Abraham bar Chiyya, one of the great leaders of Spanish Jewry during the twelfth century, declared: "Those who hope that the קָדִישׁ of their children will benefit them after death are hoping in vain." What did Rabbi Abraham bar Chiyya mean by his statement? To whom was his criticism directed? Why? How might the saying of the קָדִישׁ prayer help a child honor the memory of his parents?

The English version of the קָדִישׁ יָתוֹם in the *Union Prayer Book* included the following paragraph:

The departed, whom we now remember, have entered into the peace of life eternal. They still live on earth in the acts of goodness they performed and in the hearts of those who cherish their memory. May the beauty of their life abide among us as a loving benediction.

What do you think is meant by the phrase: "They still live on earth in the acts of goodness they performed and in the hearts of those who cherish their memory"? How might the saying of קָדִישׁ help us "cherish their memory"?

It is interesting to note that the קָדִישׁ יָתוֹם contains no mention of death, immortality, or life in either Gehenom or Heaven. Look at it carefully. What is its theme? Why did it become a mourners' prayer? How is a prayer of praise for God — one that voices the hope for the "establishment of God's Kingdom" — appropriate for the mourners' prayer?

In the sixteenth century, Abraham Hurwitz wrote the following about the קָדִישׁ.

... The קָדִישׁ is not a prayer of the son that the father may be brought up from *Sheol* but a recognition of the parent's merit, since through its recital the child best vindicates (claims honor for) the memory of his parent by causing the congregation to respond to him with the praise "Amen. May His great name be blessed now and forever."

Would you agree with Abraham Hurwitz? How does a praise of God, said in the memory of a parent, honor him or her?

The Rabbis' Kaddish

The fourth version of the קַדִּישׁ is known as the קַדִּישׁ דְּרַבָּנָן (*Kaddish derabanan*), rabbis' Kaddish. It is recited after the study of Torah or Talmud. The following paragraph is added after the third paragraph of our version.

עַל יִשְׂרָאֵל וְעַל רַבָּנָן, וְעַל תַּלְמִידֵיהוֹן, וְעַל כָּל תַּלְמִידֵי תַלְמִידֵיהוֹן, וְעַל כָּל מָאן דְּעָסְקִין בְּאוֹרַיְתָא, דִּי בְאַתְרָא הָדֵין, וְדִי בְכָל אֲתַר וַאֲתַר. יְהֵא לְהוֹן וּלְכוֹן שְׁלָמָא רַבָּא, חִנָּא וְחִסְדָּא וְרַחֲמִין, וְחַיִּין אֲרִיכִין, וּמְזוֹנָא רְוִיחָא, וּפוּרְקָנָא מִן קֳדָם אֲבוּהוֹן דִּי בִשְׁמַיָּא וְאַרְעָא, וְאִמְרוּ אָמֵן.

Unto Israel and unto the rabbis and their students, and to all the students of their students, and to all who study the Torah in this or in any other place, to you and to them may there be abundant peace, grace, lovingkindness, mercy, long life, plenty to eat, and salvation from God who is in heaven. And let us say, Amen.

The Funeral Kaddish

The fifth version of the קַדִּישׁ is the only one which mentions death or eternal life. It is called קַדִּישׁ לְהִתְחַדְתָּא (*Kaddish lehitchadeta*), the Kaddish of renewal. It is said by the mourner at the grave just after the burial, and it includes the words: "May God's great name be magnified and sanctified in the world that is to be created anew, where God will make the dead live again and raise them up unto life eternal — where God will rebuild the city of Jerusalem and establish the Temple in its midst, and destroy false worship from the earth, and restore the worship of the true God. O may the Holy One, blessed be He, rule in power and glory....."

The קַדִּישׁ לְהִתְחַדְתָּא may be one of the last versions of the קַדִּישׁ prayer written. It is the only one to make mention of the rebuilding of Jerusalem and the Temple. Its authors believed that the coming of the messianic days would also bring with them a new world with the possibility of all the dead being brought back to life.

Do Jews Believe in Life after Death?

As we have noticed, the mention of life after death is only found in the fifth version of the קַדִּישׁ prayer called קַדִּישׁ לְהִתְחַדְתָּא. We have already discussed some aspects of the Jewish belief in life after death. See the Gevurot starting on page 72.

There have always been a variety of views within Jewish life about immortality or עוֹלָם הַבָּא (*olam haba*), the world to come. The closest that Jews have come to a binding statement on the subject is found in the *Thirteen Principles of Faith* drawn up by Moses Maimonides. He wrote:

> I believe with perfect faith that there will be a revival of the dead at the time when it shall please the Creator, blessed be His name and exalted be His name forever and ever.

Maimonides' *Thirteen Principles of Faith* have been printed in most prayer books for the past eight hundred years, and most Jews have accepted them as the most important beliefs of Judaism.

Disagreement and Controversy

There are, however, many Jews who do not believe in the עוֹלָם הַבָּא, the world to come, and who reject the idea that there is a life after death. They argue that the Hebrew Bible makes no mention of it and that it is a foreign idea to Judaism. In the Book of Job, we are told: "He that goes down to the grave will not come up again" (Job 7:9), and the author of Ecclesiastes writes: "The dust returns to the earth from where it came, and the spirit returns to God who gave it." (Ecclesiastes 12:7) In another place the same author tells us: "There is no work, no advice, no knowledge, no wisdom in the grave." (Ecclesiastes 9:10)

What do the statements of Job and Ecclesiastes say about death and immortality? Is there a life after death for them? Do you think they would agree with the observation made by Moses Montefiore in 1903: "As to what happens to us after death, we have no conception and we form no theory." Would you agree with Montefiore's statement?

Reform Judaism eliminated mention of the "resurrection of the dead" from the prayer book. It does, however, say the following about life after death: "Death is not the end; the earthly body vanishes, the immortal spirit lives on with God." How does that view compare with those of Job and Ecclesiastes?

You may wish to look at the views on immortality found in *Gates of Prayer*, pp. 622–628, and also at *Bechol Levavcha*, page 150. Which of those prayers do you find more in harmony with your own view of immortality, and why?

Gehenom — Hell

We have already mentioned Gehenom. What is it? Do Jews believe in hell and heaven?

The Hebrew Bible mentions two places which might be considered hell. One is Gehenom. The name גֵּיא בֶן הִנּוֹם (*Ge ben Hinom*) means "the valley of the son of Henom." It was a place, near Jerusalem, where idolators sacrificed human beings. For this reason the valley was known as a place of torture, suffering, and bloodshed. We are not sure when, but gradually it was associated with punishment after a wicked life. It apparently became common to say that a wicked person would suffer like those who had suffered in גֵּיהִנּוֹם (*Gehenom*).

Another name for hell in the Bible is שְׁאוֹל (*Sheol*). We are not sure what שְׁאוֹל originally meant. It is likely that it referred to the grave or to the realm of death.

The existence of a גֵּיהִנּוֹם was debated by the talmudic rabbis. Here is a part of their argument.

Yannai and Shimon ben Lakish say: "There is no גֵּיהִנּוֹם, but the sun will burn up the wicked." The rest of the rabbis say: "There will be a גֵּיהִנּוֹם." Judah bar Ilai said: "There will be neither a consuming sun nor a גֵּיהִנּוֹם but, rather, a fire issuing from the wicked will burn them up."

(Nedarim 8b)

Why did ancient people make a connection between destruction by fire (sun) and wickedness? Do you think it is still possible to speak in terms of a hell for those who are unethical in their lives?

Usually, just before the mourners' Kaddish is recited a brief prayer about life or immortality is read. Following you will find some examples. Compare and contrast them. Discuss them, asking the question: "Does this prayer say what I believe and feel?" When you are called upon to do the Kaddish section of your service, you may wish to use one of the following or you may want to write your own Kaddish.

I

In death, only the body dies. The spirit lives through God's love and mercy. Our loved ones continue to be with us when we remember their deeds and the precious times we shared with them. Now, their kindness, the beautiful words they spoke, and their inspiration give us courage and direction along life's path.

II

You, O God, have placed human beings on earth and have given them minds to seek truth and hearts to know love and beauty, and surely You will not abandon us in death. Dust we are, and to dust we return, but the spirit which You have breathed into us must return to You, the Fountainhead of all spirits. Teach us to know that death is but the door to eternal life.

III

The Lord gives, the Lord takes away, blessed be the name of the Lord.

Death comes upon us just as the leaf falls from the tree when its day is done. Yet, the deeds of loving and righteous human beings enrich the lives of others just as the fallen leaf enriches the soil beneath. Cherishing the lives of those who have contributed so much to us, we praise God for their existence by saying the Kaddish.

IV

God is the Source of life, the Fountain of all good. He has given us dear ones and we rejoice in their love, grow strong through their care, and are enriched by their influence. The sorrow of their loss is the price we pay for the days and years of their love and affection.

Death is not the end; the earthly body vanishes, but the immortal spirit lives on with God. In our hearts, also, our loved ones never die. Their love and memory are a lasting inspiration, moving us to noble deeds and blessing us evermore.

Adon Olam

He is the eternal Lord who ruled Before any thing was created. At the time when all was made by His will, He was called Ruler.	אֲדוֹן עוֹלָם אֲשֶׁר מָלַךְ בְּטֶרֶם כָּל יְצִיר נִבְרָא. לְעֵת נַעֲשָׂה בְחֶפְצוֹ כֹּל אֲזַי מֶלֶךְ שְׁמוֹ נִקְרָא.
And at the end, when all shall cease to be, God, alone, shall still be King. He was, He is, and He shall be In glorious eternity.	וְאַחֲרֵי כִּכְלוֹת הַכֹּל לְבַדּוֹ יִמְלֹךְ נוֹרָא. וְהוּא הָיָה וְהוּא הֹוֶה וְהוּא יִהְיֶה בְּתִפְאָרָה.
He is One, and there is no other To compare to Him or to place beside Him. He is without beginning, without end. All power and rule belong to Him.	וְהוּא אֶחָד וְאֵין שֵׁנִי לְהַמְשִׁיל לוֹ לְהַחְבִּירָה. בְּלִי רֵאשִׁית בְּלִי תַכְלִית וְלוֹ הָעֹז וְהַמִּשְׂרָה.
He is my God, my living Redeemer, My Stronghold in times of trouble. He is my Guide and my Refuge, My Share of joy in the day I call.	וְהוּא אֵלִי וְחַי גֹּאֲלִי וְצוּר חֶבְלִי בְּעֵת צָרָה. וְהוּא נִסִּי וּמָנוֹס לִי מְנָת כּוֹסִי בְּיוֹם אֶקְרָא.
To Him I entrust my spirit When I sleep and when I wake. As long as my soul is within my body The Lord is with me, and I am not afraid.	בְּיָדוֹ אַפְקִיד רוּחִי בְּעֵת אִישָׁן וְאָעִירָה. וְעִם רוּחִי גְוִיָּתִי יְיָ לִי וְלֹא אִירָא.

Commentary

The אֲדוֹן עוֹלָם (*Adon Olam*) is one of the best loved and known of all Jewish songs. We are not sure when it was written. Some say it was composed by the great Spanish Jewish poet, Solomon ibn Gabirol, during the eleventh century C.E. Others say that the אֲדוֹן עוֹלָם was written much earlier, perhaps at the time Jews lived under Moslem rule in Babylonia. For the past six centuries, it has been included in the prayer book, and it has become one of the most popular of all Jewish songs.

The theme of אֲדוֹן עוֹלָם is the greatness and eternity of God. Actually, its verses contain a definition of God. Look at them carefully. What do they tell us about the Jewish understanding of God? How would you compare the definition of God in the song with the Christian understanding of God?

There are many different musical settings of אֲדוֹן עוֹלָם. Since it was sung on Shabbat, at Kol Nidre on Yom Kippur, at the daily service by those gathered about the bed of a dying person, and by Moroccan Jews at weddings, its music reflects a variety of moods and meanings.

Make a collection of as many different musical versions of אֲדוֹן עוֹלָם *as you can find. Compare and contrast them, and try to relate them to the times and cultures in which they were created.*

En Kelohenu

There is none like our God, אֵין כֵּאלֹהֵינוּ.
None like our Lord, אֵין כַּאדוֹנֵינוּ.
None like our King, אֵין כְּמַלְכֵּנוּ.
None like our Savior. אֵין כְּמוֹשִׁיעֵנוּ.

Who is like our God? מִי כֵאלֹהֵינוּ?
Who is like our Lord? מִי כַאדוֹנֵינוּ?
Who is like our King? מִי כְמַלְכֵּנוּ?
Who is like our Savior? מִי כְמוֹשִׁיעֵנוּ?

Let us give thanks to our God, נוֹדֶה לֵאלֹהֵינוּ.
Thanks to our Lord, נוֹדֶה לַאדוֹנֵינוּ.
Thanks to our King, נוֹדֶה לְמַלְכֵּנוּ.
Thanks to our Savior. נוֹדֶה לְמוֹשִׁיעֵנוּ.

Blessed be our God. בָּרוּךְ אֱלֹהֵינוּ.
Blessed be our Lord. בָּרוּךְ אֲדוֹנֵינוּ.
Blessed be our King. בָּרוּךְ מַלְכֵּנוּ.
Blessed be our Savior. בָּרוּךְ מוֹשִׁיעֵנוּ.

You are our God. אַתָּה הוּא אֱלֹהֵינוּ.
You are our Lord. אַתָּה הוּא אֲדוֹנֵינוּ.
You are our King. אַתָּה הוּא מַלְכֵּנוּ.
You are our Savior. אַתָּה הוּא מוֹשִׁיעֵנוּ.

Commentary

Like the אֲדוֹן עוֹלָם, the אֵין כֵּאלֹהֵינוּ (En Kelohenu) is one of the most popular songs sung at worship services. It was composed about the eighth century C.E. and has been included in Jewish prayer ever since. Originally, it began with the second stanza and was then followed with אֵין כֵּאלֹהֵינוּ. Later someone reversed the stanzas. Some say this was done so that when the first letters of the first three stanzas were combined they would spell אָמֵן (amen).

Yigdal

יִגְדַּל אֱלֹהִים חַי וְיִשְׁתַּבַּח נִמְצָא וְאֵין עֵת אֶל מְצִיאוּתוֹ.

Magnify and bless the living God who is beyond time and eternity.

אֶחָד וְאֵין יָחִיד כְּיִחוּדוֹ נֶעְלָם וְגַם אֵין סוֹף לְאַחְדּוּתוֹ.

He is one, yet there is no unity like His oneness, His oneness is mysterious and measureless.

אֵין לוֹ דְמוּת הַגּוּף, וְאֵינוֹ גוּף לֹא נַעֲרוֹךְ אֵלָיו קְדֻשָּׁתוֹ.

He has neither form nor body, and nothing can encompass His holiness.

קַדְמוֹן לְכָל דָּבָר אֲשֶׁר נִבְרָא, רִאשׁוֹן וְאֵין רֵאשִׁית לְרֵאשִׁיתוֹ.

He was before all that was created. He was first, yet He is without beginning.

הִנּוֹ אֲדוֹן עוֹלָם, לְכָל נוֹצָר יוֹרֶה גְדֻלָּתוֹ וּמַלְכוּתוֹ.

He is the Lord of all, the creator of everything, His kingdom and power rule everything.

שֶׁפַע נְבוּאָתוֹ נְתָנוֹ אֶל אַנְשֵׁי סְגֻלָּתוֹ וְתִפְאַרְתּוֹ.

He gave His prophecy through those He loved and chose.

לֹא קָם בְּיִשְׂרָאֵל כְּמֹשֶׁה עוֹד נָבִיא וּמַבִּיט אֶת תְּמוּנָתוֹ.

There has never been a prophet like Moses in Israel, who saw God face to face.

תּוֹרַת אֱמֶת נָתַן לְעַמּוֹ אֵל עַל יַד נְבִיאוֹ נֶאֱמַן בֵּיתוֹ.

God gave the Torah of truth to His people through Moses, His faithful servant.

לֹא יַחֲלִיף הָאֵל וְלֹא יָמִיר דָּתוֹ, לְעוֹלָמִים, לְזוּלָתוֹ.

He will not change or replace His law forever.

צוֹפֶה וְיוֹדֵעַ סְתָרֵינוּ מַבִּיט לְסוֹף דָּבָר בְּקַדְמָתוֹ.

All our secrets are known to Him. He knows the beginning and end of all things.

גּוֹמֵל לְאִישׁ חֶסֶד כְּמִפְעָלוֹ נוֹתֵן לְרָשָׁע רַע כְּרִשְׁעָתוֹ.

He grants a reward to each man according to his deeds and punishes the wicked according to his evil.

יִשְׁלַח לְקֵץ יָמִין מְשִׁיחֵנוּ לִפְדּוֹת מְחַכֵּי קֵץ יְשׁוּעָתוֹ.

In the end of days He will send redemption and will lead all who wait to His salvation.

מֵתִים יְחַיֶּה אֵל בְּרֹב חַסְדּוֹ בָּרוּךְ עֲדֵי עַד שֵׁם תְּהִלָּתוֹ.

Out of His great goodness He sustains all life. Blessed be His name forever and ever.

Commentary

It is said that יִגְדַּל (*Yigdal*) was written sometime in the fourteenth century and was based on the *Thirteen Principles* of Moses Maimonides. The *Thirteen Principles* were considered so important that they were included in most prayer books. Look them up (*Daily Prayer Book*, Joseph H. Hertz, Bloch Publishing Co., 1955, pp. 248–255), and compare them to the יִגְדַּל. The יִגְדַּל was more than a song for the Jewish people. It was recited at the beginning of each daily service as a statement of belief.

Some people have asked why did Maimonides include thirteen principles and not more or less? What is the significance of thirteen? There are several interesting answers. Among them are: the numerical value of the word אֶחָד (*echad*), referring to the *one* God, (א = 1, ח = 8, and ד = 4) is 13; the Bar and Bat Mitzvah age of 13; the Torah mentions thirteen powers of God ((Exodus 34:6–7). What relationship might these explanations have to the *Thirteen Principles*?

155

Kiddush for Shabbat Day

I

וְשָׁמְרוּ בְנֵי יִשְׂרָאֵל אֶת הַשַּׁבָּת, לַעֲשׂוֹת אֶת הַשַּׁבָּת לְדֹרֹתָם בְּרִית עוֹלָם. בֵּינִי וּבֵין בְּנֵי יִשְׂרָאֵל אוֹת הִיא לְעֹלָם. כִּי שֵׁשֶׁת יָמִים עָשָׂה יְיָ אֶת הַשָּׁמַיִם וְאֶת הָאָרֶץ, וּבַיּוֹם הַשְּׁבִיעִי שָׁבַת וַיִּנָּפַשׁ.

The people of Israel shall keep the Shabbat, observing the Shabbat throughout the ages as a covenant for all time. It shall be a sign for all time between Me and the people of Israel. For in six days the Lord made heaven and earth, and on the seventh day He ceased from work and was refreshed.

II

זָכוֹר אֶת יוֹם הַשַּׁבָּת לְקַדְּשׁוֹ. שֵׁשֶׁת יָמִים תַּעֲבֹד וְעָשִׂיתָ כָּל מְלַאכְתֶּךָ. וְיוֹם הַשְּׁבִיעִי שַׁבָּת לַיְיָ אֱלֹהֶיךָ. לֹא תַעֲשֶׂה כָל מְלָאכָה—אַתָּה וּבִנְךָ וּבִתֶּךָ, עַבְדְּךָ וַאֲמָתְךָ וּבְהֶמְתֶּךָ, וְגֵרְךָ אֲשֶׁר בִּשְׁעָרֶיךָ. כִּי שֵׁשֶׁת יָמִים עָשָׂה יְיָ אֶת הַשָּׁמַיִם וְאֶת הָאָרֶץ, אֶת הַיָּם, וְאֶת כָּל אֲשֶׁר בָּם, וַיָּנַח בַּיּוֹם הַשְּׁבִיעִי. עַל כֵּן בֵּרַךְ יְיָ אֶת יוֹם הַשַּׁבָּת וַיְקַדְּשֵׁהוּ.

Remember the Shabbat and keep it holy. Six days you shall labor and do all your work, but the seventh day is a Shabbat of the Lord your God. You shall not do any work — you, your son or daughter, your male or female slave, or your cattle, or the stranger who is within your settlements. For in six days the Lord made heaven and earth and sea, and all that is in them, and He rested on the seventh day. Therefore the Lord blessed the Shabbat and hallowed it.

III

בָּרוּךְ אַתָּה, יְיָ אֱלֹהֵינוּ, מֶלֶךְ הָעוֹלָם, בּוֹרֵא פְּרִי הַגָּפֶן.

Be praised, O Lord our God, Ruler of the universe, Creator of the fruit of the vine.

IV

בָּרוּךְ אַתָּה, יְיָ אֱלֹהֵינוּ, מֶלֶךְ הָעוֹלָם, הַמּוֹצִיא לֶחֶם מִן הָאָרֶץ.

Be praised, O Lord our God, Ruler of the universe, who brings forth bread from the earth.

Commentary

Wine is a symbol of the joy of the Shabbat celebration. It is shared three times on the Shabbat. First, when the Shabbat is welcomed with the קִדּוּשׁ (*Kiddush*) on Friday evening; then, at the conclusion of Shabbat morning worship; and, finally, at הַבְדָּלָה (*Havdalah*), the ceremony which concludes the Shabbat.

The קִדּוּשׁ לְיוֹם שַׁבָּת (*Kiddush leyom Shabbat*), Kiddush for Shabbat day, is also known as קְדֻשָּׁה רַבָּה (*Kedushah Rabbah*), The Great Kiddush. We are not sure how it came to be known by that name, but we do know that the first two paragraphs were added to the blessing over the wine in order to give the Kiddush importance. For an explanation of the first paragraph of the קִדּוּשׁ, known as *Veshamru*, see page 86. The first paragraph is taken from Exodus 31:16–17, and the second is from Exodus 20:8–11.

In the third paragraph, we have the בְּרָכָה for wine, קִדּוּשׁ, and in the fourth, the בְּרָכָה for bread, הַמּוֹצִיא (*Hamotzi*). According to tradition, the blessings for bread and wine are derived from the following words found in Psalms 104:14.

מַצְמִיחַ חָצִיר לַבְּהֵמָה וְעֵשֶׂב לַעֲבֹדַת הָאָדָם;
לְהוֹצִיא לֶחֶם מִן הָאָרֶץ וְיַיִן יְשַׂמַּח לְבַב אֱנוֹשׁ.

Who causes the grass to spring up for the cattle,
And herb for the service of man;
To bring forth bread out of the earth,
And wine that makes glad the heart of man.

Praising God

The קִדּוּשׁ and הַמּוֹצִיא are praises of God.

Judah ha-Levi, who lived in Spain between 1085 and 1140, once commented on the meaning of "praising God" before eating and drinking. He wrote: "Preparing for a pleasure doubles the enjoyment." (*Kuzari*) How is a בְּרָכָה before drinking wine or eating bread a form of "preparation"? In what ways can a בְּרָכָה help us to "double the enjoyment" of the wine, or bread, or anything else we may eat?

Dr. Ernst Simon, who once taught education at the Hebrew University in Jerusalem, Israel, once told the following story about his son.

Once, when my son was four years old, he happened to see some beautiful flowers and said to me: "Abba, I am happy with these flowers. What is the proper benediction (בְּרָכָה) for them?" Though a small child, he expressed a universal human sentiment. Children can love and enjoy flowers just as deeply as adults can, perhaps even more so. But this child was a little Jew who had already learned in his parents' home that nothing is eaten or experienced without a בְּרָכָה a benediction. Hence it was natural for him to seek a specific Jewish religious formulation to express a general human emotion.

(*On the Meaning of Prayer*,
by Ernst Simon)

Other Reasons

Prayer is one of the things which distinguishes human beings from animals. This is especially true of the הַמּוֹצִיא the prayer before eating bread. Animals simply eat when food is placed before them. Human beings can pause, give thought to the incredible process through which food reaches them, and give thanks to God.

There are those who believe that, in saying the בְּרָכָה for wine and bread, we remind ourselves of how dependent we are upon nature, other human beings, and upon God. Others argue that, when a Jew says a בְּרָכָה he reaffirms his identity with the Jewish people and its faith.

Which of these views appeal to you?

FINALLY, WHAT IS PRAYER?

Asking difficult religious questions can sometimes lead to loud arguments and even angry attacks. Why we pray and what we believe about God are very personal matters and, sometimes, "very touchy" subjects! That, however, should not drive us to silence or to avoiding such issues. Through a sensitive and open discussion, we can learn from one another and increase our understanding of God and prayer.

Each of us is a highly unique individual. We are different from one another in our talents, interests, and abilities. Some of us are satisfied with what we believe, others are still struggling with doubts and difficult questions. As individuals we see the world, its wonder, and human history from a variety of perspectives. It should not surprise us, then, to discover that Jews today, and throughout the ages, have developed a number of very different definitions of prayer. This chapter includes some of the most important of these various approaches to the meaning of prayer.

Prayer Is Natural

Some people believe that prayer is as natural a response to the universe as the growth of a flower toward the sun. Just as a flower, even on a cloudy day, will turn toward the light as a source of its growth, so too the human spirit reaches out to a sustaining Spirit in the universe. Prayer, in this sense, is something that all human beings do whether they recognize it or not. When a person pauses to observe beauty, or feels hope in a moment of sadness, or reaches out for strength in a time of trouble — that may be called prayer.

Some scientists believe that the evolution and development of all life are responses to a creative spirit at work in the universe. Dr. Edmond Sinnot, former director of the Sheffield Scientific School at Yale University, has written:

> If there were not something in the universe that draws us, as the moon draws the sea, man's high aspirations would have no meaning. Tides prove the moon is *there*, even though clouds may cover it.... Aspiration is an expression of something deeper than intellect; a

> ### An Instinct
>
> Prayer is a universal phenomenon in the soul-life of man. It is the soul's reaction to the terrors and joys, the uncertainties and dreams of life. "The reason why we pray," says William James, "is simply that we cannot help praying." It is an instinct that springs eternally from man's unquenchable faith in a living God....
>
> (Rabbi Joseph H. Hertz, *Daily Prayer Book*)

profound certainty that beyond man's body and beyond his mind there is a spiritual content in the universe with which his own spirit can from time to time communicate and from which he can draw strength and comfort ... this sense of Presence, this central, orienting core of things, is what we mean by God.
(*The Bridge of Life*, pp. 214–215)

The belief that prayer is a natural aspiration or response to the universe is expressed throughout Jewish literature.

The author of Psalm 19 went so far as to exclaim that the heavens, and day and night, declared the glory of God. Other similar expressions may be found throughout the Book of Psalms (see, especially, Psalms 36:6–10, 84:2–13, 96, 98, 104, and 148). Your discussion group may wish to compare and contrast the following statements about prayer. What do they have in common with Dr. Sinnot's understanding of prayer as "aspiration"? Do you find these statements and the argument that prayer is a "natural response to the universe" satisfying and/or convincing?

I

We are formed by the same forces — chemical, physical, and spiritual — which hold the stars in their orbit, thrust up the mountains, scoop out the seas, bring the rose to bloom, teach the hawk to fly, the horse to neigh. "If I climb up unto the heavens, behold Thou art there, and, if I go to the ends of the earth, behold Thou art there." (Psalms 139:8)

Prayer is not the lonely cry of a "tailless monkey playing ape to his dreams," nor a shout into an empty void answered only by its own echo. Prayer is the spirit within us reaching out to the Spirit of the universe, and prayer is that Spirit responding to us.

(*Prayer and Its Expression*,
by Rabbi Robert I. Kahn)

II

It is not you alone who pray, or we, or those others; all things pray and all things pour forth their souls. The heavens pray, the earth prays, every creature and every living thing. In all life, there is longing. Creation is itself but a longing, a kind of prayer to the Almighty. What are the clouds, the rising and the setting of the sun, the soft radiance of the moon, and the gentleness of the night? What are the flashes of the human mind and the storms of the human heart? They are all prayers — the outpouring of boundless longing for God.

(Micah Joseph Ben Gurion Berdichevski [1865–1921], translation by Rabbi Aharon Opher)

III

Every plant and bush, every grain of sand and clod of earth, everything in which life is revealed or hidden, the smallest and the biggest in creation — longs and yearns and reaches out toward its celestial Source. And, at every moment, all these cravings are gathered up and absorbed by man who is himself lifted up by the longing for holiness within him. It is during prayer that all these pent-up desires and yearnings are released. Through his prayer, man unites in himself all being and lifts all creation up to the Fountainhead of blessing and life.

(*Jewish Thought*
by Abraham Isaac Kook)

We Need Help

Human beings often feel fear and loneliness. We encounter times of sickness, hunger, oppression, failure, and death. In such moments of trial and pain, prayer can be an expression of our need for help. Such expressions are found throughout the Book of Psalms and the traditional prayer book. Here are a few examples.

I

Heal us, O Lord, and we shall be healed. Save us and we shall be saved.

(Amidah)

II

O, Master of the Universe! Redeem, help, save, and assist Your people from disease, the sword, famine, want, and all evils which trouble the world.

(Ketubot 8a)

III

Give ear, O God, to my prayer;
And hide not Yourself from my supplication.
Attend to me, and answer me;
I am filled with sorrow and will cry out;
Because of the voice of the enemy,
Because of the oppression of the wicked;
For they cast mischief upon me,
And in anger they persecute me.

(Psalms 55:2–4)

IV

O, my God, rescue me out of the hand of the wicked,
Out of the grasp of the unrighteous and ruthless man.
For You are my hope;
O Lord God, my trust from my youth.

(Psalms 71:4–5)

Each of the above prayers is based upon a trust, hope, and faith that God can and will help those who call out in prayer. Those who voice such prayers believe that God is a שׁוֹמֵעַ תְּפִילָה (*Shomea Tefilah*), a Power who hears our prayers and may answer them. The immediate and difficult question to be faced, by one who believes in God as a שׁוֹמֵעַ תְּפִילָה, is: "Does God really hear and answer prayer?" Those who have faith in

God as a שׁוֹמֵעַ תְּפִילָה have developed a variety of answers to that question. Your discussion group may wish to explore the following ones. How do they differ? Which comes closest to your own belief?

I

Is it superstition to believe that God hears prayer and answers us? Yes, if we believe that whenever we say something or do something magical then God must jump to our command. But, it is not superstitious to hope that, if we call, He will hear. What would stop Him from hearing us? Why should He not hear? Magic tries to accomplish something against God. Prayer tries to tell Him something, leaving it to Him to do what He wishes. Magic accomplishes something or tries to. Prayer is itself accomplishment.

To be heard by God is to be forgiven of our errors and changed into better people. Prayer does not insure that we get what we want, but only what God wants. It cannot cure cancer or win races, but it can change lives. It has.

(*Challenge to Confirmands*, by Rabbi Arnold Wolf)

II

Perhaps an analogy will help. Like all analogies, it is not perfect and therefore should not be pressed too far. It tends to make God seem too mechanical and distant, yet it may clarify what we mean in asserting that the proper kind of prayer is answered. Each of us has a series of faucets in his home. These faucets are the terminal points of water pipes which are connected to mains, going back ultimately to a pumping station. When we feel thirsty and want a drink of water, what happens? We proceed to a faucet, turn it on, and help ourselves. Has the engineer at the pumping station met our needs? Obviously so, but not in the sense that he is aware of our thirst whenever we feel it. He has constructed and maintained an ingenious system of pipes and valves which makes it possible for us to have water — provided we understand the system and our relationship to it, provided we fulfill our responsibility of operating the system correctly. If we merely stand before the faucet, piteously begging for a drink but doing nothing to activate the system, our thirst will never be slaked.

Similarly, God has initiated and maintains an incredibly complicated system through which most of our physical and spiritual needs may be satisfied. Here again, however, we must become knowledgeable as to how the system operates and must meet our responsibilities in activating it. In a sense, God has answered our prayers even before we utter them, even before we are aware of them. He sustains the system, keeping it in good working order, whether we pray or not. Our prayers affect, not His support of the system, but whether or not we shall reap full benefit from it. Prayer is the experience through which we remind ourselves of how our most urgent needs can be met and activate ourselves to "turn the faucet." In this sense, mature prayer is always answered.

(*Wings of the Morning*, by Rabbi Roland B. Gittelsohn)

III

Thus, at the core of prayer is its richest content — the awareness that there is a God to whom man responds. But out of this comes the frightening question — does God respond to man? "Praised be Thou, O God, who hearest prayer." What sense does this statement make? If by response we mean a reply, a "Yes, I will" or "No, I won't," then there is no response. God does not answer our requests.

I stood in a hospital room where a young woman was feeding her mother, a victim of a heart attack. Suddenly the mother began to gasp for breath. Nurses were summoned. Within seconds, doctors rushed into the room to attempt to save the patient. The daughter was taken to an adjoining room where she pleaded with me, "Rabbi, how do I pray?" Then she moaned again and again, "God, help my mother to live." But the mother died. Did God deny the prayer? It would be cruel to say this. Yet, even if we know in advance that such a prayer cannot help the patient, it must nevertheless be spoken because the grief-stricken person must express his desperate need for help. Sometimes, as in this instance, prayers are altogether nonrational. The one who prays does not ask in his anguish, "Is this reasonable?" He only knows his grief and

A Soldier Fulfilling Orders

he must release it. How wisely the rabbis said, "The heart knows its own bitterness." Anguish demands expression, and, however unreasonable it may be, it must not be denied.

But, if God does not reply, what kind of response can we expect? — the response which God gave to the suffering and questing Job, "I am God." Whatever exists responds to us. The flower responds to my touch. The violin responds to the bow. The tide responds to the tug of the moon. At Gloucester in Massachusetts, I climbed down the ancient boulders, witnesses of the Ice Age, and sat alone as the tide began to pound against the rocks, slowly engulfing them. That tide came in at the exact moment which had been ordained for it at that place. It was responding. And God responds to man. How? By disclosing Himself to us. God hears prayer, not by fulfilling our requirements, not by satisfying our needs, but by making Himself known to us as a living reality in our lives. When we pray we become aware, like Moses who sought to know who God was, that God "is what He is."

("The Need to Pray" in
The Theological Foundations of Prayer,
by Rabbi David Polish)

Professor Yeshaya Leibowitz is a scientist, philosopher, and traditional Jew who lives in Jerusalem. He teaches organic chemistry and neurophysiology at the Hebrew University, and he is one of Israel's best known and most controversial figures. Professor Leibowitz is a practicing, praying, and observant Jew who argues that prayer is not reasonable and that human beings cannot praise or influence God. Nevertheless, Professor Leibowitz prays three times a day with devotion.

In an interview, with Paula Hirth, which appeared in *Israel Magazine*, Professor Leibowitz was asked to explain why he prayed.

Q: Can you honestly, every day, say something you do not believe?

LEIBOWITZ: Why not? The prayer is not my prayer — it is prescribed. Our prayer is not meant to be an expression of my feelings, it has nothing to do with my feelings. I have no need to inform God about my needs — I am simply fulfilling the obligation of prayer, just as a soldier has to obey orders. It is impossible for man to praise God, and you can't influence God — if you believe in God and not in an idol. Therefore, the prayer, in Judaism, does not express human needs; it is a prescribed form of worship of God.

By "the prayer," Professor Leibowitz means the עֲמִידָה. For him, prayer is an obligation and responsibility. It is a מִצְוָה. The idea that prayer is an obligation which each Jew must fulfill is expressed many times in Jewish literature. In the *Zohar*, a book which first appeared in thirteenth-century Spain but which Jewish mystics claim was revealed by God to Rabbi Shimon bar Yochai (100–160 C.E.), we are told: "A man should be like a servant before his master when he stands up to recite the Amidah." The great Jewish philosopher, Moses Maimonides, also stressed that prayer was a מִצְוָה, an obligation. In his *Sefer Hamitzvot*, he wrote: "To pray to God daily is a positive מִצְוָה, as it is said: 'And you shall serve the Lord your God.' (Exodus 23:25) The oral tradition teaches that this *service* is prayer. . . . The obligation in this מִצְוָה is for every person to pray every day according to his ability."

161

What do Professor Leibowitz, the *Zohar*, and Maimonides all have in common? What does it mean to pray as if you are a "servant"? Does that make sense to you? What are the positive aspects of their arguments? What can be gained by viewing prayer as an obligation, a מִצְוָה, or something that we must do? What are some of the dangers in such an approach? How does this definition of prayer compare with the others in this chapter?

To Change Ourselves

Quite opposite from Professor Leibowitz's argument, that prayer "has nothing to do with my feelings," is the belief, held by many, that the purpose of prayer is to change ourselves.

Dr. Emil L. Fackenheim, in his book *Paths to Jewish Belief*, writes: "We pray not to change God's purposes but our own — so as to make them conform to God's. Having thus changed them, we become willing to act as God's co-workers. And this too is part of God's will. But it is not done for us. We can only do it ourselves — through prayer."

The Hebrew verb לְהִתְפַּלֵּל (*lehitpalel*), to pray, may be translated as to judge or to examine oneself. Prayer is meant to be a time of honest self-searching where we struggle with the gap between what we say and do — between our actions and our ideals. This kind of prayer is meant to bother and trouble a person. It should make us ashamed of our selfishness, aware of our apathy, embarrassed by our callous indifference. And it should force us to see the opportunities we may have wasted or the rich potentials we may have squandered. Some examples will help to clarify how this purpose of prayer can function in our experience.

When, for instance, we read: "In loving kindness You sustain the living," we may be moved to ask ourselves: "What have I done as a partner of God in helping to feed the hungry, care for the sick or the aged?" When we pray: "Grant peace . . . to all who worship You," we ought to be asking: "What have I done to make peace possible within my family, among friends, and in my community?" In other words, by using the prayers of Jewish tradition, we may challenge ourselves with questions which can, if taken seriously, change our behavior.

The Challenges We Face

Prayer is a perspective from which to behold, from which to respond to, the challenges we face. Man in prayer does not seek to impose his will upon God; he seeks to impose God's will and mercy upon himself. Prayer is necessary to make us aware of our failures, backsliding, transgressions, sins.

(Rabbi Abraham J. Heschel, *On Prayer*)

Your discussion group may wish to take a prayer from *Bechol Levavcha* and make a list of the questions we might ask ourselves if we wanted to use the prayer as a means for judging our ethical behavior and challenging ourselves to be better, more sensitive, human beings.

Try an experiment! Have each member of your discussion group prepare a series of questions and/or comments alongside a prayer. Then use the prayers and comments in a service. Afterwards, discuss how our prayer experience might help us to change our attitudes and relationships with others and the world. An example using the last section of the הוֹדָאָה follows.

Let all that lives give thanks to You.	How aware have I been of the beauty of earth? Have I given thanks for what I have eaten and enjoyed?
Let all faithfully praise Your name, O God, our Salvation and Help.	Have I praised God with helping others in need or saving them from pain? What have I done to make the world a happier and better place in which to live?
Be praised, O Lord. Your name is goodness, and it is pleasant to give thanks to You.	We are faithful to God when we are sensitive and loving with His creatures and creation. How good and pleasant have I been with friends and family? Can I really give thanks to God without being more grateful to others?

A Means of Jewish Identity

When we recite the words אֱלֹהֵינוּ וֵאלֹהֵי אֲבוֹתֵינוּ, Our God and God of our fathers, we identify ourselves with Jews of all ages and throughout the world. Speaking personally, when I enter a synagogue or join with other Jews in prayer, a special dimension is added to my life. In those moments, I renew my connection with centuries of Jewish experience and tradition. Since the prayer book is filled with the words of the prophets and the writings of rabbis and poets, I become a part of my people's engagement with God. For me, Jewish worship is the bridge which links me to the past, the present, and the future of the Jewish people. It is a reaffirmation of my identity as a Jew.

Jewish tradition has always emphasized the importance of community prayer. While it did not forbid private prayer, it taught that a human being is not only an individual, but also a participant in a community. Rabbi Milton Steinberg, in his book *Basic Judaism*, captures this emphasis of Jewish tradition when he writes: "But a Jew is also an Israelite, a fellow in the Jewish people. Wherefore Judaism has established a schedule of times and seasons at which he shall come to God in this capacity."

Your discussion group ought to discuss the variety of ways in which Jewish prayer helps us to express our Jewish identity and feelings as Jews. For instance, you may wish to examine the use of Hebrew, the participation in a מִנְיָן (minyan), the use of a common prayer book, the reading of Torah, the recitation of prayers composed thousands of years ago, and the wearing of a כִּפָּה (kipah), and טַלִּית (talit). How do these aid us in expressing our Jewishness and our devotion to the Jewish tradition and people?

> **Between Jew and Jew**
>
> Can prayer still be meaningful and relevant to the modern Jew? Prayer is the bridge between God and man, but it can also be the bridge between Jew and Jew. וְטַהֵר לִבֵּנוּ (vetaher libenu), and purify our hearts — these words are known to most Jews, if not from the prayer book, then as the text of a *horah*. Even at the time of the greatest estrangement between the *chalutzim* and the traditionalists, the *chalutzim* could still express in the language of dance what the pious Jews expressed in the language of prayer. From the Torah to *chalutziut*, there is a continuous stream of religious consciousness which has bound together all our habitations and generations. Prayer can create a unity of experience which transcends the boundaries of time and space and bridges the diversity of conviction.
>
> (Ernst Simon, *Prayer: A Study in the History and Psychology of Religion*)

To Enlarge Sensitivity

There is a story told about a chasidic rebbe who was always late to his synagogue for the daily שַׁחֲרִית (*shacharit*), morning prayers. One morning, a few of his students asked him: "Rebbe, why do you come so late each morning?" He was quiet for a moment as if afraid to answer. Then he explained: "I cannot help myself! When I awaken each morning, I immediately recite the morning prayer. I say מוֹדָה אֲנִי לְפָנֶיךָ (*Modeh ani lefanecha*), I give thanks to You. Having said those words, I cannot go on. I tremble, and I ask myself — 'who is the *I*, and who is the *You*?' The *I* is a tiny and passing creature of clay; the *You* is the eternal Creator of the universe. The contrast amazes me, and soon I am lost in wonder and silence before the vast beauty and order of the world. That is why I am late, each morning, in arriving at the synagogue."

Like that chasidic rebbe, prayer for many people is a powerful and poetic way through which human beings enlarge their vision and deepen their sensitivities to the wonder, awe, and beauty of the universe. We cannot always stand in the midst of a beautiful forest or at the top of a mountain. Yet prayer allows us the opportunity to attune ourselves to the feelings we might have had at such special moments. It also provides us with insights through which to open our hearts to new sacred experiences and recognitions. We may, for instance, in the midst of our prayer, realize more deeply than ever before the meaning and mystery of the love we share with others, or the health of our body, or the wonderous capacities of our mind. Prayer is meant to enlarge and open our sensitivities to the world and to ourselves. The author of Psalm 8 knew this when he prayed:

> How glorious is Your name in all the earth!
> When I behold Your heavens, the work of
>   Your fingers,
> The moon and the stars, which You have established;
> What is man, that You are mindful of him?
> And the son of man that You consider him?

Many psalms (see especially Psalms 19, 24, 93, 95–98, and 104) are filled with poetic expressions of reverence for God and the wonder of life. Our prayer book, as we have discovered, contains countless meditations which seek to capture our relationship with the Life-Power pervading all nature. Prayer, in this sense, is meant to enlarge our awareness and enrich our perception. It should open us to the divine margin which energizes all existence.

Your discussion group may wish to compare and contrast the statements about prayer found on page 165. Select a prayer from Bechol Levavcha, *or one of the suggested psalms, and read it after you have studied the quotations from Rabbi Heschel, Rabbi Greenberg, and Rabbi Weinberg. How did the prayer-writer or the Psalmist express wonder and mystery? How do their words help us to new insights and awareness — to a deeper appreciation of ourselves?*

In Conclusion — A Story

Far away from the highways of civilization there was a small village. In it were all the trades and crafts essential to the community except one. There was no watchmaker. As a result, over the years, all the clocks in the village became inaccurate. Many of their owners, therefore, stopped using them.

One day a watchmaker came to the village. He was greeted with much excitement. Everyone rushed to him with his clock. He carefully examined all the clocks before him and then told their owners: "I am sorry, I can fix only those which have been kept running. The others are too corroded with rust. They are ruined beyond repair."

Our ability to pray and derive meaning out of prayer demands effort and skill. *Prayer is an art*, and its success, as in all art, depends upon the artist. The cultivation of prayer requires the constant exercise of our spiritual powers and capacities.

The age in which we live challenges us with many difficult questions about ourselves and the world in which we live. Should we conform to the crowd? What is our connection with the cosmos into which we were born? How can we achieve self-fulfillment? How can we face the fears we have and express the joys we feel? What is our responsibility to our people and to all human beings? Living with such questions we require prayer. We need sacred moments set aside for struggling toward renewed perspective and faith.

We cannot afford to let our capacities for prayer become corroded by neglect. Our lives are too precious, and our tasks as partners with God in creation are too important. The Torah teaches: "Choose life!" Yet, life is constantly evolving and confronting us with novel choices. It is not enough just to exist. The vital question before us is how to exist. For us, prayer can be the indispensible art through which we probe our place in the universe, purify our souls in the white-heat of self-scrutiny, and link our lives to the goals, values, and visions of our people.

To Pray Is . . . .

To pray is to take notice of the wonder, to regain a sense of the mystery that animates all beings, the divine margin in all attainments. Prayer is our humble answer to the inconceivable surprise of living. . . . It is so embarrassing to live! How strange we are in the world, and how presumptuous our doings! Only one response can maintain us: gratefulness for witnessing the wonder, for the gift of our unearned right to serve, to adore, and to fulfill. It is gratefulness which makes the soul great.

(Abraham Joshua Heschel, *Man's Quest for God*)

To pray is to feel and to give expression to a deep sense of gratitude. No intelligent, healthy, normal human being should take for granted, or accept without conscious, grateful acknowledgment, the innumerable blessings which God in His infinite love bestows upon him daily — the blessings of parents and loved ones, of friends and country, of health and understanding.

(Simon Greenberg, *Sabbath and Festival Prayer Book*)

Prayer is awareness not only of God but of oneself as well. God is what He is and we are what we are whether we recognize and welcome it or not. Prayer is joyous recognition and deliberate thankful acceptance of what we are.

(Dudley Weinberg, *The Efficacy of Prayer*)

A SELECTED BIBLIOGRAPHY

BOOKS ON PRAYER

Philip Arian and Azriel Eisenberg, *The Story of the Prayer Book*, Prayer Book Press, Hartford, 1968.

Jack Bemporad, ed., *The Theological Foundations of Prayer* UAHC, New York, 1967.

Solomon B. Freehof, *The Small Sanctuary*, UAHC, New York, 1942.

Joel Grishaver, *Shema Is for Real*, Olin-Sang-Ruby Union Institute, Chicago, 1973.

Abraham Joshua Heschel, *Man's Quest for God*, Charles Scribner's, New York, 1954.

A. Z. Idelsohn, *Jewish Liturgy and Its Development*, Sacred Music Press, New York, 1932.

B. S. Jacobson, *Meditations on the Siddur*, Sinai Publishing, Tel Aviv, Israel, 1966.

Abraham Kon, *Prayer*, Soncino Press, London, Jerusalem, New York, 1971.

Bernard Martin, *Prayer in Judaism*, Basic Books, Inc., New York, 1968.

Abraham E. Millgram, *Jewish Worship*, Jewish Publication Society of America, Philadelphia, 1971.

Elie Munk, *The World of Prayer*, Philipp Feldheim Publisher, New York, 1954.

Jakob J. Petuchowski, *Understanding Jewish Prayer*, Ktav Publishing House, New York, 1972.

PRAYER BOOKS

Avodat Yisrael (with Commentary, in Hebrew), Orstel Ltd. Israel, 1928.

Daily Prayer Book, Philip Birnbaum, Hebrew Publishing Co., New York, 1949.

Daily Prayer Book, Joseph H. Hertz, Bloch Publishing Co., New York, 1955.

Gates of Prayer, Central Conference of American Rabbis, New York, 1975.

Sabbath and Festival Prayer Book, Rabbinical Assembly of America, New York, 1946.

Service of the Heart, Union of Liberal and Progressive Synagogues, London, 1967.

The Union Prayer Book, Central Conference of American Rabbis, New York, 1961.

GLOSSARY

The Hebrew words are listed below in the order in which they appear in the text.
For all prayers, the *Commentary* reference pages are also listed.

Talit. Prayer shawl.	Page 2	טַלִית
Tzitzit. Fringes.	2	צִיצִית
Mitzvah, Mitzvot (pl.). Commandment(s).	2	מִצְוָה, מִצְווֹת
Kipah. Skullcap.	3, 163	כִּפָּה
Shacharit. Morning service.	3, 164	שַׁחֲרִית
Minchah. Afternoon service.	3	מִנְחָה
Maariv. Evening service.	3	מַעֲרִיב
Echad. One.	4, 155	אֶחָד
Shema. "Hear [O Israel]."	4, 37	שְׁמַע
Talit Katan. Small talit.	4	טַלִית קָטָן
Arba Kanfot. Four corners (small four-fringed garment).	4	אַרְבַּע כַּנְפוֹת
Kavanah. Devotion, purpose.	6, 91	כַּוָּנָה
Lehitpalel. To pray.	7, 162	לְהִתְפַּלֵּל
Pesuke Dezimrah. "Verses of Song" or "Benedictions of Praise."	8, 10	פְּסוּקֵי דְזִמְרָה
Berachah, Berachot (pl.). Blessing(s).	11	בְּרָכָה, בְּרָכוֹת
Birchot Hanehenin. Blessings before partaking of pleasures.	11	בִּרְכוֹת הַנֶּהֱנִין
Birchot Hamitzvot. Blessings before doing a mitzvah.	11	בִּרְכוֹת הַמִּצְווֹת
Birchot Hapratiyot. Blessings recited before personal or private occasions.	11	בִּרְכוֹת הַפְּרָטִיּוֹת
Baruch She'amar. "Praised Be the One Who Spoke."	13	בָּרוּךְ שֶׁאָמַר
Rachamim. Compassion.	14	רַחֲמִים
Harachaman. The Merciful One.	14	הָרַחֲמָן
Neshamah Tehorah. Pure soul.	15	נְשָׁמָה טְהוֹרָה
Sefer Tehilim. Book of Psalms.	19, 72	סֵפֶר תְּהִלִים
Nishmat. "The Soul of [Everything That Lives]."	20	נִשְׁמַת
Barechu. "Praise [the Lord]."	24	בָּרְכוּ
Yotzer. "Creator."	24, 26	יוֹצֵר
Ahavah Rabbah. "[With] Great Love."	24, 30	אַהֲבָה רַבָּה
Veahavta. "You Shall Love [the Lord]."	24, 41	וְאָהַבְתָּ
Geulah. "Redemption."	24, 46, 55	גְּאוּלָה
Minyan. Quorum (ten adult male Jews, the minimum for congregational prayer).	25, 163	מִנְיָן
Edah. Congregation.	25	עֵדָה
Adat. Congregation of.	25	עֲדַת
El Baruch. "The Blessed God."	29	אֵל בָּרוּךְ
Veyached Livavenu. "And unite our hearts." (From "Ahavah Rabbah.")	31	וְיַחֵד לְבָבֵנוּ
Ahavat Olam. "Eternal Love."	33	אַהֲבַת עוֹלָם
Mitzvot Beyn Adam	33	מִצְווֹת בֵּין אָדָם

167

Term	Page	Hebrew
Lamakom. Commandments between the individual and God.		לַמָּקוֹם
Mitzvot Beyn Adam Lechavero. Commandments between the individual and his fellow man.	33	מִצְווֹת בֵּין אָדָם לַחֲבֵרוֹ
Ayd. Witness.	37	עֵד
Shema. Perhaps.	38	שֶׁמָּא
Acher. Another.	38	אַחֵר
Kiddush Hashem. Sanctification of God's name.	39	קִדּוּשׁ הַשֵׁם
Shomer Yisrael. "Guardian of Israel."	40	שׁוֹמֵר יִשְׂרָאֵל
Mezuzah. A small case of metal or wood containing a roll of parchment upon which are inscribed the first two passages of the Shema.	41	מְזוּזָה
Tefilin. Phylacteries (two black leather boxes fastened to leather straps, containing four portions from the Torah).	41	תְּפִילִין
Levavcha. Your heart.	42	לְבָבְךָ
Lev. Heart.	42	לֵב
Yetzer Hatov. The power for goodness.	42	יֵצֶר הַטּוֹב
Yetzer Hara. The power for evil.	42	יֵצֶר הָרָע
Nefesh. Soul.	43, 66	נֶפֶשׁ
Vedibarta Bum. "And speak of them." (From "Veahavta.")	44	וְדִבַּרְתָּ בָּם
Kedoshim. (Pl. of Kadosh.) Holy, different, distinct, special, sacred.	44	קְדוֹשִׁים
Kiddushin. Marriage ceremony.	45, 79	קִדּוּשִׁין
Mi Chamochah Ba'elim. "Who is like You among the mighty?" (From the Amidah "Geulah.")	47	מִי כָמֹכָה בָּאֵלִם
Amidah. Standing (the Eighteen Benedictions recited while standing).	50	עֲמִידָה
Chazan. Cantor.	50	חַזָּן
Shemoneh-Esreh. Eighteen Benedictions (the popular name for the Amidah).	50	שְׁמוֹנֶה־עֶשְׂרֵה
Tefilah. Prayer (another name for the Amidah).	50	תְּפִילָה
Tefilat Sheva. The seven prayers (the Shabbat and holiday Amidah).	50	תְּפִילַת שֶׁבַע
Daat. "Knowledge."	52	דַּעַת
Teshuvah. "Repentance."	53	תְּשׁוּבָה
Shuv. Return.	53	שׁוּב
Selichah. "Forgiveness."	54	סְלִיחָה
Goel. Redeemer.	55	גּוֹאֵל
Refuah. "Healing."	56	רְפוּאָה
Bikur Cholim. Visiting the sick.	56	בִּקּוּר חוֹלִים
Mevarech Hashanim. "Who Blesses the Years."	57	מְבָרֵךְ הַשָּׁנִים
Kibbutz Galuyot. "Gathering of Exiles."	58	קִבּוּץ גָּלֻיּוֹת
Galut. Exile.	58	גָּלוּת
Tzedakah Umishpat. "Righteousness and Justice."	59	צְדָקָה וּמִשְׁפָּט
Machnia Zedim. "Humbling the Arrogant."	60	מַכְנִיעַ זֵדִים

AL HATZADIKIM. "For the Righteous."	61	עַל הַצַּדִּיקִים
TZADIK. Righteous.	61	צַדִּיק
BONEH YERUSHALAYIM. "Rebuilding Jerusalem."	63	בּוֹנֵה יְרוּשָׁלַיִם
KEREN YESHUAH. "The Messianic Hope."	64	קֶרֶן יְשׁוּעָה
ET TZEMACH DAVID. "A descendant of David." (From "Keren Yeshuah.")	64	אֶת צֶמַח דָּוִד
MASHIACH. The anointed one; messiah.	64	מָשִׁיחַ
SHOMEA TEFILAH. "Who Hears Prayer."	66	שׁוֹמֵעַ תְּפִלָּה
AVOT. "Fathers" or "Patriarchs."	68	אָבוֹת
ELOHE AVOTENU. "God of our fathers." (From "Avot.")	68	אֱלֹהֵי אֲבוֹתֵינוּ
ELOHENU. Our God.	68, 102	אֱלֹהֵינוּ
ZECHUT AVOT. The merit of the fathers.	70	זְכוּת אָבוֹת
GEVUROT. "[God's] Power."	72	גְּבוּרוֹת
MECHALKEL CHAYIM BECHESED. "Who in loving kindness sustains the living." (From "Gevurot.")	73	מְכַלְכֵּל חַיִּים בְּחֶסֶד
MECHAYEH HAMETIM. "Who revives the dead." (From "Gevurot.")	74	מְחַיֵּה הַמֵּתִים
LEHACHAYOT HAMETIM. "To revive the dead." (From "Gevurot.")	74	לְהַחֲיוֹת הַמֵּתִים
MECHAYEH HAKOL. "Who sustains all life." (From "Gevurot.")	74	מְחַיֵּה הַכֹּל
NOTEA BETOCHENU CHAYE OLAM. Who has implanted within us eternal life. (From "Gevurot.")	74	נוֹטֵעַ בְּתוֹכֵינוּ חַיֵּי עוֹלָם
KEDUSHAH. "Holiness."	78	קְדֻשָּׁה
KADOSH. Sacred. (See KEDOSHIM).	79	קָדוֹשׁ
KIDDUSH. The blessing over wine.	79, 157	קִדּוּשׁ
SEFER HAMITZVOT. The Book of Commandments.	80	סֵפֶר הַמִּצְווֹת
KEDUSHAT HAYOM. "The Sanctification of the Day."	82	קְדֻשַּׁת הַיּוֹם
MENUCHATENU. "Our rest." (From "Kedushat Hayom.")	84	מְנוּחָתֵינוּ
NESHAMAH YETERAH. An extra portion of soul.	84	נְשָׁמָה יְתֵרָה
ZACHOR ET YOM HASHABBAT LEKADSHO. Remember the Shabbat day to keep it holy.	85	זָכוֹר אֶת יוֹם הַשַּׁבָּת לְקַדְּשׁוֹ
VESHAMRU. "And they shall observe." (From "Kiddush leyom Shabbat.")	86, 156	וְשָׁמְרוּ
OT. Sign.	86	אוֹת
AVODAH. "Worship."	87	עֲבוֹדָה
AVELEI TZION. Mourners of Zion.	89	אֲבֵלֵי צִיּוֹן
KOTEL MAARAVI. Western Wall.	90	כֹּתֶל מַעֲרָבִי
HODAAH. "Thanksgiving."	93	הוֹדָאָה
MODIM. "We Offer Thanks."	93	מוֹדִים
BIRKAT SHALOM. "Blessing of Peace."	97	בִּרְכַּת שָׁלוֹם
SIM SHALOM. "Grant Us Peace."	97	שִׂים שָׁלוֹם
SHALOM RAV. "Abundant Peace."	100	שָׁלוֹם רָב

Term	Page	Hebrew
Elohai Netzor. "My God, Keep [My Tongue from Evil]."	101	אֱלֹהַי נְצוֹר
Keriat Hatorah. The Reading of Torah.	106	קְרִיאַת הַתּוֹרָה
Parashah, Parashiyot (pl.). Section(s) (the weekly Torah portion).	106, 108	פָּרָשָׁה, פָּרָשִׁיּוֹת
Torah Shebichtav. The written Torah.	110	תּוֹרָה שֶׁבִּכְתָב
Torah Shebe'al Peh. The oral Torah.	110	תּוֹרָה שֶׁבְּעַל פֶּה
En Kamocha. "There are no [gods] that can compare to You." (From "At the Ark.")	112	אֵין כָּמוֹךָ
Mishkan. Sanctuary.	114	מִשְׁכָּן
Baruch Shenatan. "Praised be the One who has given." (From "At the Ark.")	115	בָּרוּךְ שֶׁנָּתַן
Echad Elohenu. "Our God is One." (From "Taking the Torah from the Ark.")	116	אֶחָד אֱלֹהֵינוּ
Gadlu. Magnify.	116	גַּדְּלוּ
Talmud Torah Keneged Kulam. The study of Torah comes before everything.	118	תַּלְמוּד תּוֹרָה כְּנֶגֶד כֻּלָּם
Kohen, Kohanim (pl.). Priest(s).	121, 120	כֹּהֵן, כֹּהֲנִים
Levi, Leviim (pl.). Levite(s).	121, 120	לֵוִי, לְוִיִּם
Yisrael, Yisre'elim (pl.). Israelite(s).	121, 120	יִשְׂרָאֵל, יִשְׂרְאֵלִים
Aliyah. "Going up" to read from the Torah, also immigration to Israel.	121	עֲלִיָּה
Aliyah Leregel. Pilgrimage to Jerusalem for the festivals of Pesach, Shavuot, and Sukot.	121	עֲלִיָּה לְרֶגֶל
Oleh. One who "goes up" to read the Torah, also an immigrant to Israel.	121	עוֹלֶה
Baal Kore. The trained reader of Torah.	121	בַּעַל קוֹרֵא
Meturgeman. Translator.	122	מְתוּרְגְּמָן
Derashah. Sermon.	122	דְּרָשָׁה
Kera. Biblical verse.	122	קְרָא
Natan. Gave.	123	נָתַן
Noten. Gives.	123	נוֹתֵן
Tanach. The Hebrew Bible.	124	תַּנַ"ךְ
Torah. The Five Books of Moses.	124	תּוֹרָה
Neviim. Prophets.	124	נְבִיאִים
Ketuvim. Writings.	124	כְּתוּבִים
Haftarah. A selected reading from the Prophets read after the Torah portion.	124	הַפְטָרָה
Ve'al Haneviim. "And for the prophets." (From "The Haftarah Blessings," part iv.)	127	וְעַל הַנְּבִיאִים
Rosh Chodesh. The New Month.	131	רֹאשׁ חֹדֶשׁ
Adar Sheni. Adar II.	132	אֲדָר שֵׁנִי
Chaverim Kol Yisrael. Israel is one united people.	133	חֲבֵרִים כָּל יִשְׂרָאֵל
Hagbahah. Lifting the Torah.	137	הַגְבָּהָה
Yad. Torah pointer.	137	יָד
Rimonim. Torah crowns.	137	רִמּוֹנִים
Etz Chaim. A tree of life.	137	עֵץ חַיִּים
Gelilah. The rolling of the Torah.	137	גְּלִילָה
Siyum Haavodah. Conclusion of the service.	139	סִיּוּם הָעֲבוֹדָה

Aleynu. "It Is Our Duty."	140, 141	עָלֵינוּ
Varik. "And emptiness." (From "Aleynu.")	143	וָרִיק
Kaddish. "Sanctification."	145, 146	קַדִּישׁ
Chatzi Kaddish. Half Kaddish.	146	חֲצִי קַדִּישׁ
Kaddish Shalem. Full Kaddish.	146	קַדִּישׁ שָׁלֵם
Kaddish Titkabel. Kaddish of Acceptance (another name for Kaddish Shalem).	146	קַדִּישׁ תִּתְקַבֵּל
Kaddish Yatom. Mourner's Kaddish.	146	קַדִּישׁ יָתוֹם
Kaddish Derabanan. Rabbi's Kaddish.	148	קַדִּישׁ דְּרַבָּנָן
Kaddish Lehitchadeta. Kaddish of Renewal.	148	קַדִּישׁ לְהִתְחַדְּתָא
Olam Haba. The world to come.	148	עוֹלָם הַבָּא
Ge Ben Hinom. The valley of the son of Henom.	149	גֵּיא בֶן הִנֹּם
Gehenom. Hell.	149	גֵּיהִנּוֹם
Sheol. Hell.	149	שְׁאוֹל
Adon Olam. "Eternal Lord."	151	אֲדוֹן עוֹלָם
En Kelohenu. "There is None like Our God."	153	אֵין כֵּאלֹהֵינוּ
Yigdal. [May He be] "Magnified."	155	יִגְדַּל
Havdalah. The ceremony which concludes the Shabbat.	157	הַבְדָּלָה
Kiddush Leyom Shabbat. Kiddush for Shabbat Day.	157	קִדּוּשׁ לְיוֹם שַׁבָּת
Kedushah Rabbah. The Great Kiddush.	157	קְדֻשָׁה רַבָּה
Hamotzi. "Who Brings Forth" (the blessing for bread).	157	הַמּוֹצִיא
Vetaher Libenu. "And purify our hearts." (From "Kedushat Hayom.")	164	וְטַהֵר לִבֵּנוּ
Modeh Ani Lefanecha. "I Give Thanks to You."	164	מוֹדֶה אֲנִי לְפָנֶיךָ

IN TRIBUTE

*T*o RALPH DAVIS who, for a quarter century, has served the Union of American Hebrew Congregations with distinction as its Director of Publications.

His genius brought the blessing of Jewish books to generations of our children.

His sensitivity to the meaning and purpose of every author's work helped to enliven Jewish ideas and values for readers of all ages.

His well-refined esthetic sense added a garment of beauty to the written word.

On this, his 25th anniversary of creative service to the UAHC, we pay tribute to him as an expression of our respect and affection.

Matthew H. Ross
CHAIRMAN OF THE BOARD

Rabbi Alexander M. Schindler
PRESIDENT

September 18, 1975
13 Tishri 5736

COMMISSION ON JEWISH EDUCATION
OF THE
UNION OF AMERICAN HEBREW CONGREGATIONS
AND THE
CENTRAL CONFERENCE OF AMERICAN RABBIS
AS OF 1976

Chairman
JACOB P. RUDIN

Vice Chairman
MARTIN S. ROZENBERG

Honorary Chairman
SOLOMON B. FREEHOF

DR. D. G. AXELROTH	ROLAND B. GITTELSOHN	MRS. CECIL B. RUDNICK
MORTON A. BAUMAN	SAMUEL C. GLASNER	DR. LENORE SANDEL
HERBERT M. BAUMGARD	DAVID S. HACHEN	FREDERICK C. SCHWARTZ
ALAN D. BENNETT	JACK HOROWITZ	SYLVAN D. SCHWARTZMAN
LEO BERGMAN	BERNARD KLIGFELD	L. WILLIAM SPEAR
MORRISON DAVID BIAL	HAROLD I. KRANTZLER	MARVIN S. WALTS
ERIC FELDHEIM	MRS. DAVID M. LEVITT	HEINZ WARSCHAUER
HARVEY J. FIELDS	LOUIS LISTER	SUE WEISKOPF
LEON C. FRAM	STANLEY MEISELS	ISAIAH ZELDIN
STUART GERTMAN	SALLY PRIESAND	

Ex Officio

MATTHEW ROSS
ALEXANDER M. SCHINDLER

WILLIAM C. CUTTER	ABRAHAM SEGAL
JOSEPH B. GLASER	SADIE SEGAL
ARTHUR J. LELYVELD	BERNARD M. ZLOTOWITZ

UNION EDUCATION SERIES
Edited by

Director of Publications
RALPH DAVIS

Editor of Keeping Posted
EDITH SAMUEL